Editorial Director: Jere L. Calmes
Cover Design: Beth Hansen-Winter
Production and Composition: Eliot House Productions

© 2003 by Entrepreneur Media Inc.
All rights reserved.
Reproduction or translation of any part of this work beyond that permitted by Section 107 or 108 of the 1976 United States Copyright Act without permission of the copyright owner is unlawful. Requests for permission or further information should be addressed to the Business Products Division, Entrepreneur Media Inc.

This publication is designed to provide accurate and authoritative information in regard to the subject matter covered. It is sold with the understanding that the publisher is not engaged in rendering legal, accounting, or other professional services. If legal advice or other expert assistance is required, the services of a competent professional person should be sought.

Library of Congress Cataloging-in-Publication Data

Tracy, Brian.
Many miles to go: a modern parable for business success/by Brian Tracy.—1st ed.
p. cm.
ISBN 1-891984-99-3
1. Success in business. I. Title.
HF5386.T8142 2003
650.1—dc21 2003041046

Printed in Canada

10 09 08 07 06 05 04 03 10 9 8 7 6 5 4 3 2 1

D1038035

many mi
to go

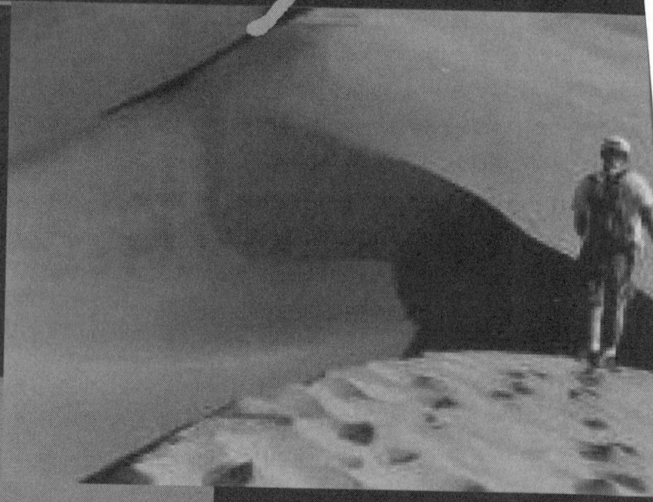

A Modern Parable for Business Success

Brian Tr

Entrepreneur Press

Table of Contents

Dedication v

Foreword *Caution: This Book Will Change Your Life* by Harvey Mackay vii

Introduction *Why Are Some People So Successful?* xi

SECTION I

The Vision and Dream

CHAPTER 1 The Call of the Open Road 3

CHAPTER 2 The Preparation 11

SECTION II

Starting Out—Just Do It!

CHAPTER 3 The First Step: Vancouver to Montreal 17

CHAPTER 4 The First Crisis 23

CHAPTER 5 Setting Off Once More 29

CHAPTER 6 Getting Down to Business 35

SECTION III

The Real Journey Begins at Last

CHAPTER 7 Setting Out 43

CHAPTER 8 Our Tour de France 47

CHAPTER 9 The Spanish Railways 69

CHAPTER 10 Gibraltar Days 83
CHAPTER 11 The Turning Point 101

SECTION IV
The Dawn of Reality
CHAPTER 12 Morocco and the Atlas Mountains 107
CHAPTER 13 The Best-Laid Plans of Mice and Men 121
CHAPTER 14 A Change of Pace 131
CHAPTER 15 You Will Die in the Desert 137
CHAPTER 16 Algeria and the Sahara 147

SECTION V
Never Give Up
CHAPTER 17 Sahara Crossing: The First Attempt 157
CHAPTER 18 Sahara Crossing: The Second Attempt 167
CHAPTER 19 Third Time Lucky 187

SECTION VI
The Greatest Desert on Earth
CHAPTER 20 The Convoy 203
CHAPTER 21 The Crossing 209
CHAPTER 22 One Oil Barrel at a Time 221
CHAPTER 23 Bordji-Perez 235
CHAPTER 24 Running the Border 245
CHAPTER 25 A Very Close Call 259

SECTION VII
Reflections
CHAPTER 26 Lessons for Life 267

APPENDIX Becoming Unstoppable 275

About the Author 281
Index 287

Dedication

To Christina, a great adventurer of the heart and mind. You have come so far and done so well, and you have so many wonderful experiences ahead of you. I am so proud of you.

Don't Quit

When things go wrong, as they sometimes will,
When the road you're trudging seems all uphill,
When funds are low and the debts are high,
And you want to smile, but you have to sigh,
When care is pressing you down a bit,
Rest, if you must, but don't you quit.

Life is queer with its twists and turns,
As every one of us sometimes learns,
And many a failure turns about,
When he might have won had he stuck it out;
Don't give up though the pace seems slow,
You may succeed with another blow.

Success is failure turned inside out,
The silver tint of the clouds of doubt,
And you never can tell how close you are,
It may be near when it seems so far;
So stick to the fight when you're hardest hit,
It's when things seem worst that you must not quit.

—Author Unknown

Caution: This Book Will Change Your Life

YOU ARE ABOUT TO EMBARK ON AN EXCITING JOURNEY of exploration into the depths of the most fascinating person you will ever know: yourself.

Life is a journey, and every part of life is a small journey, complete in itself. You begin with a destination, either clear or fuzzy, travel with the inevitable ups and downs, and finally you arrive at your destination, which may or may not be what you had in mind. Your experiences along the way, and how you react to them, are what make you who you are and determine who you will become.

Learn from Experience

The more experiences you have, and the more you learn from them, the faster you become all you are capable of becoming. The bad news is, we tend to learn more from the mistakes and detours than from the miles of smooth road. The good news is we can have Brian Tracy as our traveling companion.

You have extraordinary intelligence, talent, ability, and skill you can develop and direct toward accomplishing exceptional things and making a real difference in the world. This book will show you how to tap into them.

Timeless Truths

I've known Brian Tracy for several years. He is one of the most respected speakers and consultants in America, and perhaps the world. (I ought to know; we've shared the platform on several occasions, and I've sat in the first row taking notes.) His books, articles, audio and video programs, and seminars have been published in 35 countries and 20 different languages. Brian has the unique ability to draw timeless truths and principles from his experiences, and then share them with others in such a clear and simple way that their lives and thinking are changed forever.

One Common Goal

Everyone wants to be successful. Everyone wants to be healthy and happy, do meaningful work, and achieve financial independence. Everyone wants to make a difference in the world, be significant, and have a positive impact on those around him or her. Everyone wants to do something wonderful with his or her life.

Luckily for most of us, success is not a matter of background, intelligence, or native ability. It's not our family, friends, or contacts who enable us to do extraordinary things. Instead, it is our ability to get the very best out of ourselves under almost all conditions and circumstances. It is your ability, as Theodore Roosevelt said, to "Do what you can with what you have, right where you are."

The Success Formula

The great success formula has always been the same. First, decide exactly what you want and where you want to go. Second, set a deadline and make a plan to get there. (Remember, a goal is just a dream with a deadline.) Third, take action on your plan; do something every day to move toward your goal. Finally, resolve in advance that you will persist until you succeed, that you will never, ever give up.

This formula has worked for almost everyone who has ever tried it. It is simple, but not easy. It will require the very most you can give and the best qualities you can develop. In developing and following this formula, you will evolve and grow to become an extraordinary person.

Learn from the Experts

One more thing: learn from the experts. You will not live long enough to figure it all out for yourself. And what a waste it would be to try, when you can learn from others who have gone before. Ben Franklin once said, "Men can either buy their wisdom or borrow it from others. The great tragedy is that most men prefer to buy it, to pay full price in terms of time and treasure."

Over and over, I have found that a single piece of information—a single idea at the right time, in the right situation—can make all the difference. I have also learned that the great truths are simple. They are not found in complex formulas that require a rocket scientist to interpret. They are contained in basic ideas and principles virtually anyone can understand and apply. Your greatest goal in life should be to acquire as many of them as possible and then use them to help you do the things you want to do and become the person you want to become.

Fasten Your Seat Belt

Before you start reading this book, fasten your seat belt; it's a real page-turner. As you join Brian and his friend Geoff on their journey, and face the challenges they face, you will find yourself learning about life at a more rapid rate than you may have thought possible. You will see yourself and your own story in almost every page.

As Brian says, "Everyone has a Sahara to cross." You and I move in and out of crises on a regular basis. The turbulence and turmoil of life are inevitable and unavoidable. The only part of the equation you control is how you respond. As Epictetus, the Roman philosopher, once said, "Circumstances do not make the man; they merely reveal him to himself."

At the end of this book, you will be a different person, a better person, a wiser person. In fact, you may never be the same person again.

Bon voyage.

—Harvey MacKay

Why Are Some People so Successful?

> "I have learned that success is to be measured not so much by the position that one has reached in life as by the obstacles which he has overcome while trying to succeed."
> —BOOKER T. WASHINGTON

HAVE YOU EVER WONDERED WHY some people are more successful than others? Why is it that some people enjoy better health, happier relationships, and greater success in their careers and achieve financial independence—if not great wealth—and others do not? What is it that enables some people to accomplish remarkable things and enjoy wonderful lives while so many others feel frustrated and disappointed?

These questions were important to me when I started out in life. I came from humble beginnings. My parents were good people, but often out of work. Growing up, we never seemed to have enough money for anything. Our family theme song was, "We can't afford it!"

I didn't graduate from high school. I didn't quit or drop out, but I was in the half of the class that made the top half possible. At the commencement ceremony, instead of a diploma, I got a simple "Leaving Certificate."

A Poor Start

My first full-time job was as a dishwasher in a small hotel. I started at 4 P.M. and often worked into the early hours of the morning. When I lost that job, I got one washing cars on a car lot. When I lost that job, I got a job with a janitorial service washing floors late into the night. I began to think that washing things was going to be in my future.

With a limited education, I seemed to have a limited future as well. I worked in a sawmill stacking lumber, first on the afternoon shift and then later on the graveyard shift, which meant getting off at 7 A.M. I pumped gas and worked at odd jobs. I worked in the bush with a chainsaw on a logging crew, sometimes 12 hours a day, enduring black flies, dust, diesel fuel, and 90-degree heat. I even dug wells for a while. That's where you start at ground level and work *down.* And when you succeed, you *fail,* because when you find water, they fire you. It was not a great incentive system.

Learning the Hard Way

I was homeless before it was respectable. I lived in my car in the winter and slept next to it in the summer. I worked in hotels and restaurants, washing pots and pans in the winter and working on ranches and farms in the summer. I worked in construction as a laborer and in factories putting nuts on bolts, hour after hour.

I worked on a ship—a Norwegian freighter in the North Atlantic—as a galley boy, the lowest man on the nautical totem pole. I worked and drifted from odd job to odd job for years, continually asking and wondering, "Why are some people more successful than others?"

Lessons Learned

My life is different now. I live in a beautiful house on a golf course in Southern California. I have a healthy, happy family and a successful business with operations throughout the United States, and Canada, and in a dozen foreign countries. And all this happened for me because I finally found the answers.

After years of searching, I met a wise and wealthy man who sat me down and told me the key to success. He also explained the reasons for failure and underachievement in life. As he spoke, I immediately recognized the truth in what he said. And his discovery about success was quite simple, as all great truths seem to be.

What he told me was this: "*The key to success is for you to set one big, challenging goal and then pay any price, overcome any obstacle, and persist through any difficulty until you finally achieve it.*"

Program Yourself for Success

By achieving one important goal, you create a pattern, a template for success in your subconscious mind. Ever after you will be automatically directed and driven toward repeating that success in other things you attempt. By overcoming adversity and achieving one great goal in any area, you program yourself for success in other areas as well.

In other words, *you learn to succeed by succeeding. The more you achieve, the more you can achieve.* Each success, especially the first one, builds your confidence and belief that you will be successful next time.

Nothing Can Stop You

The fact is that you can accomplish almost any goal you set for yourself if you persist long enough and work hard enough. The only one who can stop you is you. And you learn to persist by *persisting* in the face of great adversity when everyone around you is quitting and every fiber of your being screams at you to quit.

When you subject certain chemicals to intense heat, they crystallize and form a completely new substance, a composition in which the crystallization process is irreversible. A lump of coal, for example, becomes a diamond under intense prolonged heat and pressure.

In the same way, you become a person of great strength by persevering in the crucible of intense difficulty until you finally succeed. Each time you force yourself to persevere, rather than give up, your character "crystallizes" at a new, higher level. Eventually, you reach the point where you become *unstoppable.*

The Ultimate Aim of Life

Aristotle, the Greek philosopher, said that the ultimate aim of life is the development of character. A person of character is one in whom the great virtues of courage, persistence, compassion, generosity, integrity, tenacity, and perseverance have crystallized and become permanent. Your life and thinking are now built around an unshakable set of principles that you will not compromise under any circumstances.

The development of character is not easy. It often takes an entire lifetime. This is why every extraordinary achievement in life seems to be a result of thousands of ordinary efforts, backed by courage and persistence, that no one ever sees or appreciates.

As the poet Henry Wadsworth Longfellow once wrote,

Those heights by great men, won and kept,
Were not achieved by sudden flight;
But they, while their companions slept,
Were toiling upwards in the night.

Shape Your Own Character

When you complete a major task, overcome a great obstacle, or achieve an important goal, you experience the emotions of exhilaration, joy, satisfaction, happiness, and personal pride. These experiences establish a pattern, or conditioned response, in your subconscious mind. Forever after, you will be motivated to do the same things that brought you success in the past so you can once more enjoy those same feelings.

You develop into a superior person by practicing the qualities you most want to have whenever they are called for. You learn to be brave by being brave. You learn to persist by persisting. You learn to overcome by overcoming. The quality of character you develop is in direct proportion to the amount or intensity of these qualities demanded by the difficult situation, *multiplied* by the length of time you demonstrate these qualities in the face of adversity.

Entrepreneurs and business people become successful as a direct result of trying and failing over and over again, and then picking themselves up and pressing on. Each time they refuse to be stopped by a setback or disappointment, they reinforce the qualities within themselves that enable them to persist even longer next time.

Eventually, they reach a state of mind where they become unstoppable. Failure for them is not an option. They become like forces of nature, irresistible and unmovable. They reach the point *in their own minds* where they cannot conceive of any outcome except final victory. This state of mind must be your goal as well.

Unlimited Potential

Here is some good news: you have within you, *right now*, everything you could ever need or want to be a great success in any area of your life you consider important.

You have within you, right now, deep reserves of potential and ability that, properly harnessed and channeled, will enable you to accomplish extraordinary things with your life. The only real limits on what you can do, have, or be are self-imposed. They do not exist outside of you.

Once you make a clear, unequivocal decision to cast off all your mental limitations and throw your whole heart into the accomplishment of some great goal, your ultimate success is virtually guaranteed, as long as you don't stop.

Looking Back

But I am getting ahead of myself. We learn most of our important lessons in life from experience, by looking back at what happened to us. We evaluate those experiences and ideally, extract ideas and insights to apply to the future.

The turning point in my life came many years ago, although I did not recognize it at the time. Afterwards I felt I could accomplish just about anything if I wanted it badly enough and was willing to work long and hard for it. This is also true for you.

I have spent many years traveling around the world, but the "crucible experience" of my life was my first big trip, my first great journey into the unknown. In a very positive way, I never recovered from it. The experiences I had and the lessons I learned were burned into my brain and affected my outlook on life forever after. I have never been the same since the Sahara crossing.

The Never-Ending Story

This story is about a trip. It is a story for people who travel and enjoy it, and for those who want to travel but never seize the opportunity. It is for anyone who sets out toward a distant goal and enjoys the steps they take to get there as much as the arrival. The more inclined you are to look upon *life* and *success* as a journey, the more likely it is that you will actually enjoy your life—every step of the way.

My heartfelt desire is that you will not only understand this story about traveling but also feel, at least in part, like a member of the team, making progress from place to place and covering as much ground as possible in order to achieve the goal. You will also see the parallels with your own journey through life, and some of the lessons you have learned from your experience.

The True Traveler

Traveling, in its purest form—that is, separate from occupational, recreational, educational, and social excursions—has been described by the author John Steinbeck as the "urge to be someplace else," but there is more to it than that.

True traveling is the desire to wake in the morning and see the mist on the road, knowing that the miles ahead will be brand new and consist of people, places, and experiences completely unpredictable and unknowable. It is the feeling of detachment and freedom from the environment, while being at the same time so involved with it physically and emotionally that the body tingles with eagerness and anticipation. The overwhelming sensation of a true traveler is the joyous exhilaration that comes through motion—not once, but over and over again—and creates a state of continual elation and, underneath, a contentment and peace bordering on paradise.

There are only a few true travelers, and none of them are full time. Like malaria, the traveling "bug" enters the bloodstream, often through a tiny prick in the consciousness—a book, song, or poem—and builds up in the body silently. Then one day the fever strikes with an intensity that causes an incredible dissatisfaction with routine and normal living.

The cost of traveling is high. To be a true traveler means severing bonds, leaving behind friends, family and security, and casting one's fate into the teeth of the unknown. Not many people dare to pay this price. Those who answer the "call of the road" and are mentally suited to it, are among the happiest people on earth; they do not need to die to know what heaven is.

Those who do not dare to leave their security and social obligations behind always carry with them the vague feeling that they have missed something important. Throughout their lives, they will be troubled by recurring periods of uneasiness they can't explain to themselves or anyone else. They need not die to have a taste of hell.

The Traveling Life

The traveling life, though costly, is so enriching emotionally and intellectually that it does not, and cannot, last for long periods. A period of traveling usually leaves the traveler spent and fulfilled, quite prepared to accept the regularity of a quiet life in exchange for the demanding and exhausting uncertainty of the road.

The traveling life is essentially an individual one, best embarked upon alone or with a close companion with whom one is in complete accord—and this is asking a lot.

Any true traveler reading this account understands clearly what I'm trying to say. I was a young man when I came to these conclusions, but years of practical experience have only reconfirmed their essential truth.

If you feel the call, "the lure of little voices, all a' begging you to go," don't fight it or be afraid of it. Take hold of it with both hands and kick yourself free. Live it until you really get to know yourself—and then go back, if you can. It's not an easy life, even if you do it right. It can be deadly difficult if you do it wrong. But, if you're meant for it, it's surely the greatest life on earth.

Seeking Adventure

My friends Geoff and Bob and I left home seeking changes and challenges to be endured at the time and bragged about later. When viewed by romantic souls, these hard times become glorious "adventures." Over the miles, we learned a lot about traveling and about Europe and Africa, living, and life. Each lesson we learned came from personal and often painful physical experience, and each benefit we gained came from the practical application of that lesson.

We grew up as ordinary children, in that we each thought of ourselves as rather *extraordinary*. We were young men with high moral ideals and romantic ideas about how people should behave and how things should be done, on the basis of what we'd read and been taught.

For example, we considered reminders like "be strong," "be brave," and "keep smiling" to be fine and noble and applicable to any difficulty; that is, until we found ourselves sitting in the Sahara by an empty road in 120 degrees of bake-oven heat, with 2,000 miles between us and our destination. Just about then, we began to wonder about the merits of noble ideals. And the situation had not the slightest resemblance to an adventure.

Out of this and countless other experiences, many of them a good deal worse, came a gradual realization that *a large gulf exists between the Pollyanna platitudes and reality.*

Three Ways to Read this Book

There are three ways you can read this book. The first is to read it as a travel adventure. In writing this narrative that spans two years of the most impressionable time of my life, I have tried to be purely objective, relying on our many unusual experiences to make the story worthwhile reading. This assumes that a vivid account of three young men who set a goal 17,000 miles away, and then went about getting there, would be sufficiently interesting to justify the writing of it.

However, I also have laced the narrative with my own philosophical observations. As I neared the completion of this story, I discovered truths so universal they can be removed entirely from the context to stand alone as lessons applicable to any situation. So this tale of traveling to and through Africa assumes an added dimension of timeless truths that can be applied to many other areas of life.

Second, this story can be read as an account of a *search for truth.* It begins with innocence, marked by questions and curiosity. When the search begins in earnest, many obstacles arise, most notably that of ignorance—of how to pursue the quest. The search takes us over vast stretches of barren terrain and across several borders. There are times when knowledge and experience are concentrated into short bursts of enlightenment and understanding.

There is confusion and dishonesty. There are dangers and hardships. There is the necessity for courage and perseverance, flexibility and ingenuity. There is the need for assistance from other people and the eventual realization that no one does it alone in the journey through life.

When the truth finally dawns, it is overwhelming and requires a violent rearrangement of previous beliefs, leaving us older and wiser, and with an understanding of what it really means to suffer.

A Gradual Transformation

The third way this story can be read is as a biography of a person going through a complete metamorphosis. There is the conception, the prenatal preparation, and then the birth. There is a childhood, a troubled and long one. There is adolescence, confused and uncertain, a young maturity, and a striving middle age, complete with disillusion and resolute plodding along a straight line. At last comes old age, and in this instance, an empty, exhausted arrival at the "other side."

"The world is so constructed, that if you wish to enjoy its pleasures, you must also endure its pains. Whether you like it or not, you cannot have one without the other."
—Swami Brahmananda

Whichever way you look at it—as a story about traveling, a search for truth, or a biography—one thing is clear. It is entirely true. And as we saw it, it was absolutely necessary and unavoidable. Geoff, Bob, and I did it, as many others have and will, and it doesn't matter who you are—sooner or later, *everyone has a Sahara to cross.*

SECTION I

The Vision and the Dream

> "Dream lofty dreams, and as you dream, so shall you become. Your vision is your promise of what you shall one day be; your ideal is the prophecy of what you shall one day unveil."
>
> —JAMES ALLEN

EVERY GREAT ACHIEVEMENT begins with a vision, a dream of something exciting or different, a feeling that inspires and motivates you to aim higher and beyond anything you have ever achieved before.

What is your vision for your life? Imagine for a moment that you have no limitations on what you can be or do. Assume you have all the time and money, all the knowledge and experience, all the skills and resources, and all the friends and contacts. If you could have anything in your life, what would it be?

Project forward five years and imagine that your life is now *perfect* in every way. What does it look like? What are you doing? Who is with you? Who is no longer there? Describe your ideal future as if it were perfect in every respect.

Dream Big Dreams

Allow yourself to "dream big dreams." Decide what's right before you decide what's possible. Imagine your future as ideal in every respect and remember: Whatever others have done, within reason, you can probably do as well.

Once you've decided where you're going, the only question you ask is, How do I get there? How do you get from where you are today to where you want to be? And remember, *failure is not an option.*

"Man, alone, has the power to transform his thoughts into physical reality; man, alone, can dream and make his dreams come true."
—Napoleon Hill

CHAPTER 1

The Call of the Open Road

> "The entrepreneur is essentially a visualizer and an actualizer. He can visualize something, and when he visualizes it, he sees exactly how to make it happen."
> —Robert L. Schwartz

Some people are born to stay at home. Others are born to travel. It is not easy to distinguish them from each other, but the things we dream about and plan toward are good indications of our preferences.

When Geoff and I were 16, we were already talking about how quickly we would be on the road when our schooling was finished. One day I found a poem in the school library, one that forever spoke of our aims and ambitions and the attitude we would adopt toward our lives, and later, our traveling. Perhaps we already felt this way, but no one had ever summed it up quite as well as Robert W. Service in "The Lone Trail":

The trails of the world be countless, and most of the trails be tried;
You tread on the heels of the many, till you come where the ways divide;

And one lies safe in the sunlight, and the other is dreary and wan,
But you look aslant at the Lone Trail, and the Lone Trail lures you on.

That was the general idea. The doing of something different, not necessarily for the sake of being different, but because we thought the best way to express our individuality, and the only way we could really enjoy life, was to refuse to be satisfied with the commonplace. But to do that you have to pay a price, of sorts, as the poem goes on to say:

Bid good-bye to sweetheart, bid good-bye to friend,
The Lone Trail, the Lone Trail follow to the end.
Tarry not and fear not, chosen of the true;
Lover of the Lone Trail, the Lone Trail waits for you.

Of course, at 16, we really didn't know what the poet was talking about; but it sounded good and whatever he meant, we agreed with it wholeheartedly.

The Open Road

The call of the road first sounded for us when we were 17; drawing us to the north woods for the summer to fight fires on various forestry crews. When we were 18, the call came from Southern California and Mexico with a craving to taste tequila and see Hollywood. Within a year after leaving high school, we had worn out two cars in the high country around Vancouver, and in British Columbia. In the summer of 1962, the call came from the East, luring us over the Rocky Mountains to the prairies and beyond.

That fall Geoff went off to the university, completing his second semester in May 1963. I was working the graveyard shift at a local sawmill at that time, and was quite content, when he came by my apartment one morning and woke me up. He had come to say good-bye.

"Where are you going?" I asked sleepily.

"To Winnipeg," he replied. "I'm going to work there for the summer."

"Yeah, when are you going to settle down and start becoming a respectable citizen?"

"Next year, for sure."

"Well, you can start being a good citizen right now by letting me go back to sleep. When are you leaving?"

"Now."

"What?!"

"Right now. I'm on my way out of town."

"Humph! You'd better write when you get an address. I might join you later this summer."

"I'll be expecting you. So long."

With a honk and a happy wave, he steered out of the parking lot in his battered Pontiac and turned onto Georgia Street, heading for the trans-Canada highway leading eastward.

Wait for Me

It was the end of July before I caught up with him. I rolled into Winnipeg after a sweep through British Columbia and northern Alberta, down through Saskatchewan to Regina, and then east into Manitoba and the queen city of the province. Winnipeg was 1,600 miles from Vancouver and represented the farthest we'd been from home.

I found Geoff working a construction job at the airport. That night we decided that since we had already come this far, we might as well see Toronto, 1,600 miles farther, before we settled down. A week later, in response to a telegram, Tom Culbert, our best friend from Vancouver, hitchhiked out to join us. Geoff quit his job. We pooled our finances, loaded our few clothes into my 1951 Chevy, and were on our way.

Keep On Going

We had mapped out a route that would take us south and east below the Great Lakes via Chicago and up to Detroit, over the border and on to Toronto, then back. But as the miles rolled past under us, we became infected with the enchanting lure of the open road.

"We might never get another chance," we told ourselves. Our route and destination began changing every day or two. We had little money but found we could get by on one meal a day. This enabled us to pay for gas the rest of the trip.

In the next month we drove through Minneapolis, Chicago, and Cincinnati, down into the southern United States to Miami, Florida, up the Atlantic seaboard through Philadelphia, Washington, D.C., New York, Montreal, and Toronto, and finally above the Great Lakes and back to Winnipeg.

Four weeks later, after a total of 17 states, six provinces, and 12,000 miles, we wearily arrived back in Vancouver, thoroughly glutted with faraway places and more than ready to settle down.

Settling Down

I had worked for the first year after leaving school and concluded that higher education was something much to be desired if I didn't want to sweat for a living for the rest of my days. I enrolled in a series of courses a week later and got a job on the night shift at a sawmill to earn the funds I had neglected to set aside in the previous year. Geoff found a similar job in a plywood mill and decided to concentrate on working for a year; he planned to return to his education the following fall.

We had traveled on a starvation budget, sleeping in the old Chevy when it rained and in parks and fields when it didn't, and eating very little in order to save what money we had for gasoline. Often we drove for two or three days at a stretch, living on cigarettes and nervous energy. We mistook the fatigue resulting from a month of this to be satiation with travel. The thought of giving up a life with a definite purpose and a future to do it again was out of the question. However, we made one concession.

City by the Bay

On Thanksgiving weekend in October 1963, when we had three days free of school and work, we fueled up the Chevy and drove 1,100 miles south to see San Francisco. It took 22 hours of steady motoring to get there, and after a rollicking, happy day and a half, 22 hours to get back. We finally gave up fooling ourselves.

We were hooked on traveling. The complacency that had marked our attitude after our return from the East had turned sour. We spoke about it often and decided that we had exhausted North America as a place to tour. We had loved every minute of it, but now wanted to see something different, unusual, and more challenging. But where?

The Next Destination

The obvious answer was Europe, the old world, the land of our forefathers. But everyone who traveled went to Europe. Many of our friends had already been and returned, and others were preparing to go. We wanted to do something different from them.

No, Europe was not the answer. Later perhaps, but not the first time we set foot off the North American continent. We discussed variations and alternatives for a long time before finally deciding. Africa!

It filled all the requirements. Just to think of it—the Dark Continent. Black Africa, pygmies, Zulus, lions, elephants, savagery, splendor, tribal dances, exotic jungles, and adventure. Our imaginations leaped and bounded with a thousand different images and fantasies.

Of course it never occurred to us to ask why no one else was going to Africa. That was our first mistake. We would eventually find that out at great price.

It seems that all great ventures begin with a dream—a fantasy—and usually require great risks and the willingness to *"go boldly where no one has ever gone before."*

Keep It Confidential

There seemed little point in discussing our decision with anyone. We had learned from past experience that nothing kills an idea so completely as endless discussion, idle chatter, and empty speculation. Besides, no one among our acquaintances knew anything about Africa and so we kept our plan to ourselves. This is a good rule at the beginning of any new venture.

In the following weeks, without more than an occasional chat on a possible route, the thought of Africa became the focal point of our lives. This ambition stood as an exciting pillar of assurance. No matter how bored or disgruntled we became, we could always look inward and chuckle, "It won't be for much longer; we'll soon be on our way to Africa."

What Is Your Personal Mission?

You have been put on this earth to do something wonderful with your life. What is it? What is that one thing you are meant to do, that one great accomplishment that will benefit both yourself and others? One of the most important things you ever do is to ask and answer this question.

You have within you enormous untapped resources of talent and ability—just waiting to be harnessed and challenged toward some great good. You must refuse to "go to your grave with your music still in you."

Be honest with yourself. Don't fall into the trap of selling yourself short and settling for less than you're truly capable of. You were born for greatness. You are here to make a difference with your life in some way.

What do you really want? If you could be or do or have *anything* in life, what would it be? Allow yourself to dream, and then go to work to make your dreams come true.

> "Have you built your castles in the air? Good! That's where they should be built. Now, go to work and build foundations under them."
>
> —Henry David Thoreau

CHAPTER 2

The Preparation

> "When schemes are laid out in advance, it is surprising how often the circumstances will fit in with them."
>
> —WILLIAM OSLER

BECAUSE OF MY SCHOOL and the need to put aside enough money for our trip, we set a tentative departure date for late August 1964. Then, early in the year, Geoff's sister, Pamela, announced her engagement and intention to marry on September 19th. So we decided to attend the wedding and leave for Africa on September 20th.That would give us ample time to pay off an accumulation of small debts and build a healthy bank account.

In April 1964 we brought our good friend, Bob MacDonald, into the planning. Before then we had largely contented ourselves with glorious fantasies and romantic speculation. Bob was a big, robust fellow with an easy laugh and outgoing personality with whom we played football and drank beer on the weekends. He naturally wanted to know what we had done toward preparing for our departure. It dawned on us that we had not done much beyond talking about it during the last three months. He made us realize it was time we got down to business.

Preparing in Earnest

Our preparations went from fanciful chat to serious steps toward the great adventure. We formed a club, the *Bon Vivants*, and made the Dark Continent our first project. We began writing to every travel bureau whose address we could unearth for information on Africa. In the following months we received a mass of information, but unfortunately it consisted largely of brochures on luxury hotels, expensive cruises, guided tours, all-inclusive safaris, and jet and ocean-liner fares—all far beyond our humble means. There were, however, some useful bits of information, and these we gleaned and set aside for future reference.

We began a series of inoculations to withstand the assaults of smallpox, tetanus, yellow fever, cholera, typhus, poliomyelitis, and black water fever. After three months of regular visits to the health center, we felt confident we would never contract another disease. We even took an industrial first aid course from St John's Ambulance to be prepared in case of an accident. This knowledge later proved to be vital.

Show Me the Money

To finance our travels we opened a bank account and started depositing \$5 each per week. In April we increased the sum to \$10 and subsequently raised the amount \$5 a month for the rest of the time we were in North Vancouver. For the three weeks before departure in September, the ante was \$35 a week, which brought the account to almost \$2,000 by the time we left. It seemed like a lot at the time, but once underway the money didn't last long. (In 2003 dollars, this would be about \$10,000.)

I later learned that every new venture ends up costing about twice as much as you thought and taking three times longer. These projections are especially true in starting any new business or introducing any new product or service. They certainly proved true for traveling.

There Is a Party Here Tonight

During July and August the Bon Vivants rented a furnished five-bedroom house in the neighborhood where we'd grown up and gone to school. It became the social center of our group. By mid-July 11 of us were living there. In late August we invited all our friends to a going-away party.

Over 200 people came and the band played until the early hours of the morning. The whole house shook with music and laughter. The sun was high in the sky before the last guests departed.

The restoration of the house to its original—or even better—condition, took a week of hard work and cost over $200. It was cheap at twice the price. Our adult lives had begun.

The Master Skill of Success

Your ability to set goals and make plans for their accomplishment is the "master skill" of success. This ability, developed through practice, will do more to assure your eventual success than anything else you ever learn.

The 10/90 rule says that, "The first 10 percent of time you spend planning and organizing will often account for 90 percent of the value of the entire process."

Here is a powerful but simple method I've learned for setting and achieving goals:

1. *Decide exactly what you want.* Clarity is the starting point of great success.
2. *Write it down in detail and set a deadline.* Set subdeadlines if necessary.
3. *Target the additional knowledge, skills, and abilities you will need to achieve your goal*—and how you will acquire them.

4. *Determine the obstacles and difficulties you will have to overcome to reach your goal,* and organize them in order of size and importance.
5. *Identify the people, groups, and organizations whose help you will require,* and decide what you will have to do for them to earn their assistance.
6. *Make a detailed plan, broken down by activity and organized by priority and sequence.* What is most important? What must be done first? What must be done before something else is done?
7. *Take action on your plan immediately.* Do something every day to move toward your goal. Get going and keep going.

At each stage of your life, whenever you are confronted with the need to make new choices and set new goals, sit down and think them through using these seven steps. Always think on paper and be willing to revise your plans when you get new information. Keep working on your plans until they are complete. Then, execute them boldly.

> "Our goals can only be reached through a vehicle of a plan, in which we must fervently believe, and upon which we must vigorously act. There is no other route to success."
> —Stephen A. Brennen

SECTION II

Starting Out—Just Do It!

> "Create a definite plan for carrying out your desire and begin at once, whether you are ready or not, to put your plan into action."
>
> —NAPOLEON HILL

"A JOURNEY OF A THOUSAND LEAGUES begins with a single step," wrote Confucius. A thousand dreams die unborn every day because the dreamer lacks the courage to take the first step, in faith, with no guarantees of success.

The great difference between high achievement and failure in life is contained in your willingness to launch in the direction of your goal, even when your information is still incomplete.

There are no guarantees in life, and we know that if every question must be answered, if every obstacle must first be overcome—then nothing will ever get done.

Decide what you want, write it down, make a plan, and then—take action. "*Leap and the net will appear!*"

"Our grand business is not to see what lies dimly at a distance but to do what lies clearly at hand."
—Thomas Carlyle

CHAPTER 3

The First Step: Vancouver to Montreal

> "Act as if it were impossible to fail, and it shall be."
> —Dorothea Brande

On a Sunday evening at 10 p.m., three weeks after the party, in a cold drizzling rain, we bid our families and friends our last good-byes, severing the final ties with our youth and 20 years of life. I turned the old 1948 Chevy eastward, and we left Vancouver behind us in the night. It was September 20, 1964.

I learned later that every successful enterprise, great or small, begins with a leap of faith, a driving into the dark—the unknown. Nature is kind to us; she never lets us see too far ahead. If we really knew all the difficulties, disappointments, temporary failures, and heartaches we would experience, most of us would not start out at all. This applies to new businesses, careers, marriage, having children—and almost every other human endeavor.

Off to See the World

That was the beginning. It was rather anticlimactic after a year of planning and looking forward to the big moment. For a long time we were understandably silent, each wrapped up in his own thoughts as we drove into the night. We were off to see the world.

We drove all night, stopping for gas or coffee occasionally (the Chevy burned a quart of oil every 50 miles), but more or less driving steadily north, then east across the Rocky Mountains. The magnificent unspoiled beauty of Rodgers Pass was behind us the next morning when the sun rose through the clouds over Banff, Alberta, where we stopped for breakfast. We arrived in Calgary early in the afternoon and checked into the YMCA for the night.

On our way across the country, we stopped in Regina and stayed with friends for two days. We checked into a motel in Winnipeg for two more nights, and then turned south into the States toward the Great Lakes. The weather was bad—nothing but howling winds and icy rains most of the way.

Sudden Emergency

The tank-like Chevy we had bought for the trip was riding very low on its springs and using an alarming quantity of gas and oil, but by and large the car held together quite well. We only had one emergency, and that was on our way to Chicago through Iowa. The brakes failed altogether.

Bob first discovered this problem as we drove about 50 miles an hour in the rain, late at night, and on a curve. He yelped, "The brakes are gone!"

"Pump them up! Pump them up!" we shouted.

"I've been pumping them for the last hour! There's nothing left to pump!"

He geared down to second and shut off the engine, bringing the car to a jerky halt a quarter of a mile later. The brake cylinder was dry and we were 85 miles from the next large town. The highway was dark and empty and the cold wind howled across the silent cornfields on both sides.

Pressing On

Since there was no traffic on the road, we decided to drive the car carefully until we found an open service station where we could buy some brake fluid. It was 11:30 at night when I got behind the wheel.

It seemed like the entire state was asleep. Town after quiet town slipped past the rain-spattered Chevy as we crept along, peering down the darkened side streets looking for the lights of a service station. Finally, about two hours later, we came to the outskirts of Dubuque, a large town with considerable traffic, even at that hour.

After helplessly coasting through two red lights with no garage in sight, we became more cautious, driving in first gear, and approaching intersections as furtively as thieves.

Then, coming down a slight grade, we arrived at a busy cross street. A steady stream of traffic passed ahead of us, and a red light faced us. The Chevy was already in first gear with the engine cut, but we could see we wouldn't stop in time to avoid coasting right into the traffic.

When in Doubt, Improvise

At just about the same moment we all had the same idea and leaped out of all four doors into the street. Throwing every bit of weight we could muster, feet skidding along the wet pavement, we gradually brought the beast to a halt. Six feet in front of us an express bus roared through the intersection, whipping us with windy spray. Delighted at our newfound *brakes*, we congratulated each other and climbed back inside.

Twice more this course of action became necessary before we found an all-night service station and refilled the thirsty brake cylinder. From the looks on the faces of passing motorists, we deduced that this sort of thing wasn't done too often in Dubuque, Iowa. But we had no further difficulties with the vehicle after that.

Keep On Going

For the next two days we drove steadily, not stopping to sleep at all. After half a day in Chicago we drove out and followed Lake Michigan through Gary, Indiana, and on up the expressway to Detroit. There we crossed back into Canada, and continued through Windsor to Toronto and another night at the YMCA. The following evening we rumbled into Montreal, 3,200 miles from Vancouver, and the end of the first leg of our long trip to Africa.

Before starting this adventure we had made several long trips without sleeping, driving nonstop to save time. Sometimes we traded off when one of us began falling asleep. This experience, to which we gave little thought at the time, of driving for two or three days without sleep even when we were so tired we began to hallucinate would serve us well in the months ahead. It may have saved our lives.

Right on Target

We had made Montreal our first objective, to be accomplished within ten days and with a minimum of expense. It took us nine days and cost just $200 for everything, including gasoline and oil (and brake fluid!), food, motels and YMCAs, and beer. The weather was bad but our spirits were high and we rolled into Montreal singing, all four of us in the front seat. It was a grand beginning.

From Montreal our next objective was to get to London, England—the cheapest way possible. For three days we tramped the waterfront seeking a Europe-bound ship needing crewmembers. However, with winter in the air, there were few ships in the inland port, and they had no vacancies for unskilled seamen. It soon became obvious we weren't going to get a job that would save us the cost of the fare.

After discussing it for awhile, we agreed that not only was it too late in the year to find a job on a boat, it was also too late to start for Africa, even if we did manage to get to Europe. We decided to work somewhere for the winter and set off in the spring. The question was, where?

The First Real Lessons

For you to accomplish any big goal you will have to learn certain lessons and gain new knowledge and experience. You begin to learn at an accelerated rate the moment you launch a new venture.

We only learn when it costs us money or emotion, or both. There seems to be no other way. We have to pay for anything worthwhile. And we never get our lessons on the cheap.

The key to maximizing the value that an experience holds for you is to look into any setback or obstacle for the valuable lesson or benefit it contains. Why has this happened? What can you learn that will make you smarter next time? If you look for the good—the valuable lesson—you always seem to find something.

Here is a great mental exercise to help you take and keep full control over your mind and emotions. No matter what goes wrong, focus on the future rather than the past. Think about what you are trying to accomplish and where you want to go. Learn from the past and then let it go.

> "Leap, and the net will appear."
> —Robin Crow

To improve your ability to think and react effectively, think about the solution rather than the problem. Consider what concrete action you can take right now rather than what happened or who is to blame. Keep asking, What's the solution? What's the next step? What do we do now?

CHAPTER 4

The First Crisis

> "How many a man has thrown up his hands at a time when a little more effort, a little more patience, would have achieved success?"
> —ELBERT HUBBARD

OUR INABLILITY TO FIND JOBS in Montreal in order to earn money to work our way to Europe as we had planned triggered the first crisis on our trip. One of the guys, who had only come along for the adventure, decided to quit and hitchhike home. The other two—my fellow Bon Vivants Geoff and Bob—decided to stop looking for jobs on a ship and instead used their limited funds to purchase passage on a freighter headed for England.

I was upset with this decision, especially since they had obviously discussed and decided upon it separate from me. We argued and I tried to talk them out of it. I told them *quitting is a habit.* If they quit now, they would always quit each time they met resistance and disappointment. They would establish a pattern for failure rather than one for success. It was a matter of principle that we not give up at the first sign of resistance to our plans.

Parting of the Ways

But their minds were made up. They were impatient to get to Europe and not interested in finding another way. We went to the bank, withdrew all the money we had so carefully accumulated over the previous year and split it three ways. They used half their money to book passage on a freighter that took a small number of paying passengers. They left the next day. Our partnership was officially dissolved, just two weeks after starting out.

I later learned that *partnerships are the worst of all forms of business relationships.* They start off with high hopes and usually end with dashed expectations, ruined friendships, and mutual recriminations. One of the partners is always more dedicated and harder working, while the others contribute less and less yet demand an equal share of profits.

Reevaluating the Situation

I decided it was too late in the year to go to Africa and resolved to stay in Montreal for the winter. I got a job as a construction laborer in an office high-rise, where I carryed materials for the carpenters and joiners all day. I later worked in a factory on a production line, screwing nuts onto bolts hour after hour.

Because of my limited means and savings, I rented a tiny one-room apartment with a foldout bed and small kitchen. The temperature that winter fell to 35 degrees below zero, and life seemed very bleak indeed.

Here I was, 20 years old, 3,200 miles from my family, with no intention of going back home. I had failed in high school, fooling around and working as a dishwasher in a small hotel rather than studying. I was uneducated, unskilled, and regularly unemployed. And I wanted to go to Africa. This was not a great start in life.

My Great Revelation

I still remember that fateful night, sitting alone at my little kitchen table, with the cold winter wind howling outside. It suddenly dawned on me that *everything and anything I ever accomplished in life was up to me. I was completely responsible.* No one was ever going to do anything for me. If I did not take charge of my life and make changes, nothing was ever going to change. I would remain an underpaid laborer, pinching pennies and worrying about money the rest of my life.

It was an incredible revelation! I determined right then and there that my future would be different from my past. I wrote out a series of goals for myself and resolved to take action on them. That realization that night was the turning point in my life.

The next day I bought a book and began to study French to prepare for my travels in France and Africa. I started taking karate lessons three times per week. I read every book I could get on subjects that interested me. I began my lifelong commitment to personal development and success. I was responsible.

Back On the Road Again

Five months later, at the end of February, I packed all my belongings in an old trunk and shipped them to Halifax, the biggest port on the Atlantic coast. I then spent several chilly days on the road hitchhiking my way across the Maritime Provinces to Halifax and once more checked into the local YMCA.

My goal was to get a job on a ship, work my way to England, rejoin my friends, and set off once more for Africa. I got up early that cold winter morning and began scouring the waterfront, visiting every ship from one end of the harbor to the other and asking if they needed a crewman for the crossing to England.

By the end of the day, after hours of plodding from dock to dock, I had gone to each ship on the waterfront and been turned down every time. There was not a single ship going to England that needed anyone for the voyage. Tired and dejected, I trudged up the long hill back to the warmth of the YMCA, wondering what I would do now.

A Lucky Break

Then something remarkable happened. Just as I reached the front of the YMCA, I turned and looked back one last time toward the waterfront. From that vantage point, I saw two ships load cargo at a dock somewhat apart from the others in the harbor. I hadn't seen them before; they were the only two ships I hadn't visited to look for a job.

It was already late in the afternoon and I was tired and hungry. I stood on the sidewalk and looked longingly at the welcoming warmth and beckoning comfort of the YMCA. Then I forced myself to turn away and trudge down the long hill to the two ships and give it one more try.

The first ship was going down the east coast of the U.S., but the second one—the Norwegian freighter Nordpohl—was going to Manchester, England, and yes, they had an opening for a galley boy. The job was mine if I could be on board and ready to depart by 8 P.M, just two hours away!

I was ecstatic! I had a job. My last shot had paid off. My goal and dream of working my way across the Atlantic on a ship, was realized. Could I be ready to depart in two hours? You bet.

The Persistence Test

I learned a vital and *life-changing* lesson from this experience: *your greatest success, breakthrough, or lucky break often comes one step beyond where you are ready to quit.* It is almost as though nature places a final "persistence test" in your path just to see how badly you want it. As the poem says:

And you never can tell how close you are,
It may be near when it seems so far.
So stick to the fight when you're hardest hit,
It's when things seem worst that you must not quit.

I hurried down to the train depot to retrieve my trunk, went back to the YMCA to collect my things, and at 8 P.M.—right on schedule—was on board the Nordpohl as it cast its lines and headed out into the Atlantic. I stood on the bow of the ship as the city of Halifax disappeared into the night. I was off to see the world!

Testing Time

Life is a continuous succession of problems, large and small. Like the waves of the ocean, they never stop coming. The only thing you can control with problems is how you respond to them. Are you positive or negative, constructive or destructive? Do you treat them as stumbling blocks or stepping stones?

Most people quit at the first crisis. They collapse, like tents with the center poles removed. They give up and retreat back to their comfort zones where there are low levels of challenge and accomplishment. This tendency to quit becomes a conditioned response to trouble and a difficult habit to break.

> "Never give up then, for that is just the time that the tide will turn."
> —Harriet Beecher Stowe

But this is not for you. You should view every problem, setback, or crisis as a "test" sent to teach you something you need to know to be more successful in the future. You should look within it for the valuable lesson it contains. It is always there.

Resolve *in advance* that no matter what happens, you will never give up. You will bounce rather than break. You will keep on keeping on until you eventually succeed.

CHAPTER 5

Setting Off Once More

> "Life is a series of steps. Things are done gradually. Once in a while there is a giant step, but most of the time we are taking small, seemingly insignificant steps on the stairway of life."
>
> —Ralph Ransom

The Atlantic crossing took six weeks, including a stop to take on cargo in St. John, New Brunswick. For most of the five weeks at sea we were in a storm of hundred-foot swells and sweeping, icy rains, and worked nonstop to feed the crew and swab the galley. The crew was a rough mixture of multiple nationalities and languages and not your typical college graduates. The time at sea with these men was a great introduction to what I was to experience later on my journey.

At the end of March 1965 I signed off in Manchester, got my pay, collected my belongings, and took a train up to Coventry in the English Midlands to once more join up with Geoff and Bob. It had been a long, cold winter for me in Montreal after we decided to go our separate ways.

Quitting Becomes a Habit

My friends had taken a ship to Amsterdam in the first week of October and arrived in England four weeks later. They had then set off for Africa by themselves, taking the ferry from Dover to Calais and trying to hitchhike across France. But French drivers don't stop for hitchhikers. After several hours of standing by the side of the road waving their thumbs they quit again—just as I had predicted some months ago in Montreal.

Like most people they didn't know that *quitting is an insidious habit. It grows so slowly that one is unaware of its enticements until it is deeply ingrained and it cuts off all hope of success and great achievement.*

Discouraged, they took the ferry back to England and made their way up to Coventry to visit friends of Geoff's family. They ended up staying there through the winter working as lifeguards at the public swimming pool.

Spring, Glorious Spring

Now spring was in the air. The country was lovely and green, as the travel posters show, and early flowers brightened the tiny thatched-cottage villages along the railway route. There was a magic sparkle in the air that one could feel dancing along the skin, bringing with it restlessness and an urge to be out doing things. As the train rumbled across the English countryside toward Coventry, I thought how strange it was that we would plan and anticipate for over a year, set off boldly, and then do almost nothing for six months.

I suppose the launch had been the important thing—that first step of cutting loose, casting off, and leaving familiar ways far behind. Many friends and acquaintances from school and work in Vancouver had started getting married and settling into careers. A pattern of day-to-day living had begun to form; the grip of adulthood and maturity was tightening.

But we had broken the pattern. We were like colts shaking off the traces, running free, and kicking up our heels, secure in knowing that when we tired of the open pasture we could always return to the security and stability of the lives we left behind.

It didn't matter if we stopped somewhere for the winter; we were free and unfettered by responsibility and the necessity to account for our present and future. Surely in a year or two we would have to return like prodigal sons and earn our places in our well-ordered society. But we couldn't be satisfied with one place until we'd grown tired of looking at the others; that wouldn't be for a long time.

Begin with no Guarantees

I learned later that the most important thing to do with a new goal is to begin with no guarantee of success. Once you start off toward an unknown destination, everything will change anyway. New avenues and opportunities open up for you—openings you could not have seen had you not been in forward motion. The best rule is always: Leap and the net will appear.

Once the train arrived in Coventry, I got a taxi that took me to the Stoke Hill Guild House late that afternoon. I soon found my friends' narrow, cement-floored room. It was locked and my friends were nowhere on the grounds among the other working people coming from jobs in the mills and factories of Coventry. So I climbed in the window and made myself comfortable. I drifted peacefully off to sleep as the sun went down. It had been a long trip.

Three hours later, Bob and Geoff crashed in singing and startled me awake with their drunken rendition of "She loves you, yeah, yeah, yeah." Bob was halfway into bed with his cute girlfriend when he saw me sitting there blinking at the sudden light and noise. His face broke into a mile-wide grin and we embraced with a joyous whoop. Geoff was right behind him and in a bubbling outburst we laughed, asked questions, and tried to catch up on five months. It was like old home week.

Catching Up

After we had calmed down a bit I told them about my life at sea and the bully on the ship who had turned out not to be so tough after all. Bob got out his suitcase and showed me his picture from the newspaper after he had won the third-place ribbon in the "Mr. Coventry" bodybuilding contest that January. Suddenly there came a harsh rap on the door.

It was a pair of English Bobbies investigating a report that an Austin van had smashed through a barrier in a nearby automatic parking lot. The license number was suspiciously identical to that of the van driven by Geoff and Bob. It turned out they hadn't had a shilling for the automatic gate release and in their inebriated state had said, "What the hell!" and driven right through it. After long arguments, denials, and promises to pay in the morning the police departed and we all had a good laugh.

Planning and discussion were wisely put off until morning when clearer heads would prevail.

Saying Goodbyes

Once again we were on our way to Africa. The boys had many goodbyes to make after five months in Coventry and we had a lot of beers together to catch up on. But three days later, everything was wrapped up, the van was sold, and we caught the morning train for London. Most of our luggage, including the big trunk I had brought from Montreal, was sent to store with my aunt in Potter's Bar, a hamlet north of London.

We arrived at Easton Station at noon and began the 20-minute walk to Russell Square, an area known for its inexpensive bed and breakfast hotels. We took turns lugging the two overstuffed suitcases and inquired until we found a hotel with vacancy for three and a landlady with some imagination with regard to price. After a little haggling she agreed to give us a reduction if one of us would sleep on the floor in the room with one double bed. That was no hardship for three stout lads on their way to Africa.

Reevaluating and Regrouping

Your ability to think and apply your mind to your situation is the greatest power you have. The more often you stop the clock to assess and reassess your situation when it is constantly changing and your knowledge is incomplete, the better decisions you will make.

Whenever you experience resistance or temporary failure, ask yourself, What are my assumptions? What am I assuming to be true that might not be at all? How can I test these assumptions? What changes will I have to make if they are wrong?

Try to keep your ego out of it. Focus on what rather than who is right. Be prepared to admit you could be dead wrong about your current course of action. The person who discovers he or she is on the wrong road and turns back quickly is the one who makes the most progress.

> "It's not easy but you have to be willing to make mistakes. And the earlier you make those mistakes, the better."
>
> —Jane Cahill Pfeiffer

CHAPTER 6

Getting Down to Business

> "An intelligent plan is the first step to success. The man who plans knows where he is going, knows what progress he is making, and has a pretty good idea when he will arrive."
> —Basil S. Walsh

We had left the actual planning of a route and mode of transportation to and through Africa until we were a little closer to the objective. One lesson in our previous traveling had repeated itself time and time again: *Be clear about the goal but be flexible about the process of achieving it.* Sure, you must set reasonable goals as ultimate aims and work toward achieving those goals, but you shouldn't decide on the exact intermediate steps. *Each step toward an objective modifies and influences the following steps.* The greater the number of unknowns in the situation, the more flexibility you need to deal with things that arise. We had avoided making specific plans since we were almost totally ignorant of the road ahead.

Keep an Open Mind

I later learned that the willingness to continually reevaluate plans, especially when you experience resistance, disappointment, or temporary failure, can be critical to long-term success. The ability to consider the possibility that you could be wrong or misinformed is the mark of a superior mind.

This attitude of accepting change and adapting to difficulties gave us a certain resilience and buoyancy that made it almost impossible for us to become downhearted or discouraged at the unexpected twists and turns of fate. We would simply bounce back and try something new.

Our first objective had been to leave Vancouver with as much money as possible. The second had been to cross Canada to Montreal and spend as little money as possible. The third had been to reach London with a minimum of expense. Our fourth was to reach the crown colony of Gibraltar on the doorstep of the African continent. There we would decide on our fifth objective.

Our One-Page Map

The next day we sat down in a small teashop with an atlas. It contained a one-page map of Africa that included Europe as well. We used this single page to work out a tentative route for our journey. We would travel through France and Spain to Gibraltar, sail across the straits to Morocco, traverse the Atlas Mountains into the Sahara, and cross the desert to Senegal.

From there we would follow the hump of Africa around and into Lagos, Nigeria, the modern capital of British influence in West Africa. Once in Lagos we could decide whether to head directly south or through central Africa and then south through Kenya and Tanzania. Our ultimate goal was Johannesburg, South Africa. It seemed quite straightforward.

The Lure of Self-Delusion

We knew the decision would be dictated by conditions beyond our control; however, we had no idea how much what we had innocently planned would differ from the reality.

We made the dreadful error of superimposing our experiences in North America onto our travel plans in Africa. We assumed "roads were roads" and the lines on the little map were as drivable as roads in North America. We thought we could travel anywhere without hindrance. I later learned that *unexamined assumptions lie at the root of most problems in life.*

Once our route was planned we discussed what mode of conveyance we would use. There were several methods available. Bob had found that the cheapest way to travel from London to Johannesburg was by plane—it would cost just $300 each, which was all we had. We considered flying to South Africa and returning to Europe by land via Cairo, but disregarded it as too expensive. We rejected the idea of going by ship for the same reason. We therefore decided we would travel from London to Johannesburg by land—all the way.

Unexamined Assumptions

Since our little map clearly showed roads through Africa it was evident that many people had already driven across the continent. We reasoned—falsely—that there couldn't be much challenge in following the footsteps of countless others. However our limited funds made a vehicle too expensive. Besides, we wanted to make the trip in a way that would bring us some fame and glory. What about bicycles?

Bicycles, we reasoned, were cheap to buy, repair, and operate. Our limited speed and the necessity to live off the land would enable us to gain a greater understanding of the countries we passed through. An added benefit was that we would become physically hardened by pedaling all day and sleeping out each night. And we'd never heard of anyone making such a trip on a bicycle. There was no way of telling how much acclaim we could receive. We might even set a record or win a prize. We all agreed bicycles were the answer.

Taking Action Immediately

There were two places we could buy bicycles—either in London, or in Gibraltar after hitchhiking across France and Spain. The main argument for Gibraltar was that Africa was our objective and we should get there with a minimum of delay. However, we needed time to train for the trip across Africa. We therefore decided, with our limited knowledge, we would become accustomed to traveling on bicycles in the civilized countries of France and Spain and set out to buy them in London that very day.

This was another decision that probably saved us from our own innocence and ignorance. We were forced to use our wits by our limited resources. Just as in starting a new business, *bootstrapping your way up on your profits from sales is usually better than starting with too much money.* Starting with limited means forces you to fall back on your natural intelligence and ingenuity when you experience the inevitable disappointments that accompany attempts to do anything new or different. As a result, you quickly develop the resilience and tenacity necessary to succeed later. Buying bicycles did this for us.

The Common Pool

When we arrived in London our combined savings totaled just over $1,000. We pooled the entire amount into what we called "the company." Every purchase and expense from then on was paid out of this cash pool. This common objective caused us to subordinate personal desires and pettiness to the common good. We agreed to be "one for all, and all for one!"

Everything we bought or did was agreed upon unanimously. Anything any of us had we all had, right down to underwear and razor blades. We would have many heated discussions and disagreements in the days and miles ahead, but personal ownership never entered into them. After a while we no longer talked in terms of "I" and "me," but rather "we" and "the Bon Vivants."

We bought three used bicycles, three rucksacks, a kettle, a tiny stove, a frying pan, some cutlery, a few dishes, and a little brown teapot. We chose a few clothes from each of our belongings that fit us all: a pair each of tennis shoes and jeans, socks, T-shirts, underwear, and three warm sweaters. A shaving kit, three towels, three books, and a radio completed the outfit. Dressed in woolen caps and high-collared plastic rain jackets, we felt well attired for our crossing of Europe. So we divided the load evenly, tied it onto our bicycles, and pedaled out of London towards Potter's Bar to visit my aunt.

Ready to Go

Geoff was then 20 years old and weighed a solid 180 pounds. Bob was a little taller and heavier with a solid 184 pounds, spread over his raw-boned frame. I was the oldest and heaviest at 21 and 185 pounds. We should have known better than to choose bicycles. But in those days, we were hopelessly optimistic.

We were bursting with energy and eagerness, puffed up with ambition and high ideal, and strong and joyous at being at last on our way to Africa, the ultimate in high adventure. In those first carefree days there was nowhere we couldn't go and nothing we couldn't do. We were indomitable supermen, world-beaters on our way to Africa.

Potter's Bar

We had sent the things we couldn't take with us to the rail depot in Potter's Bar where my Aunt Barbara lived. We were hoping she would have a place to store them and perhaps somewhere we could sleep the night. We were in luck on both accounts. Although she was unsure at first which of us three strapping lads was her nephew since she had not seen me since I was 13, she readily threw open her little garage to us and offered us a place to sleep. After bringing the trunk and suitcases from the depot and storing them away, we sat down to explain our plans and intentions to "conquer Africa." We were tired from our 20-mile ride from London but talked until midnight before going to bed in her little guest room.

The next morning we promised faithfully to return no later than October for a longer visit, then waved good-bye and rode toward Dover and France.

Flexibility Is the Key

The most important quality you can develop to assure great success in times of change and turbulence is flexibility.

Be open to new information. Be willing to accept feedback and self-correct. Admit that you could be wrong and that there may be a better way.

> "Many a one has succeeded only because he has failed after repeated efforts. If he had never met defeat, he would never have known any great victory."
> —Orison Swett Marden

A famous military axiom says, "No strategy survives first contact with the enemy."

No plan, no matter how detailed, survives first contact with reality. Your job is to be clear about your goal, and flexible about the process of attaining it.

SECTION III

The Real Journey Begins at Last

> "To win without risk is to triumph without glory."
> —PIERRE CORNEILLE

SHAKESPEARE WROTE, "What's past is merely prelude." What we know for sure, at each stage of our lives, is that what's coming is more important than what has gone before.

Author Laurence Durrell once wrote, "I do not write for people who have never asked themselves, 'When does real life begin?'"

This life is not a rehearsal for something else. Successful, happy people live intensely in the moment, the "now" of life and reality. They have learned to combine a long-term vision with a short-term focus. They are dreamers with their feet firmly planted in the reality of the current situation.

To achieve something you've never achieved before, you must do something you've never done before. You must become someone you've never been before. As Goethe said, "To have more, we must first be more."

The great majority of people want their success and happiness on the cheap without paying full price for it in advance as nature demands. This continual striving after something for nothing—of achievement without expense—leads to frustration, failure, and impoverishment of spirit.

The good news is that nature is exceedingly generous. If you are willing to pay the price and put something in before you get something out, you will eventually enjoy rewards out of all proportion to your efforts.

You will also become a person of character, competence, pride, and self-respect. You'll become the kind of person you always dreamed of being, one others look up to and admire.

"If we did all the things we are capable of doing, we would literally astound ourselves."
—Thomas Edison

CHAPTER 7

Setting Out

> "The power which resides in man is new in nature, and none but he knows what that is which he can do, nor does he know until he has tried."
>
> —Ralph Waldo Emerson

The distance by land by the shortest route from London to Gibraltar is approximately 1,600 miles. Allowing for our inexperience with traveling long distances by bicycle, we optimistically reckoned we could average 80 miles a day. That would put us in Gibraltar by the end of April. However, there were several variables we failed to take into consideration—the first and worst being the hills located directly in our line of travel.

We covered 30 miles on the first day of that terrible trip to Gibraltar, and collapsed in an irrigation ditch south of London, exhausted and famished, just before sundown. Our legs were rubbery with fatigue and we smelled of sweat and exhaust fumes, our hair was dried like straw, and our faces were streaked with dirt and grime. The day had been a battle from the first flat tire, but we had won, and surely tomorrow would be a good deal easier.

Cautiously, worried about being arrested for trespassing, we built a lean-to with our groundsheet and camouflaged it with twigs and grass; we hid our bicycles in the bushes nearby.

We managed to work an element of drama into everything we did and proceeded as though there was a plot afoot to thwart our adventure. We assumed people would look at us when we went into stores to buy food and say under their breaths to their friends, "I wonder where those young men with the air of mystery are going?"

It is more likely they said something like, "Bums! Every year more and more bums on the road. What's the country coming to?"

After a supper of bread and cheese, followed by Geoff's tea made over a smoky fire, we sat wearily for a few minutes before crawling into our sleeping bags and going to sleep. Tomorrow would surely be better.

Back On the Road

We woke the next morning feeling stiff, cold, dirty, and hungry. It took two hours of pedaling to work the pain out of our thighs and shoulders. Geoff said something like, "Muscle ache means muscle development" to try to encourage us. Bob and I refused to speak to him for the next ten miles.

And the hunger! Until you've sweated yourself sick with pain and lack of nourishment on a bicycle, you don't know what hunger is. We stopped in the evenings trembling with weakness and woke in the mornings from the knife twisted into our empty bellies. Once we stopped at a cafe for breakfast and ate the entire menu twice. After that we couldn't trust ourselves in places selling hot food and were forced to buy supplies for supper and breakfast at small grocery stores. The all-consuming hunger was a constant companion. It was another factor we had not taken into consideration when we chose bicycles.

Dover to Calais

Three days after saying good-bye to Aunt Barbara we rode into Dover and along the White Cliffs to the ferry terminal. During the crossing to Calais we thumbed through our French-English dictionary, looking up and writing down words we thought we would need. We would soon need lots of them.

It wasn't long before we learned that the travel book tenet "everyone speaks English" was wrong. Not even the members of the crew on the ferry spoke any English. We rode from the extreme north to the far south of France and never met a single French person who spoke English. I guess they hadn't read the same travel books.

We realized a working knowledge of French was not just an asset; it was a necessity. Fortunately I had begun studying French in earnest back in Montreal in October. My understanding and eventual fluency in the language as we drove deeper into Africa proved to be a valuable asset. It probably saved our lives later on, but I'm getting ahead of myself.

You Can Learn What You Need to Learn

Later in life, I learned the biggest mental block to learning a new language or acquiring a new skill is the fear of looking or sounding foolish during the time between unfamiliarity and mastery. This rule has served me all my life: *Whatever is worth doing well is worth doing poorly at first; it's often worth doing poorly several times.*

The power is always on the side of the person with superior knowledge and skills. The law of requisite variety says that, "In any group of people, the individual having the highest integrated level of knowledge and skill will tend to rise to dominate and lead all other individuals in that group." Your job is to become that person.

The good news is that *you can learn anything you need to learn to achieve any goal you set for yourself.* Your personal boundaries are determined more by inner limitations than outer circumstances. The only real limits on your potential are the ones you impose on yourself by your own thinking. When you change your thinking, you change your life.

New Situations Require New Attitudes

Frustrated expectations lie at the root of most unhappiness. To survive and thrive in new situations you must keep your mind open and always be willing to question your expectations. Are they realistic and based on new information?

The good news is that you are extremely adaptable to change and circumstance. You can learn to cope with any situation if you decide to.

One of the most helpful exercises you can do is to separate "facts" from "problems." A fact is just like the weather. It cannot be changed. You don't waste a minute of energy or emotion railing against "facts." Instead you accept and adjust to them, and get on with your life.

A problem is different from a fact. It is a situation you can do something about. It is amenable to a solution.

The key to happiness, success, and personal effectiveness is for you to focus on the *solutions* to the problems in your life. Think about the future and what you want and where you are going. Success comes from focusing on those things you can do something about.

And remember, you can learn anything necessary to achieve any goal you set for yourself, even if it's getting across France and Spain to Gibraltar.

> "Nobody succeeds beyond his or her wildest expectations unless he or she begins with some wild expectations."
> —Ralph Charell

CHAPTER 8

Our Tour de France

> "The most important thing in life is not the triumph but the struggle. The essential thing is not to have conquered but to have fought well."
> —Baron Pierre de Coubertin

April in France can be lovely, I am sure. Through the sweat and rain of those arduous days, I glimpsed many indications of a wonderful potential. The promise of summer was everywhere in the rolling green hills, early buttercups along the grassy shoulders, and swallows singing and flying in from the south. However, the gusting winds and drenching rains that swept across the open road and sent piercing chills through our thin jeans and down our uncovered necks were a reminder that winter was not long past and summer was not yet here.

The Roads All Run Uphill

The roads in France don't follow the lay of the land. The hills are not high and it was obviously more practical to build roads straight from town to town and over hills and plains with few curves to offset their directness. A motorist in northern France can thus make good time between towns and over long distances. And the roads are built for motorists.

On a bicycle it is a different bucket of sweat. The law of averages says that for every amount of uphill there must be an equal and opposite amount of downhill, but somehow it didn't seem to work out that way on the roads we traveled. We should have recovered the time we lost on the ascent on the descent. But more often than not, the downhill rides were into the wind; if the descent was gradual, it would be as difficult pedaling as it was on a level stretch.

I learned that in any new venture, the roads are all uphill, and the wind is always in your face. Murphy's Laws apply with a vengeance: *Anything that can go wrong will go wrong. Of all the things that can go wrong, the worst possible thing will go wrong at the worst possible time and cost the greatest amount of money.* Murphy was our constant companion.

Keep On Going

As we approached the uphill stretches (and there were so many), we'd pedal furiously in third gear, then second, and then first. The thrusts came slower and slower, the muscles along the tops of our thighs burned, and our breaths came in painful gasps. Our forward momentum would cease and the bikes would come to a halt. We would then jump off and push the bikes the rest of the way up the hill, finally arriving at the top pouring with sweat.

We were often strung out over a mile and used the hilltops as places to stop until the third man caught up. Then we'd remount and attack the next hill. We rode hour after hour, doggedly trying to make a reasonable average of kilometers covered for each day.

We were exhausted each night and slept long and soundly in forests and fields along the road despite the rain and discomfort. Around 10 A.M. we would break camp and get back on our bicycles, stiff but rested, and always in good spirits. This refreshed feeling and the good spirits would last until the third hill, after which it once more became determined slogging and unending miles of hard work. The stiffness abated by noon, only to come seeping back shortly after and stay with us for the duration of the day's ride.

The Battle Against the Road

The wet, windswept road became an enemy to be conquered. The diminishing distances between us and the towns ahead became our measures of victory and achievement. We had by now realized that bicycles were not the ideal solution to our transportation problems, but we had named our poison and neither the road nor the bicycles were going to defeat us. We were the Bon Vivants; we were undefeatable and going to Africa.

If those cold, windy, pain-wracked days were some of the worst of our lives, they were also some of the best. When we stopped in the late afternoon to camp, usually in a small clump of trees not far off the road, the first thing we did was to build a fire. The second was to open the bottle of wine purchased in the last town. The fire warmed our faces and dried our clothes and the wine took care of the rest.

By the time supper was cooked, the magic warmth of the wine tingled its happy way into our tired brains and back down again, flowing through our bodies like music and erasing the day in its soothing passage. With dinner eaten and the fire crackling and dancing, a joyous feeling and peaceful content settled over our camp. We laughed, loafed, and dreamed and felt truly sorry for anyone who could never feel as wonderfully happy and genuinely fulfilled as we were—out on the open road and on our way to Africa.

There is often a fine line between the best of times and the worst of times, between pleasure and pain, joy and sorrow. As the author G.K.

Chesterton once wrote, "An adventure is merely an inconvenience, rightly considered." Of course it often takes a lot of imagination to see difficult situation as an adventure, but that's what imagination is for.

Making a Virtue of Necessity

We couldn't afford to stay in hotels and after a few nights of camping had no interest in being anywhere but in the element we had chosen—cool crisp nights, happy hours, laughter unto tears, and unspeakable joy. Never had we been so cheerful and easy to laugh, eaten so well and enjoyed it so much, and had nights so restful and appreciated. The treasured camping in the evenings almost made us forget the conditions of the day.

But then came the mornings, breakfast, and another day of stinging sweat and aching backs. The intensity of the pleasure of the wine-soaked evenings by the little fires was made possible only by the grueling labor and pain of the long days that preceded them.

Rough and Ready Looking

We must have looked a bit unusual as we bicycled our way along roads, across farm country, and through tiny villages with our faces unshaven and machetes jutting out of our bulging rucksacks. People often came to their windows and doors to follow us silently with their eyes until we were far down the road.

When we stopped to buy food in the larger towns we were often asked where we were from and where we were going. When people learned our destination was Africa, they would say that was very far, hot, or dangerous, but they always seemed to approve. People liked the idea that we were going somewhere else, no matter why, as if the going itself were an answer to something.

You will find people will often encourage you in a risky venture as long as it means nothing to them. It would be different if you invited them to come along. The acid test of their approval or commitment, whether it's in life or business, is to invite them to participate or invest their own money. That's when you learn how deep their feelings are.

The Direct Route

Our route was planned as the shortest distance between London and Gibraltar; even a few miles difference in one route compared to another meant extra hours of toil. We rode south to Boulogne, then to Abbeville, and on through Beauvais to arrive in Chartres on the fifth day of pedaling.

We cashed a traveler's check in a small bank in Chartres and then sat down on the curb outside to assess our position. It was not encouraging. The wind, rain, hunger, muscular aches, and pains had all combined to keep our speed so low that we were only averaging 40 miles a day. We had only $750 of our original $1,000 left and still had a long way to go to Gibraltar.

The bicycles and equipment had cost a lot, but what was gobbling our funds was paying for food. Although we were limiting ourselves to only two meals per day, those meals had to be enormous and nutritious. Meat, eggs, cheese, bread, milk, and vegetables for three ravenous fellows was inordinately expensive in France. At our rate of speed, we couldn't possibly finish the first part of our trip in less than another four weeks, and by that time we'd be very low on cash.

The Tipping Point

What really upset us was a genial motorcyclist—an American—who stopped to chat. It turned out he had left London that morning and covered the same ground in eight hours that we had covered in five days. We smiled through our tears.

This was a valuable lesson: a person who is properly equipped and knows what he is doing can cover greater distance faster and easier than the most determined but inexperienced person can under the same circumstance. This is why businesses started by experienced entrepreneurs have a 90 percent success rate and those started by inexperienced people fail 90 percent of the time. There is simply no replacement for having done it before—for knowledge and experience.

We finally calculated that it would be cheaper to take a train than continue on bicycles. We hoped that once into the south of France the wind would be gone and the weather would be considerably more pleasant for bicycling. We would make better time and enjoy the traveling—something we were having a rather tough time doing in the rain.

The Orleans Challenge

To save money and justify taking a train we made ourselves a deal. It was then noon; if we could be in Orleans, 71 kilometers further south, in time to catch the 10:25 southbound train from Paris that night, we would have earned the train ride and there would be nothing on our consciences.

"How's that for an idea, fellows?"

"What?"

"Oh, come on now, it's not that far."

"Yes, I know. I'm just as tired as you are."

"It's a matter of pride, that's why."

We eventually all agreed it was a fine idea and headed out for Orleans. We had already bicycled 20 kilometers that day and the rain hadn't let up for a second. If we made it on time, we deserved to travel a while by train.

All afternoon we punished ourselves, pedaling into the icy wind, knuckles white on the handlebars from the cold, eyes narrowed against the lash of the fine spray, chests burning with the exertion, and legs screaming silently from the pain that gradually spread up into the back and shoulders and worked its way down the arms into the wrists.

Our jeans were soaked through. We were chilled to the bone. But there was no way to justify a stop and no place to stop even if we could. The hours marched by with the milestones jeering at our creeping pace. At 40 kilometers from Orleans, we were on our last legs. With 30 kilometers to go we no longer dared to stop at the top of hills for fear our exhausted bodies would refuse to continue. We would reach the end of the upgrades and just keep on trudging with the bicycles until we had enough breath to throw our legs over and take up the silent count of pedal strokes once more.

At 20 kilometers to go we knew there was no stopping us. We ignored the incessant honking of passing motorists as the bikes wandered into the road, as well as the hollow twisting knots of hunger in the gut and everything but the road directly in front of the wheel. Like silent, relentless robots we forced the hateful pedals down.

The Good Samaritan

Just after dusk a yellow Citroën passed us, beeping its horn as it sped by and slowing and stopping on the road ahead. As we rode our bedraggled way past the car, a well-dressed man got out and motioned for us to stop.

Unable to get off our bikes, we straddled them weakly and waited to hear his troubles. He was very gracious and led us to understand that he lived in Orleans and would take our gear in with him to make our loads a little lighter.

We were too exhausted to argue or be suspicious. We just nodded in mute agreement and dropped the bicycles unceremoniously in the street in our fumbling haste to throw our backpacks into the opened trunk. There was no discussion about honest intentions or ulterior motives. We thanked him and stood watching as his car disappeared into the night. Geoff stuffed the address into his pocket and picked up his bike and climbed on wordlessly. We followed suit and began the silent cadence once more.

When you're at your wits end and your load is no longer bearable, some bit of relief will come to your aid. The burden remains, but at least you can continue. "Act boldly and unseen forces will come to your aid."

Lights and Music

Our ravenous hunger and mind-numbing fatigue made the last ten kilometers of the day a haze of signs and arrows pointing toward "Orleans-Centre Ville." Every muscle in our bodies felt as though it were being held in place with a hot spike. The rain had stopped and the moisture on the road and electric wires caught the lights from oncoming cars and sparkled clear against the blackness of the fields. It was like riding through an alley of flashing pain and stunning motion until the road suddenly widened into four lanes and poured out into the square in the center of town.

The main street through the square was ablaze with lights and music, honking horns, and flashing headlights reflecting against the rain-damp roads and the row of gaily lit restaurants lining the boulevard. Glasses tinkled and laughter echoed from table to table. White uniformed waiters glided in and out with overfilled trays and jukeboxes blared into the crowds surging along the broad sidewalks. We stopped at the corner of the street where the entire panorama of light and excitement began and stretched for several blocks. We stared with glazed eyes and too it all happily in. It was 5:30 P.M. We had made it to Orleans on time and felt like the survivors of a massacre.

An Invitation to Dine

At that moment, one of the sons who had been in the back seat of the Citroën rode up on his bicycle, babbling in French and enthusiastically motioning us to follow him. We were halfway off our bikes and headed in the direction of the nearest cafe, numb with exhaustion and giddy from hunger, and the suggestion that we delay eating to retrieve our equipment was greeted with scowls. The boy, however, insisted and assured us it wasn't far; he suggested that food was involved. Like robots we heaved our stiffening limbs back onto the bikes and pedaled away from the city lights onto a dark side street.

We rode two more blocks to a featureless three-story house in a tightly constructed row of similar buildings whose front doors opened onto the narrow sidewalk. At the boy's eager knock, the door was opened and the bespectacled gentleman who had relieved us of our gear three hours earlier ushered us inside.

In sharp contrast to the dull facade, the entrance hall was lined with mirrors and the walls of the parlor and dining room were done in white fresco depicting spring landscapes, cherubim, and angels. The black walnut furniture was richly polished and placed elegantly around a high fireplace. A crystal chandelier dangled on a silver chain above the burnished walnut table in the dining room. The most memorable part of the whole scene was the fragrant aroma floating in from the kitchen beyond the dining room.

French Hospitality

Monsieur Allard was a pleasant, well mannered businessman and he was sure we would like a little something to eat after our ride. While his wife was busy in the kitchen, he invited us to seat our emaciated selves around the long table and tell him and his sons about our trip.

Pasting "hands across the seamanship" smiles on our grubby, unshaven faces, we labored with what words of French we knew and let them deduce the meaning. All we could think of was the food. Every distant sound from the kitchen was a clarion call of forthcoming joy.

The movement finally stopped in the kitchen and the door swung open as Madame Allard swept into the dining room with a cheery smile. We caught our breaths in anticipation as she leaned over and set a large bowl of soup in the middle of the table. I didn't know whether to laugh or cry.

Our first nourishment in 11 hours and 91 kilometers consisted of a medium-sized tureen of thin celery soup, and a two-inch diameter loaf of French bread sliced into bite-size chunks. Any one of us could have devoured the lot; however, it was for all of us, including the family of four.

Watching Our Manners

The younger son carefully distributed the bowls and Madame Allard elegantly ladled a dipper full into each one. Through gritted teeth and phony smiles we made an effort not to slurp the soup down our fronts as we rushed it into our screaming innards; we also resisted the impulse to pick up the bowl in both hands and gobble the thin contents.

Our ill-concealed hopes were in vain; the soup was not an entrée. It was the alpha and omega. After waiting long enough to ascertain that there was to be nothing more, we politely said our good-byes, edged toward the door, and shouldered our packs while grinning insincerely. As the door closed behind us, the grins disappeared in a hasty scramble for our bikes.

Food, Glorious Food

Battle stations! We went into the main street and skidded up to the first bistro we could find, then led the confused waiter to the table and explained in desperate French what we wanted. We ordered and ate everything he had. Half an hour later the table was littered with empty plates and we were out of critical condition. With a little sleep our chances for recovery seemed quite good.

The beefsteak and potatoes had stopped the hollow ache in our stomachs and rekindled a little energy, which we directed into drinking a bottle of "vin ordinaire" and watching the passing parade on the busy sidewalk. The wine soon smothered the spark of energy from the food and the long day began to catch up with us. We nodded and mumbled and conversation dropped to broken, meaningless sentences. It was time to catch our train.

The Shuttle Train

We paid the bill and dragged ourselves across the square to the Orleans train station. We bought second-class tickets to Toulouse in the south, checked the bikes with the baggage department, and took our positions on the empty platform where our train was supposed to appear.

It was right on time. Knowing nothing about the French railways, and thinking only of sleeping, we clambered into the last car and shut ourselves into the end compartment. It had only simple benches, but that made no difference to three stout lads who had been sleeping beside the road for the last few days.

Few other passengers boarded the train so we hoped to sleep through the night while traveling. Our car was still empty when the train started out of the station. We congratulated ourselves on our luck and stretched out on the padded seats to sleep.

About 11 minutes later, the train jerked to a halt and stirred Geoff and me from our half-slumbering positions on opposite benches of the narrow compartment. Feeling irritable we raised our heads above the level of the window and peered out. Across the platform, about ten yards away, we saw a long, brightly lit passenger train, full of milling, laughing people crowding in and out of busy compartments.

"I'm glad we're not on that train," Geoff mumbled, and withdrew his head. The snoring in the next compartment indicatedBob was beyond giving an opinion. I also withdrew my head and lay down to sleep once again.

A Language Problem

Seconds later the door to the next compartment opened and a gruff French voice demanded something of the sleeping Bob. He woke and mumbled incomprehensibly. Thinking it must be someone wanting to see our tickets, I took them in; Geoff followed closely behind.

The bulky, blue-uniformed and whiskered conductor seemed to think Bob should not be on this train; when we entered—blinking at the brighter light—he included us in his protests. He was babbling furiously in French and gesticulating toward the door and platform. We could understand only that he was interrupting our sleep with his chatter.

I showed him the tickets for Toulouse to placate him, but he merely punched and handed them back, all the while talking and suggesting vociferously that we were not in the right compartment. He insisted we get off the train. We told him—just as loudly—we were staying. He gave one last burst of French, and then stepped onto the platform and strode away indignantly.

"What was all that about?"

"Don't know. Don't care either. He was probably trying to get us onto another car so he'd have this for someone who tips better."

"Well, he can drop dead. We're here and we're staying."

"Geez, I'm beat. Wake me up when we get to Toulouse."

The Wrong Train

We switched off the lights and lay back to sleep on our respective benches. Outside we could hear the other train pulling away and clacking off into the night. Seconds later our train also began to move—backward in the same direction from which we'd come.

"It's going back," said Geoff without raising his head.

"No it's not. It's just transferring to another line for the trip to Toulouse."

After a brief silence, Geoff raised his head to stare out the window.

"We're passing the same refinery we passed coming out," he said as a matter of interest.

"Can't be. Must be some other refinery. There are probably lots of refineries around Orleans."

"There's the bus terminal, too," he said. "We must be going back."

"Maybe they've forgotten our bicycles. Yeah, that must be it. They've forgotten our bicycles."

Three minutes later the train pulled back into the huge, brightly lit dome of the Orleans main station and came to a halt exactly where we had boarded it. We lay silently and half asleep in the dark and listened uncaringly to the voices on the platform outside. Within five minutes the train moved once again out of the station into the darkness of the rail yards.

"That must have been it," said Geoff drowsily. "We seem to be on our way again. Funny they should forget a bicycle."

We dozed as the train clattered along under the bridges, past the bus terminal and refinery, and out into the suburbs, and then jerked to a halt 11 minutes later at the same platform as before. This time there was no other train, conductor, or other person in sight. There was only the rain, the night, and the lonely lights of the deserted transfer station.

Eight minutes later the train started back in the same direction as before. We sat up and looked dopily out the window at the passing landmarks: the refinery, bus terminal, bridges, and rail yards of the main station. The truth—the bitter truth—dawned on us.

We were on a shuttle train! The other one had been the southbound passenger train from Paris to Toulouse. The little conductor had been trying to tell us we must change trains.

Our Night in Orleans

This time when we got back to the main station I went and asked what was going on. Our suspicions were confirmed. We had missed our train. The next one headed south didn't come through until the next morning at 7:30. It was raining again and late, and we were exhausted. There was only one solution. After a brief conference, we decided to sleep right where we were on the shuttle train.

All night the computer-controlled electric train rumbled out of the station to the little platform in the suburbs, stopped for eight minutes, and then rumbled back to Orleans. Meanwhile, we slept fitfully to the rocking motion in the darkened compartment.

Occasionally, when the train stopped at the station, one of us climbed out and went into the men's washroom on the adjacent platform. Minutes later, he came out, gave a sleepy nod to the curious members of the terminal staff working through the night, and reboarded before the train rolled out of the station once more. They began to expect us as the night wore on. They always watched when someone got off and it amused them no end. It seemed that sort of thing wasn't done too often in Orleans.

The lesson I learned from this situation, which was definitely "an inconvenience rightly considered," is that *sometimes the very best thing you can do when things go wrong is—nothing.* Just accept the situation as it is and bide your time. It will often correct itself without your doing anything.

Off to Toulouse

The next morning—Sunday—we felt a bit refreshed after a moderately comfortable night and boarded the southbound train to Toulouse right on schedule to once more continue our trip to Gibraltar. The train wasn't crowded and we easily found an almost empty compartment where we could sit and watch the hills go by. We shaved and washed in the cramped toilets and arrived in Limoges that afternoon.

The weather was better already; the day was sparkling clear and the sky was dotted with puffy white cumulus clouds sweeping by on a pale blue carpet. We had one hour to wait in Limoges for the connection to Toulouse. It was a good chance to look at a few buildings, as well as find a place to eat. We joined families strolling on the quiet boulevards and reveling in the warm spring sunshine we made our way into town. The streets were deserted, the stores were shut tight for the weekend, and there didn't seem to be a place to eat anywhere.

Lunch in Limoges

After half a mile of undernourished searching and a gradual ascent of several blocks we came into a colorful square built around a fountain. Spreading from the base of the fountain in the shape of a star were five little gardens swollen with red and yellow flowers; the points of the stars were aimed at restaurants facing onto the square. The aromas wafting into the clear air, told us they were open for business.

"What are we waiting for?"

"Who's waiting?"

"Which one looks the cheapest?"

"That one."

"Well, what are we waiting for?"

"Who's waiting?"

We sat down and ordered a four-course lunch. We made it clear to the waiter that we were in a hurry since our train pulled out in 30 minutes and the next one wasn't until the following morning. The waiter nodded vigorously with a smile of perfect agreement when we explained that we had to be back to the terminal by 2 P.M. He flipped his fingers with a show of efficiency and glided away to the big kitchen in the rear.

A Train to Catch

After five minutes I got up and went to the door of the kitchen. The waiter was sitting at a table reading a newspaper. He looked up with mildly interest at my entrance.

"We must catch a train in 30 minutes," I told him, and then repeated the same message two or three ways so he would be sure to understand. "Bring the food to the table all at once, please. We are in a hurry."

"Oui, oui, Monsieur," he said. "It is coming immediately, if you will go and sit and wait."

With a burst of professionalism, he followed me back to the table with a large tureen of thin vegetable soup. He set it ceremoniously in the center of the table—as though it was the solution for everything—and sauntered to the mirrored bar, where he began chatting with the bartender.

By this time we had less than 20 minutes before we would be stuck in Limoges for the night. We called the waiter tersely back to the table and told him to bring all the food, NOW.

With a look of surprise that we should want another course when we were still slurping the soup, he hurried into the kitchen and came back, this time with a large salad bowl. He rolled his eyes as though we had just sworn in church, and then walked over to the window, sat down and stared aimlessly into the square.

"More! More!" we shouted. "Bring more! Bring it all!"

Grossly offended, the waiter returned to the table. This time I held up the menu and then my watch. "If we don't have it all in another two minutes, we'll have to leave to catch our train—and we're not paying," I told him.

He'd never heard anything so blasphemous in his whole life. However, he hurried off to the kitchen and came back with the next course.

The minutes were running out and we still wanted more— faster. We dashed through the second half of the meal by eating with both hands, paid the bill, and streaked into the street. Far away a train whistle sounded high and clear.

Sprinting through Limoges

We sprinted across the square, down the cobbled street, and cut across a newly planted lawn. Gasping and perspiring on our full stomachs, we dove through hedges and galloped along sidewalks, and caused women pushing baby strollers to leap aside. We finished with a quarter-mile run down the center of the city park and—bloated and puffing—tore across the parking lot and bolted through the wide swinging doors of the train station. People turned to stare in curious incredulity as we dodged and sidestepped our way down the busy hall, swung through the turnstile, and plunged down three levels of stairs to the platform below.

The train had just started to move. We peeled off like jet fighters, spacing ourselves. Scooping up our waiting rucksacks, we sprinted straight for the last car. I was the first inside; Bob dove in after me as the train gained speed. Geoff was now in a full sprint down the platform. We shouted at him to run faster. With a final burst of speed, he grabbed my outstretched hand and tossed his pack to Bob, who dragged him onboard just as the train sped out of the station.

We lay on the floor, gasping, and completely spent. It was a full five minutes before anyone spoke. Then Bob sagely observed, "We almost missed the train."

Yes, that seemed to be a safe assumption. Were there any more clever children like him at home? Perhaps they'd be good enough to stay there.

We found an empty compartment and rode comfortably the remainder of the way to Toulouse.

It turns out that most people you meet in life are like the waiter; they are not particularly ambitious for a variety of reasons. No one places the same value on your time as you do. Only about 2 percent of people have a "sense of urgency," and they end up at the top of every competitive organization. Just making a firm personal commitment to "do it now" and operate in "real time" can give you the winning edge in almost any competitive situation because so few people do it.

The South of France

"It's easy to fight when everything's right," said Robert W. Service; this was certainly how we felt when we came off that train in Toulouse. It was late afternoon and the sky was glistening with golden rays of warmth. The clouds were far behind us in the Loire Valley and the road ran toward the south under a sky we knew was *Mediterranean.* We could almost smell the orange blossoms and salt spray from the railroad station.

Like young tigers, we leaped on our bicycles and pedaled out of town. We followed the signs to Carcassone and the sea feeling full of confidence, enthusiasm, youth, and joy in the birds, flowers, and glorious world of excitement and adventure. Delight and exhilaration tingled through our hardening limbs, and lightened our wind-burned faces with laughter and happiness. Our hearts brimmed with song and springtime.

The knowledge that we were conquerors—and unstoppable—leaped and danced in our tumbling brains and warmed us with pride, hope, and defiance. What did we care for the elements, the rain and the cold? We were lovers in a field of flowers, eager to pluck the waving blossoms of beckoning experience and hurl defiance at everything and anything that stood in the way of our trip to Africa. We were unquenchable drinkers at the fountain of dreams and romance, insatiable eaters at the table of rugged living and challenge. It was a long way to Tipperary, but in our imaginations and hearts we were on the highroad, and halfway back already.

The Joys of Youth

In those fancy-free days, we almost welcomed the wind and the rain; we saw in them an opportunity to flaunt our strength and persistence. There in France, far from home and love and security, we were explorers and discoverers, Bon Vivants and vagabonds supreme. With each drop of sweat and painful gasp we were taking part in the battle of youth against age—the conflict between the lure of the easy chair and the lone trail.

We felt genuinely sorry for people speeding past in their cars and were sad they couldn't share our labors and revel in the satisfaction of tired bodies and kinship with the hard life. We were giving the best we had in stamina and determination, heeding the call of distant places, and striking the words "quit" and "defeat" from our vocabularies.

As three idealistic young men, we were seeing drama and romance in commonplace occurrences and looking for and finding the mysterious in everything new or unusual. We thought of ourselves as exceptional people for having taken up the gauntlet of Africa when others our age were contenting themselves with bumming around Europe.

We wanted something much more than that, but we didn't have the slightest idea what it was. We thought it was Africa, and so that vast unknown land mass became our Shangri La and the bicycles our penance and pilgrimage. We felt unstoppable.

Sunday Night by the Road

We rode another two hours that afternoon to a little place called Montgiscard, where we searched for a place to buy our evening meal and breakfast. But we had miscalculated again; it was Sunday night and nothing was open.

As a last resort, we halted at a wayside café to ask if they would sell us a few provisions. The owner was a large motherly woman who took one look at our bicycles and us and *adopted* us without another word. She took us into her warm, homey kitchen and loaded us with bread, eggs, milk, onions, and tomatoes. At her friendly insistence, we made our camp under some trees on the hill above the café and cooked an egg-and-onion omelet over a smoky fire set in the roots of a spreading oak tree.

A Clean, Well-Lit Place

The night temperature fell sharp and chilly after supper and a cold breeze ran under the groundsheet we had rigged up as an open tent. It wasn't long before the warmth and music floating up from the café below drew us like a magnet off the muddy hill.

Business in the café was good that Sunday night, and the atmosphere was even better. Most of the light came from the bright bar in one corner and the jukebox next to it. Mama was bustling back and forth from the kitchen to her guests at the bar. She was a bundle of happy efficiency and enjoyed her role as hostess like a queen at a coronation. She cheerily greeted and introduced us to the crowd, and then led us to a table and presented us with a bottle of wine. We joined the mostly older crowd of farm folk from the area in the restaurant, and felt caught up in the music and good spirits of the establishment. The gaiety and laughter in the busy room had us feeling like members of a homecoming party.

We drank Mama's bottle of wine—and one more—before making our way back up the hill. That night we slept through the rain that soaked our fireplace and half our gear. We could have slept through a blizzard.

Monday morning dawned clear and windy, with the wind coming out of the north for the first time. After breakfast and a fond good-bye to our friends at the café, we were back on the road and making exceptional time. The wind was often so strong at our backs that we had no need to pedal. All that day we rode like fools—effortlessly—with the tires singing on the pavement. We flew joyously ahead of the crisp gusts of wind and through the rolling hills and vineyards, Castelnaudery, and Carcassone, then down to the Mediterranean at Narbonne.

At Narbonne we bought our daily groceries and continued along the coast toward Spain until we found an old Roman watchtower and set up camp inside for the night.

That was the best day we had ever had on bicycles; we covered 140 kilometers without the exhaustion that had marked days when we had only traveled 60 or 70 from morning to night. I'm glad we had that day, not only because we deserved it, but also because it showed us—just once—how pleasurable traveling on a bicycle can be. We needed to temper the memory of the hard days past and boost us in the days ahead.

There Are no Free Lessons

Nature is a just employer, but she demands full measure of payment for every reward. The trials and tribulations of our bicycling trip across

France forced us to dig deep into ourselves for untapped reserves of energy and patience.

The good news is that your biggest problem or difficulty today has been sent to you at this moment to teach you something you need to know to be happier and more successful in the future.

It is often when you experience the greatest pain and strain that you are preparing for the greatest joys and pleasures. Develop an "attitude of gratitude" no matter what happens. Count your blessings. Look for the good in every situation and surprise! You'll always find it.

> "The truth is that all of us attain the greatest success and happiness possible in this life whenever we use our native capacities to their greatest extent."
> —SMILEY BLANTON

CHAPTER 9

The Spanish Railways

> "We all have possibilities we don't know about. We can do things we don't even dream we can do."
> —DALE CARNEGIE

THE NEXT DAY THE WIND had changed again; however we rode all day toward Spain with the shining Mediterranean on our left. We entered the foothills of the Pyrenees and camped the night just beyond the small town of Perpignan. On Wednesday morning we got another passport stamp at the Spanish border station of Le Perthus and began the long haul to Barcelona.

Everything in life is cycles and trends that go up and down, get better and then worse, and progress and regress. Nothing ever continues indefinitely in the same way. It's usually a matter of two steps forward, one step back, and sometimes *more* than one step back. That's why you have to be infinitely flexible. The best way to predict the future is sometimes to create it.

Barcelona Days

"Africa begins at the Pyrenees" was said a long time ago, probably by someone who'd been to both and liked neither. One thing we could attest to by the time we rode into the soot-blackened outskirts of Barcelona three days later, with our teeth rattling from the broken pavement, was that the bad roads begin at the Pyrenees. If anyone ever gets up a protest march against cobblestones, save me a banner to carry!

A check at poste restaunte, the general delivery of Europe and the rest of the world, freed us from any obligation to answer letters, since those who knew we were going through there had either run out of ink, or thought we wouldn't make it. We contented ourselves with finding a cheap place to stay for the weekend.

Living on a Limited Budget

For 42 pesetas each, per night, we found a small pension whose owners were not overly concerned with encouraging the tourist trade. Our quarters consisted of a converted closet with two sagging beds shoved together, one water spigot with a tin bowl for washing and shaving, and a large window opening onto a roof overlooking an impoverished neighborhood.

Five pesetas and a half-hour wait gave us enough hot water out of the old electric tank in the distant bathroom to brush our teeth—if we were inclined toward that sort of thing. However, all our clothes had become caked and filthy after ten days of sleeping in them every night and sweating in them during the day, so we took advantage of the *deluxe* facilities to wash them.

The wash was accompanied by the wails and protestations of the clerk at the desk, who repeatedly threatened to call the police if we didn't leave immediately and wash our clothes somewhere else. He finally gave up and went away.

Cleanliness Is Next to Godliness

The flies that seemed to cluster on us when we stopped or even slowed down in the streets indicated a little bathing wouldn't hurt us either.

After we'd scraped off some of the dirt and sweat with carbolic soap, our room—when we were in it—stopped smelling as though a rat had died in the woodwork.

We had arrived in the morning and were feeling quite like men of the world in our clean dry clothes that afternoon. It seemed only fair that since the Spaniards had built this city on our path to Africa, we should go out and give it the once over, especially since it was Good Friday—an important holiday in Catholic Spain.

The streets had been quiet all day but were now coming to life. Long rows and clusters of chairs were being set up on the main boulevards and sidewalks. People dressed in their Sunday finery poured into the large streets from the many smaller ones leading away from the center of town. All the stores except those dealing in soft drinks and pastry, were closed and the pious looks on the faces of the solemn Spaniards left no doubt but that they took their religious holidays seriously.

Gradually the multitudes of chairs filled and overflowed with people and the surrounding streets were also packed. We felt like outsiders; we weren't overly moved by the occasion, and the better-dressed natives were giving us scowls. Our jeans and T-shirts did not lend much to the holiness of the holiday.

Chaperones Everywhere

We concentrated more on catching the eyes of the Spanish damsels and received more than one blush or smile in return. But we could not meet or even get close to them; they all seemed to be surrounded by parents and jealous brothers. When they sat beautifully in their spring dresses the family group extended its tentacles of protection to the front and sides of the lovely creatures.

When they walked it was invariably with Mama and Papa on either arm, and often a brother or cousin bringing up the rear. It was a bit discouraging for us to walk around Spain's second largest city, steeped in lascivious thoughts but unable to do more than lust. Alas, that was part of the cross we had to bear to become world-beaters.

Exploring the City

Early the next morning, we got our bicycles and rode through the quiet streets to the city's outskirts along the waterfront. There were no packs this time. This was to be a pleasure tour of the low spots—and some of them were pretty low. Once away from the main streets we got into slum areas consisting of clumps of shanties built from cardboard and tin sheets and held together with chicken wire.

I remember thinking these were probably the worst living conditions I had ever seen. It was good for us to experience this; it broadened our education. Little did I know what awaited us in Africa.

The Agony of the Spanish Roads

On Easter morning we pedaled off toward Valencia and right back into the teeth of the wind. It was another day of counting pumps, burning thighs, and eyes full of fine grit from the sand between the cobbles; and of sweat and gritted teeth. The pack straps dug into our shoulders with the constant joggling and rattling of the rough road, our stomachs knotted from hunger, and our hands on the lowered handlebars became stiff and cramped. All the rigors and tribulations of bicycling set in once more.

We kept at it. One day. Two days. Three days. The wind became the enemy and it was vicious. It never let up. It lurked at every bend in the road, attacking us up and down every hill and slashing our faces with sand. It gave us no peace and no quarter; at night it took almost an hour to cook our egg-and-onion omelets over the little fires that struggled to stay alive. The wind shook us wrathfully awake every morning, drove at us all day, and howled to keep us awake throughout the night.

We grew to hate the wind and the road and bicycles that were part of the ceaseless ordeal. Outside Tarragona the wind became so strong that maximum effort was required just to keep from being blown over in a standstill. After four days we were barely a two-hour drive out of Barcelona, and the wind finally won.

Accepting the Inevitable

It was after a breakfast of an egg (the cheapest protein) and onion (the only vegetable available that early in the year) omelet (the easiest to prepare) in a rocky creek bed with the wind whistling up the rocks from the road below that we decided to reevaluate our situation.

"We're like fools banging our heads against a brick wall," said Geoff, "because it feels so good when we stop. I say we should stop now!"

"If I never ride another bicycle in my life, it'll be too soon," agreed Bob, resolutely.

"But think how tough we're getting with this life."

"Yeah, well I'm tough enough already."

"Yes, but it's a matter of pride."

"What do you mean?"

"If we quit now, think how much tougher it'll be to carry on when it gets tough in the future."

"Who's thinking about the future?"

"Well, I'm thinking about the future."

"Let's try it for another three days."

"The hell with it!"

"What about two days?"

"Oh, come on, at least one day more."

"Hey, fellows, you're not even listening. Let's discuss this."

"What's that? Vinaroz. The next town? Now slow down for just one second!"

"Where are you two going? Hold on a minute. Let's not rush off without thinking this over."

"Yes, but we haven't thought it over enough."

"Let's take a vote! Aw, for cripes sakes, wait for me!" And with that dialogue ended, off we went to the nearby train station.

Sometimes in business and in life you have to try, try again, and then try something else. In most cases, *difficulties come not to obstruct, but to instruct.* You must always be prepared to accept, adjust, and respond differently.

The Train from Vinaroz

Vinaroz was a typical Spanish town; its streets were lined with box-like clay and brick houses, except in the center, where the larger buildings rose two or three stories. Other than a mangy goat nibbling at a bit of dusty grass, the depot by the tracks at the end of town seemed deserted.

We rode across the unpaved yard to the old frame building and stomped around inside, calling hopefully, until an old man wearing the remains of a blue overcoat stuck his head through one of the barred ticket windows. He grudgingly growled the prices at us and then sold us third-class tickets to Valencia before going back to sleep. We had two hours to wait and set off to find something to eat—our universal remedy for all ailments including riding, walking, sitting, and delays caused by Spanish trains.

After eating an overpriced something in a sidewalk greasy spoon, we passed the next hour soaking up a little local culture and then pedaled back early to catch the train. We were not the only ones who were early.

Traveling Companions

A multitude that Moses would have been proud to lead was gathered in the previously empty yard in front of the tracks. There were old unshaved men in sweat-stained peasant clothing, accompanied by old women dressed in the ubiquitous black of mourning popular throughout Spain. Tired-looking husbands and wives tended bundles of family possessions and underfed children. Young men and ancient farmers milked in the crowd and the yard was cluttered with goats, chickens, dogs, mattresses, babies, baskets, vegetables, and old bicycles. Now there were also three scruffy-looking gringos to make the party complete.

Everyone sat in the hot, dry sun of midafternoon and looked tiredly at everyone else, as though waiting for a hearse to pass. A few heads turned to look at us when we rode up, and after seeing that we didn't bite, returned to staring at the dust. We gave our bicycles over to the man at the baggage counter and took our place with the others.

Moses arrived in the form of a coal-blackened, greasy-looking engineer running the old steam engine that dragged the converted cattle cars into Vinaroz 15 minutes late. His inspirational powers were astonishing. There was a mad, squalling, chaotic rush to get aboard. We hurled ourselves into the thick of it, yelling and pushing with the best of them and scrambling for places for our packs and sleeping bags in the narrow compartments. The corridors quickly filled with humanity just as the old engine gave one shrill toot and grunted its way out of the station toward Valencia.

Third Class Trains

The trip took almost seven hours and ranks as a milestone in our experience. Everyone should go to Spain, if for no other reason than to ride on a third-class train. It is a singular event in the evolution of transportation that will some day be only a memory. When the Spanish railways increase their freight-handling capabilities and make it obsolete you'll have to go to India for the same sensation.

Once in Valencia it took almost an hour to retrieve our bikes, buy tickets for San Roque (the nearest Spanish station to Gibraltar), recheck our bikes with the next baggage department, and finally get out of the station into the clear night and bright lights of downtown.

Always Ask a Cop

We used two phrases—*tenemos mucho hambre* (we are very hungry) and *no mucho dinero* (not much money)—from our Spanish language book to flag down the first policeman we saw.

He looked at our unshaven faces, down at our dirty sweaters, jeans, and ragged tennis shoes, and smiled and nodded in understanding. Motioning for us to follow him, he led us through the busy streets, past several cafés, and into a narrow lane to a small, clean, and crowded café.

Aqui no questo mucho dinero, (it doesn't cost much here) he said as he smiled and hurried off the way we'd come.

The food was good, the people pleasant, and—best of all—the price was less than half what they were charging at places near the station. When in doubt, ask a cop. If they don't know personally, they know someone who does, and they rarely lead you astray. In a civilized country the most omniscient person in any given neighborhood is the cop working the street. It was a lesson we learned early in our traveling and never forgot.

The Night Train

We were back at the depot early to board our night train. It was different from the one we'd ridden from Vinaroz; it had padding on the benches and doors on the compartments. We were among the first passengers aboard and quickly found an empty compartment. We foolishly thought that since it was so late perhaps we'd have it to ourselves and could sleep the night. At 10:48 P.M. when the train crept out of the station our compartment was still empty. Aha! Good bit of luck. Good night, amigos.

Traveling Companions

But 15 minutes later the train ground to a halt, heralding a rush of passengers from the suburban station, three of whom pushed loudly into our compartment. Disgruntled, we sat up and made space, unable to stretch out our legs any more.

It seemed the train had just started moving when it stopped again to allow another rush of Spaniards to storm aboard, three more of whom jammed into our compartment. This process continued, despite our threats and protests, until there were 12 of us packed shoulder to shoulder in the small compartment. The space between the benches was so narrow we sat with knees overlapping.

"I haven't even got enough room to scratch," said Bob. "Do you think any of them are going to get off in the night?"

"It won't make much difference if they do," I said. "Just look at that corridor."

The passageway outside was already filling up with Spaniards unable to find places to sit; it was going to get worse before it got better.

"We're lucky to have a place at all," muttered Geoff. "But it's going to be a long night."

What Can't be Cured Must be Endured

The other passengers accepted the conditions with resignation; half were already on their way to sleep. Soon we were all dozing in the muggy compartment, lulled by the typewriter-like clacking coming from the rails below as the train swayed and lurched its way through the night.

Whenever one of us got up in the night to struggle down the crowded corridor to the foul-smelling cubicle at the end of the car, he had to warn the other two before he left. They had to stand guard to halt the rush for the vacant seat. This initiated a lot of vigorous argument in Spanish and English until the third friend returned and regained his place.

It soon became extremely hot and stuffy in the airless compartment; the window was tightly shut and the corridor was full of smoke and sweat from the press of bodies. The air was so thick we could almost chew it before choking it down. The hours dragged as the train chugged its way overland toward the high country around Cordoba and we sat slumped and swaying with the rocking motion throughout the night.

The Trains in Spain

All the next day we rode across Spain, changing trains three times and traveling with two English girls part of the way; we ended up that night in a whistle stop called Rodriquez. The next train heading our direction wasn't leaving until late the following morning.

You only learn what really works by trying things that don't work. Keep questioning and evaluating. Ask, Could there be a better way? Sometimes what you need is a break—a chance to stop, stand back, and reconsider.

In Rodriquez we once again retrieved our bicycles and began our endless quest for food. As soon as we had something to eat we pedaled out of town to camp on the outskirts.

The next morning we rode in from our camping spot in the eucalyptus grove in time to catch the southbound cattle car to El Golea, where we again had to change trains. The platform superintendent in El Golea informed us our tickets would have to be upgraded to second class, at an additional charge, if we didn't want to wait until the next afternoon for the third-class train.

Battle with the Bureaucrat

The conductor of the second-class train refused to have our bicycles in his baggage car; he said they must go on the third-class train the following day. The reasons, we soon gathered, was that bicycles were a trifle demeaning for a man of his status to deal with.

We protested vigorously and after 15 minutes he finally relented while muttering and swearing at us under his breath. The bicycles were loaded into the small baggage car and we continued on our way. I felt sure this was the silliest incident I would ever experience in dealing with public officials and petty bureaucrats. In retrospect, it doesn't even receive honorable mention.

Traveling in Luxury

The second-class train consisted of only one self-contained car, with the engine in the forward section and baggage compartment in the rear. The padded passenger section occupied the center three-quarters of the car.

San Roque was two hours down the line, two comfortable hours in the modern airy coach, made even more enjoyable when compared with what we had been through for the past 48 hours since leaving Vinaroz.

We sat across from two American women who had flown from Vancouver to Madrid two days before; this set us thinking of our departure in the rain seven months back. We'd come a long way in these months, by car, foot, thumb, bicycle, and now train—not to mention 2,000 miles by ship and a few by ferry. And yet we were only two flying days away from home on a little train in Spain.

It's amazing what you can do with a little money—and what you must do when you have very little money to accomplish the same end. But there are things money can't buy. Some have to be paid for in a different type of currency—things, for instance, like memories.

First Aid to the Rescue

As we clambered out of our seats upon arrival in San Roque and grabbed our rucksacks from the overhead racks, Bob's machete slid out of its sheath and dropped onto the man below. The man bellowed in pain and held up his hand dripping with blood from a shallow two-inch cut—a mere scratch actually. Three or four passengers hurried forward as Bob stood helplessly holding the offending machete like an apprehended axe murderer.

"Get out the first-aid kit, Bob. It's in your pack, isn't it?"

I gave the distressed, bleeding Spaniard a confident smile and clapped his handkerchief from his breast pocket over the cut, then led him to the door of the car, out of sight of the other passengers. Geoff had joined Bob on the platform and the little bundle of bandages and antiseptic was ready for use in seconds.

With an efficiency that would have gladdened the heart of our first-aid instructor, we cleaned, dressed, bandaged, and taped the shallow cut tight under a roll of white gauze strips. One final pat and we boosted the confused gentleman back into the car just as it started moving and closed the door behind him. We stood there smiling professionally until the little train was out of sight.

A small crowd of about 20 people had gathered to view this scene; they stood back silently as if to "give the patient room to breath." We had the definite feeling this sort of thing wasn't done too often in San Roque.

The Last Leg to Gibraltar

Bob refastened his pack, slipped it on, and joined us where we waited with the bicycles. The last eight kilometers to Gibraltar were over a dusty farm road that wound through a range of low hills before becoming paved and descending to the border post of La Linea and "The Rock"; this was the end of the first leg of our trip to Johannesburg.

The Purpose of Pain

Nature sends us pain of all kinds—physical, emotional, and financial—to tell us to stop doing certain things and perhaps start doing other things more in keeping with what we really want. Look into every problem or pain for something good and helpful. Become an "inverse paranoid," a person convinced a great conspiracy exists—and is aimed at making you successful and happy.

Whenever God wants to send you a gift, he wraps it up in a problem. The bigger the gift, the bigger the problem it comes wrapped up in. Nature also sends you peace, pleasure, and happiness to tell you what you should do more of. So look into your greatest difficulty for the gift it contains. It's always there.

"I have always believed, and I still believe, that whatever good or bad fortune may come our way, we can always give it meaning and transform it into something of value."
—Hermann Hesse

CHAPTER 10

Gibraltar Days

> "For gold is tried in the fire and acceptable men in the furnace of adversity."
> —Sirach

A PERSON RARELY HAS THE CHANCE to witness such deliberate, childish, stupid, and yet official pigheadedness as that we experienced for three hours at the Spanish border post leading into Gibraltar.

The Spanish government, in the wake of receding British influence, was making a determined effort to establish a claim to the Rock and force the British to give it up. One of their schemes in the plan of protracted aggravation was to limit tourist traffic across the border into the colony; they accomplished this by insisting on holdups and searches that lasted for hours.

Political Pigheadedness

The Spanish police couldn't have been more irritating if they had taken lessons. One American family in front of us had to wait for three hours and then completely unload their station wagon onto tables for inspection. The police didn't even look at it before ordering them to repack the car; then in half an hour they demanded it all be unloaded again. We arrived at 2 P.M. when the family had already been there four hours; they passed into Gibraltar just ahead of us at 5 P.M. How a government could resort to that form of pettiness was beyond our limited comprehension.

Meanwhile, on the other side of the customs bay, hundreds of Spanish workers entered and departed in a steady stream, with no questions asked. We waited patiently in line for three hours before they condescended to put a chalk mark on our unopened packs and allow us through.

The blue-uniformed British officials who were one kilometer further up the road simply assured themselves we were not potential welfare applicants and stamped us through. This experience left me with definite opinions concerning who should control the colony.

Destination Achieved

It was April 20, 1965, and we had achieved our objective: London to Gibraltar in 17 days at a cost of $460. Our remaining assets consisted of $540, three very worn bicycles, three rucksacks, and about $20 worth of camping gear, not including our sleeping bags and clothes. We could see Africa looming out of the haze on the Moroccan coast, just 20 miles across the straits. We had completed the third stage in our journey.

"Hey! Brother world-beaters! The water's great! Come on, you can't sleep forever!"

I was back from an early swim in the crystal-blue water lapping the beach in our new home of Sandy Cove. Geoff and Bob were buried in their bags and I could have been talking to myself for all the reaction I was getting.

At last a voice mumbled out of the depths of one of the misshapen quilted lumps on the sand.

"Geoff? Geoff, buddy?"

"Yeah?" came the guarded reply.

"Do you hear anything, Geoff?"

"Yeah. I hate to admit it, but I think I do."

"What is it? What does it sound like?"

"I think someone's strangling a cat."

"Well, tell them to go down the beach and strangle it. About a half-mile down the beach!"

I grabbed the two sleeping bags, hefted them up, and dumped their occupants onto the warm sand. They blinked at the morning sunshine.

"Let's drown him," growled Bob.

"Let's castrate him first, then drown him," said Geoff.

We splashed and dove, yelling and laughing in the crisp salt water as we teamed up and jumped on the odd man, then jumped on the teammate and got dunked in return. For ten minutes we cavorted in the tingling surf before dragging ourselves ashore and making our way back to the sleeping bags.

Reviewing the Situation

We dried off in the warm morning sun and resumed our discussion of the previous evening about our next move. The situation was altered beyond recognition from our tentative planning in Vancouver and London. All our thinking had to be considerably revised.

There was no question about the bicycles. They had to go, and the sooner the better. We could barely stand to look at them; they had caused us so much heartache and strain—strain we could still feel in our legs after almost three weeks of hard riding.

It was time to get back onto four wheels. We realized it had been foolish to start out on bicycles in the first place, and would be doubly foolish to continue with them now. We needed a vehicle.

In Search of a Land Rover

We had arrived in Gibraltar with 180 English pounds—about $500—and full of ambition and ideals, with no idea of what was ahead in Africa. We were yet to see a reliable map of the continent and had little idea of the geography beyond Algeria and Morocco.

On the one-page map in our atlas, the Sahara Desert and tropical belt were indicated by yellow and green colors. Strewn throughout this area were several countries that we would cross when we came to them. Nothing to worry about there, we thought. That brought us back to the vehicle. What would it be?

A Land Rover was our first answer. In the little reading we had done about overland traveling the name "Land Rover" had appeared in almost every article. We had even considered buying one while we were still in Vancouver, but had decided it was too expensive for our limited budget. Now we couldn't afford not to have one, not if we were going to cross the Sahara and the rest of Africa. We hid our gear in the rocks at one end of the little beach and bicycled into town to take care of first things first—securing a Land Rover.

When in Doubt, Ask for Directions

We knew there were Land Rovers in Gibraltar, but didn't know where, so we flagged down the first one we saw and asked the driver. He said the Land Rovers in Gibraltar were mostly military vehicles, except those bought by civilians at auctions for private use. The last army auction had been five weeks before and the next one wouldn't be until July; we would have to find a vehicle for sale by a civilian. We thanked the man and pedaled into town to find a policeman.

Always ask a cop—you can't go wrong. The first bobby we spoke to gave us the name and address of a man who had sold his Land Rover the week before. We looked him up and asked if he could help us, or even sell us his vehicle. He declined our offer but gave us a few pointers for buying a Land Rover in Gibraltar. He then referred us to another man, a Mr. Earnest Harten, at the Roots Group Garage in the center of the little town at the base of the Rock.

A Used-Car Salesman

Mr. Harten was a thin, balding fellow with that confident attitude of people who deal in used cars—the one that seems to say, "Whether you buy it or not makes little difference to me, but you'll never find a better deal." However, his friendly attitude dispelled many of the doubts we had about buying a used car in a foreign country or colony.

He listened to our requirements and heart-rending story and assured us he might know someone with a Land Rover for sale. He told us to return that afternoon.

In the next three hours we looked at two light trucks, a couple of cars, and two Land Rovers, including one that was almost new and priced at 300 pounds, and another that was almost ready for the scrap heap for 90 pounds.

We had never bought a Land Rover before, but were far from babes when it came to buying used cars. Between Geoff and me, we'd bought, driven, and ruined about eight cars. There was one rule we relied on: if the body is good, the running gear will also be good, and vice versa. Simple, but true, and we'd never gone wrong with it.

We Find What We're Looking For

When we returned that afternoon, Mr. Harten greeted us with a smile and led us to the vehicle. It was not impressive; the windows were dirty, it had a canvas top, and the paint was flaking off. We walked around it critically.

"Does it run?"

"I'll start it up if you like. There we go. How's that?"

"Sounds all right."

We went over it from one end to the other, checking the water, oil, and undercarriage, and then took it for a drive. The steering was good and the brakes caught readily enough. The only complaint was the clutch. Mr. Harten assured us it would last another 5,000 miles.

We then took the Land Rover for a short test drive, parked it in the same place, and walked back to Root's Garage with Mr. Harten. He wanted 120 pounds, nothing less. That was two-thirds of all the money we had in the world. We told him we'd let him know within a day or two.

"Now we are in a fix," said Bob. "If we buy the Rover and insure it, we'll be too broke to go anywhere in it."

Facing a Dilemma

Immersed in thought, we rode back to our camp on the beach; each of us tried to think of a solution. It was a strange problem in that we were not broke, yet we had run out of money. We'd come too far to go back but couldn't go on. Behind us was Europe and before us was Africa; all we could see was Africa. One solution was right at hand and we discussed it briefly.

I learned later that *the hallmark of all successful people is that they are intensely solution- and future-oriented.* They constantly seek for ways to achieve their goals or solve their problems. They think in terms of where they are going rather than where they've been.

If we decided against buying the Land Rover, we could sell our bicycles, load everything on our backs, and set off hitchhiking. The money we had was enough to either get us back to England or into Africa. But we couldn't do both. We were stuck.

Pride and Self Reliance

"Let's be honest," we said. "We started out to achieve something, and we aren't going to achieve anything by becoming bums who wave their thumbs as if the world owes us a ride."

In our travels we had met many bums; they often had more money than the people from whom they were begging rides and accepting free meals, and we had no intention of becoming like them.

We had met fellows who bragged about having $500 in traveler's checks in their pockets and $3,000 in banks at home, but were saving on transportation by hitchhiking in order to have more money to spend on liquor and entertainment when they arrived in the big cities. We felt there was a hole in any reasoning that went against the principle of a person's responsibility to pay his or her own way.

Naturally there are sometimes unexpected circumstances that cast one on the whims of fate, but these are backward steps that must be made up before one is even again. No one has the right to base his or her actions solely on charity or on the assumption that someone else will foot the bill. Nor should they avoid doing something just because there is no one to stand as a backstop.

Independence Above All

One reason we had decided on bicycles in London was that they would give us a certain independence—freedom not enjoyed by those who feel they have no need to provide their own transportation. We had not traveled like kings, but neither had we expected to travel first class. At least we were three independent beings, taking and asking nothing from the country we traveled through. We weren't rich, but we weren't slaves to the unpredictability of the oncoming traffic either. Although going back was a grim alternative, hitchhiking—except in an emergency or in desperation—was one shade worse.

The desire or attempt to get something for nothing in any area of life is destructive to the soul and spirit of an individual. The decision to pay one's own way in full on the other hand, braces the personality and strengthens the character. Self-reliance is a source of pride and self-respect. Trying to live off of others is a source of shame. We refused to do it.

Show Me the Money

Our pressing need was for money—a cold cash injection to put the trip to Africa back on its feet. The question was, Where and how were we going to come by this elixir of life? The workforce in Gibraltar consisted of Spaniards earning an average of $15 per week. Since we ate more than that each week we quickly ruled out the idea of taking jobs. We would either have to borrow the money or give up altogether.

The word *borrowing* leaves a bad taste in the mouths of self-reliant people. It denotes debt, bankruptcy, and repossessed television sets, ruined friendships, and ne'er-do-wells. Yet it is the foundation of the western world, upon which our lives were built. It is the credit system that allows pleasure and necessity to be dealt with immediately, and repaid when possible.

Geoff and I had both bought cars and insurance on this system. We had gotten educations under the secure wing of borrowed capital. We had bought clothes and spare parts, rented homes and apartments, pulled friends out of difficulties with pregnant girlfriends, and financed chums in buying cars and paying rent—all on credit. For years we had been both recipients and benefactors of the borrowing system and could honestly say one thing: We had never left a debt unpaid.

We had been in debt before and would be again. We felt no shame toward borrowing or borrowers and were secure in our ability not only to repay but also to accept repaying as a moral and irrevocable obligation, one not to be shirked because of distance or the passing of time. We felt that, having always borrowed and repaid, we had earned the right to do it again when the occasion arose. And the occasion had arisen.

Writing for Money

That resolved, we threw our hearts into the borrowing enterprise with the enthusiasm of entrepreneurs seeking venture capital for a new start-up. For the remainder of the afternoon we sat on the beach and wrote passionate letters to friends explaining our desperate position and asking for loans, to be repaid when we reached Johannesburg and began working again.

Most of the letters were addressed to people from whom we had extracted offers to call on them if we ever ran short and needed financial assistance. So we wrote: "Well, faithful friends, this is the pinch. You can't come with us personally on this journey, but you can accompany us in spirit; you will be sharing the adventure by helping to make it possible." Just before the post office closed that evening, we sent all the letters by air express, plus two telegrams. Then there was little for us to do but wait for the replies.

A Surprise Announcement

That evening on the beach, much to our surprise, Bob announced he was cashing in his chips. He'd had enough of sweating and insecurity and was fed up. He said he would rather go back to England than sit like a fool on a lonely beach waiting for money to come so he could go out and risk his life some more.

"You can't be serious, Bob. Not after all we've been through together?"

"Come on, Bob. What good are *two* musketeers? How can you leave us when Africa is within our grasp? Look! You can almost touch the lights of Morocco."

"I'm not sold on this idea anymore. Why don't we give it up and go to the beaches in Southern France? That we can do with the money we have left."

"But Bob, we've come all this way to go to Africa. We can't just quit!"

"Think about it, Bob. Don't make up your mind tonight. It's late; and it's been a long day. We'll talk about it in the morning. What do you say?"

"I don't need to think about it anymore," he said. "I've been thinking about it since Barcelona, and have made up my mind. One third of the money is mine, and tomorrow I'll take my share and leave."

We tried to argue, using our long friendship as a lever, but it was no use. Like a bulldog he had locked onto the idea of going back to England or France and staunchly refused to budge. We dropped the subject and turned in for the night.

Our hope for a change of heart failed to materialize. The next morning, after hiding our gear in the rocks once more, we rode back to the Barclays Bank in town and cashed the remaining traveler's checks. Geoff and I glumly gave him his share of "the company"—60 pounds. He took it and went off to sell his bicycle, leaving Geoff and me alone at the bank.

Taking the Plunge

"What do we do from here?"

"I think we should buy the Land Rover and find some way to continue on our way to Africa."

"I can't envision going back. After all this, it would be ridiculous."

"Let's go and see if Harten will accept 100 pounds for the Rover."

To our surprise, Mr. Harten accepted the reduced offer. We took delivery of the Rover that afternoon and drove it back toward Sandy

Cove—our beach—to test the four-wheel drive in the sand. Coming around one of the sharp corners on the sea cliff road, we almost ran over Bob. He was riding into town to deliver his bicycle to a shop and move into a youth hostel at the far end of the main street.

We had no hard feelings toward Bob. We offered him a lift into town in *our* Land Rover, which he accepted. A few minutes later he sheepishly asked if we had any openings for a spare driver to Africa.

"I didn't think you'd buy the Rover," said Bob. "I thought you'd give it up without my share of the money, and then we would all go back together."

"Bob, old buddy, we are never going to give up. Not now, not if the money runs out, not ever—until we get to Johannesburg."

"Anyway, welcome back. We're glad to have you aboard again."

Another Great Lesson

All great achievements begin with a leap of faith, a bold step into the unknown. Great success requires an irrevocable commitment—a cutting loose from the safety and security of the tried and true. Act boldly and unseen forces will come to your aid. They always do.

That afternoon we drove up and down the sandy beach with wheels churning, engine roaring, and three light-headed world-beaters cheering wildly. After supper, which was cooked beside the vehicle on the sand, we drove into Gibraltar and got drunk for the first time in a month. The lights on the Moroccan coast seemed ten miles closer.

It is strange how our perceptions are so colored by the news of the day or moment. Something that one minute remote, distant, and difficult can suddenly seem doable, close, and even imminent after just one positive change.

The Rock of Gibraltar

The Rock of Gibralter is shaped like a disfigured pear and is cut off from the mainland by a narrow channel that is crossed by a two-lane causeway; it is like a small Anglo-Saxon island on the edge of a Spanish sea. The famous rock fills the easterly two-thirds of this area, with the city of Gibraltar draped compactly on the western base above the harbor. On the eastern side, at the bottom of the steep concrete rain catcher, a narrow winding road from the city snakes around the cliffs and ends at a sheer stone face just above the tiny beach where we set up camp.

High above the road the huge rock looms at an angle of 70 degrees and an altitude of 2,200 feet; like a cliff it cuts off the sun to the beach below at 3 P.M. every day. We found the beach to be largely deserted, except on the weekends, and so made our temporary home there.

Home Sweet Home

We reckoned it would take at least six days for people to reply to our requests for additional finances. We therefore set about filling the hours as constructively as possible; we were sure the money would come and wanted to be prepared for departure when it did.

The day after Bob's defection and subsequent return was Sunday. The beach began filling with tourists and Gibraltarians shortly after 9 A.M. Our haphazard procedure of tossing the sleeping bags on the beach each night to sleep and then tossing them back among the rocks each day was senseless if we were to be staying there six days or more. We needed something more permanent.

We chose the most ideal spot against the seawall that ran the length of the little beach to be our home. We then labored all day in the hot sun, carrying rocks from the base of the cliff to build walls that would give us a little protection from the breezes that came up every day or two, as well as some privacy. By the end of the day we had completed a three-walled enclosure about four feet high, open to the sky, and roomy enough to cook and move around in.

Passing the Time Away

We all gave up the casual smoking we'd been doing and started training a little, throwing our football back and forth and running out for passes into the water and shouting and splashing. The water was crystal clear and cool; it shimmered in the bright sun that shined all the days we spent in the tiny colony. We swam every morning, and increased the distance daily until we could do a mile. Our skin began to take on a copper tan, light at first, then darker as we spent hours in the warmth of the Mediterranean early summer. Slowly the days passed, but with no reply from our friends.

The Land Rover was put into the garage for two days to have the muffler repaired and electrical system checked. We changed the spark plugs and had the contacts cleaned. Meanwhile, we bought five five-gallon jerry cans—two for water and three for gasoline—and a small tool kit to add to the spare parts we had ordered from Roots Garage. With a little black-and-gold enamel we proudly painted the Bon Vivant emblem on both doors of the light green vehicle to add the finishing touch.

Nothing to Report

We soon developed a routine for those lonely days in Gibraltar. Every morning we inquired at the post office, the telegraph office, and bank to see if there had been any replies. "Not today, boys," or "Nothing yet," or "Maybe later on, call this afternoon," were the answers.

We had photographs taken and then took tests for our International Driving Permits and Gibraltar licenses. The health center in the main square informed us we needed yellow fever vaccinations and boosters for typhus A and tetanus. We signed the forms and paid one pound each for the shots. They were really powerful. We lay awake the entire night, moaning at the pain and numbness in our left arms and shoulders. Geoff had a tooth filled at a small clinic in town, while Bob and I took the remaining bicycles to the large shop inside the city gates and sold them for one-third the price we had paid in London. We were glad to be rid of them.

And every day, morning and evening, we made our pilgrimage to the communications offices to check for the replies that never came.

Marking Time

At night we parked the Rover and roamed the streets in search of bars with jukeboxes carrying tunes we wanted to hear again before saying good-bye to civilization. We became regular customers of several places, dropping in each evening for a glass of beer and a little chat about our impending trip. The Dollar Bar, run by old Ben and his two married daughters, became our favorite hangout. It was a hole-in-the-wall, but comfortable and always cheery.

Behold a Pale Horse starring Gregory Peck was showing at the main theater in town. We'd all seen it, but went again. We also went to the movies on other quiet nights at the military theater and the small show house in the old part of town. The days passed slowly by, one after another, and still there were no replies to our requests for money.

Waiting can be the hardest type of work; you see no progress and find no relief from anxiety. For us, the long slow days seemed to run together, with the sun rising each morning at 5 A.M. and becoming so warm by 6 A.M. that we had to abandon our sleeping bags from the heat and perspiration.

The first thing we saw in the morning was the green Land Rover with its black-and-gold emblem, standing patiently by our open "house" as if to reproach us for failing to take it to Africa, as we had promised. In town the streets were alive with colorful clothing shops run by ivory-toothed, smiling Hindus who were always good for a bartering session on our way to the post office and bank.

Look for the Good

There were flowers everywhere in Gibraltar during those bright spring days; they filled the windows and storefronts and overflowed from carts pushed by Spanish women along the narrow main street. Music blared at us from the wide doorways of the many modern stores selling duty-free radios and tape recorders, gifts, and souvenirs.

Each day we trudged hopefully to the post office, resignedly to the bank, pessimistically to the telegraph office, and then disappointedly back to the Rover and home to the beach.

If the shadow of defeat had not hovered like a cloud over us we could have enjoyed those days in Gibraltar immensely. The weather was consistently beautiful, the people were warm and friendly, the living was cheap, and the pace of life was soft and easy. But the grim specter of failure always rose to taunt us and make a mockery of our fading nonchalance. The hardest part wasn't the waiting; we could wait for anything as long as necessary. The hard thing was simply not knowing; the silence from the outside world that was neither a negation nor an affirmation of our requests.

We had worked it out in our minds so neatly and written so eloquently that it didn't seem possible our letters could be ignored. What was holding up the replies, and more important, the money? Sitting there on the beach by our Land Rover, ready to go, we felt like brides at the church with no groom in sight.

A Reply at Last

On the ninth day after mailing the letters we received a reply from my Aunt Barbara. I had asked her for 100 pounds, if she could spare it, and a certain suitcase from her garage, which she could send airfreight.

The reply was ripped open eagerly with trembling fingers:

Dear Brian,

I have forwarded your suitcase as you requested. You owe me six pounds, which I suppose I'll never see. As for your request for money, if you think I can afford to finance your aimless wanderings while you squander your youth to no good purpose, you will have to think again. You had no right going off without enough money to pay for your entire trip, and I am not prepared to rectify your mistakes. Why don't you boys take a job in Gibraltar and work for six months? You don't really care how you waste your time."

The letter continued another page and a half and ended with a mention of how nicely her geraniums were blooming this spring.

So that was it. That was what they thought about our great adventure. That was why there had been no replies, no money, no response at all. We drove back to the beach, parked, and sat in the Rover in silence. Everything had been so perfect, we thought. All the details were wrapped up and taken care of. We had found a seed called Africa, planted it, and nurtured it until it grew and was about to bear fruit. But now we lacked the money needed to reap the harvest, while the sun beat down and the fruit rotted on the branch.

The Cold Wind of Reality

How foolish we must look. Three boys playing a silly game called "Let's be men and go to Africa." Three improvident youths living in a cheap utopia made of high ideals and childish fantasies—that's what we were to everyone else; we were the only ones too dense to see it. Even a little old lady could see into our senseless dream world and hold the reality up for us to cringe before. It was like catching us shame-faced and tongue-tied with a stolen cookie. After all our hopes and plans, glorious ambitions, and eagerness to do battle with life in the Dark Continent, was this what it came down to—a triumvirate of worthless juveniles, tilting at windmills?

We wondered if they all felt that way, that this trip, so precious to us, was just a great big waste of time. That night we discussed the possibilities of driving back to England and starting over. We could sell our watches if necessary for petrol and perhaps try again in five months or so. We'd made our big try and lost and knew we couldn't stay in Gibraltar forever. Perhaps we needed to face the facts and do something a little more "realistic."

We didn't go into town that night. Instead we sat on the dark beach beside our Land Rover, gazing out at the empty sea. We felt like old men on a lonely shore, unneeded and unappreciated by an indifferent world. The lights of Morocco now seemed very faint, and distant.

"The most essential factor is persistence, the determination never to allow your energy or enthusiasm to be dampened by the discouragement that must inevitably come."
—James Whitcomb Riley

The Opinions of Others

Don't let your dreams be destroyed by the opinions of other people, including close relatives. You alone know what your goal means to you. Other people always have a different perspective. They may be well meaning in their comments and criticism, but they simply don't understand. You might listen out of respect to their words and weigh them, but the decision—and its consequences— is yours alone to bear.

CHAPTER 11

The Turning Point

> "There is only one thing for us to do, and that is to do our level best right where we are every day of our lives; to use our best judgment, and then to trust the rest to that Power which holds the forces of the universe in His hand."
>
> —Orison Swett Marden

THE NEXT DAY WAS SUNDAY and "our beach" was half full of relaxed Gibraltarians strolling along the water's edge or picnicking in the bright sunshine. With the happy laughter and tinkling music around us, we tossed off our shroud of discouragement somewhat and swam and tossed the ball around.

If we couldn't go to Africa, that didn't mean we had to cry about it. There was always tomorrow, when we could come back to Gibraltar and try again. No matter what we would keep the Land Rover and tools intact for the next try in a few months. Disappointed? Yes. Defeated? Never!

Africa would still be there in September, and this time we wouldn't make any mistakes. We had fought and lost; but the first battle didn't decide the war. We were saddened all right, but not destroyed. It was a shame we had come so far and been turned back on the very threshold, but we were only down, not out—not by a long shot.

Our Lives Transformed

On Monday morning we strode to the post office staunch as Vikings determined to accept the worst and carry on from there. Smiling bravely, we presented ourselves at poste restaunte like disciplined soldiers walking before a firing squad. There was one thin letter waiting for Geoff from a friend of his father in London whom he had met only once in his childhood and to whom he had written requesting 75 pounds. We waited patiently, like doomed men hearing the rifles cocked, as the letter was ripped open.

Geoff read it to himself, then aloud to us; suddenly the world burst into a blaze of light and music—a joyous, crashing symphony of glorious relief and reprieve. The siege was lifted; the cavalry had come thundering to the rescue. We were world-beaters again in a burst of exultation and triumph. Slapping each other on the back, laughing riotously, and jumping up and down in excitement, we made him read it again. It was brief and to the point:

Dear Geoffrey,

Your father wrote and told me you would be in London sometime this winter, and I look forward to seeing you again as a grown man. However, it will wait until you return from your journey into Africa. It is unfortunate that you have exhausted your finances, but as I was once a young man in similar circumstances, I appreciate how easy it is to under-budget, much more when you have so little idea of what to budget for.

It is a wonderful thing you boys have embarked upon; it would be a shame to abandon it for the sake of an innocent miscalculation of expenses. You must employ your youth to the full while you have the opportunity, and before you become burdened with responsibilities. To assure that you experience no further difficulties, I have ordered my bank to transfer the sum of 150 pounds to you, care of Barclays Bank, Gibraltar.

Please do not feel that you are under any pressure for repayment, and if there is anything further I can do for you, please do not hesitate to write. Please extend my regards to your two friends, and may I wish you all, Good Traveling.

Yours faithfully,
Jack S. Turing

How can a person express gratitude so great it wells up in the throat like a shower full of tears? And to a man we had never met, in a distant city, who had, in a kindly gesture of warmth and encouragement, changed our whole lives? We had come to our Rubicon at the Gates of Hercules, and a hand had reached across the miles and pushed us confidently into the current.

It was not a question of whether we would succeed, or whether it was advisable. It was the simple realization that we must have the chance; by giving it to us, to do with as we could according to our abilities, Mr. Jack S. Turing became our inspirational symbol, the banner under which we proudly entered into Africa.

Something Always Happens

This was a most important lesson for me. I had the same experience over and over again. I found that if you make a total commitment to a goal and hang on long enough, something always happens. Many people lose heart and give up just one day, one step, or one action before the breakthrough that leads to great success. It is as if nature poses a test to see how badly you really want it; it is at that moment—

of quitting or continuing—when you demonstrate what you're really made of.

"Most people give up just when they're about to achieve success. They quit on the one-yard line. They give up at the last minute of the game, one foot from a winning touchdown." —H. Ross Perot

One Thin Letter

What a difference a letter can make! One letter of rejection can dash your hopes and call into question your very purpose. It can dismiss you as a vain and foolish vagabond. One letter of acceptance then restores your faith, validates your mission, and ultimately makes the remainder of your journey possible. The special irony is that the affirmation or assistance may come from a distant relative—or even a total stranger.

"Our greatest lack is not money for any undertaking, but rather ideas. If the ideas are good, cash will somehow flow to where it is needed."
—ROBERT SCHULLER

SECTION IV

The Dawn of Reality

> "The thing that contributes to anyone's reaching the goal he wants is simply wanting that goal badly enough."
> —CHARLES E. WILSON

MOST GREAT SUCCESS IN LIFE comes just one step beyond where you are ready to quit. There is a time in your life when you feel yourself suddenly beyond caring, completely willing to accept the outcome, whatever it is. But you persist anyway. And at that moment, fate intervenes. Destiny acts. Something happens.

Every test you take and pass on your journey merely prepares you for more difficult tests and challenges. The problems and difficulties never end. They only change and become tougher as you grow and mature.

Never wish for things to be easier. Instead, wish you were stronger and better. Never seek the easy way out. Instead look for the hard way through.

Nature is kind. She never sends you a problem too big to handle. She is clever as well. She prepares you step by step, raising the bar—the requirements—gradually until you are ready for the big tests when they come.

As long as you have a clear goal and plan and are willing to be flexible in the face of changing circumstances, you will continue to move onward and upward.

You will eventually look back and be amazed at how far you have come. But it is nothing compared to how far you have yet to go.

"Nothing worthwhile comes easily. Work, continuous work, and hard work, is the only way to accomplish results that last."
—Hamilton Holt

CHAPTER 12

Morocco and the Atlas Mountains

> "A man to carry out a successful business must have imagination. He must see things in a vision, a dream of the whole thing."
> —CHARLES SCHWAB

ON THURSDAY, MAY 4, AT 2 P.M., we drove off the ferry in Tangiers and after a brief customs formality, continued into the city. The now topless Land Rover was heavily laden with cans, boxes of tinned food, equipment, and clothes; on top of the tightly packed load sat Bob and two English girls who were only riding with us as far as Tangiers. We seemed to have just about everything.

The food took up most of the space in the back and made the Rover look like an overland delivery wagon. Based on the distance, we anticipated being on the road to our next destination of Lagos, Nigeria. Thus the food buying was simplified immensely. We just bought 30 cans of each item—beans, spaghetti, meatballs, sausage, peaches, and green peas. We had 48 cans of condensed milk to go with the tea and coffee, plus bouillon cubes, sugar, salt, pepper, and garlic. The total cost, including two petrol burners for cooking, came to just under $100.

We reckoned that two meals per day, morning and evening, would be sufficient. The monotony of a diet lacking in variety of foodstuffs would be offset by the time lapse between the two meals and assure hunger enough to make anything welcome.

Somehow, we managed to be wrong in almost every calculation we made, until it almost seemed safer in the long run to make a decision and then do the closest to the opposite we could find. But in this case, planning on a two-meal daily diet, we had been quite correct. We could always supplement it with tea or bullion cubes.

My Kingdom for a Map

At a large, Spanish-type house overlooking the sea on the outskirts of the city, we dropped off the two girls and wished them luck in their proposed plans to work the summer in an orphanage. We returned to the Casbah—the main shopping area—to buy insurance for the vehicle, which we had not been able to do in Gibraltar.

At this point, we felt we should finally get a map for the coming journey. After a couple of hours of searching, we were surprised and chagrined to find there were no maps of Africa and the Sahara Desert available in Tangiers.

We knew a map was essential. We tried the Michelin Tire Company offices and asked if they had one of Africa. The receptionist had no idea and went back to speak to her boss, a Monsieur Tourneau.

Monsieur Tourneau politely informed us that Michelin did not sell maps, only tires. We thanked him politely and went back to the car. As we sat there mulling over our situation, he suddenly appeared, looked at us searchingly, and then handed us a map and walked away.

I still remember that moment, that exact time and place in the warm afternoon in the parking lot. We suspected something important had just happened. We opened the map, which was two feet by three feet, and gazed at a miracle of the modern world.

A Modern Miracle

It was Michelin Map Number 953, covering Africa from the Mediterranean across Morocco, Algeria, and south almost 3,000 miles. It was incredible, a work of art. It detailed every city, town, and landmark across the Sahara and into sub-Saharan Africa. It had obviously been drawn and upgraded over many years, when the French governed much of Africa. In the weeks ahead, it turned out to be an incredible blessing. I cannot imagine how we could have survived without it. It definitely saved our lives.

This was a vital life lesson. I was able to find later that usually any map or plan is better than none. And if it is complete enough, as this map was, it can make the critical difference between victory and defeat. It is amazing how many otherwise talented and intelligent people underachieve and fail in life because of poor or nonexistent planning and preparation. Sometimes the first 10 percent of the time you invest in doing your homework determines 90 percent of the value of everything that happens afterwards.

Two hours and $48 later—insured for the entirety of the continent of Africa for three months—we were traveling on the southbound road to Rabat and singing "It won't be long, no, it won't be long."

Mechanical Difficulties

We were right; it wasn't long. Just 12 kilometers out of Tangiers we began learning interesting things about our beloved Land Rover. For example, the radiator was no good. In fact, it was bubbling, boiling, steaming, and pouring water all over the road.

A couple of minutes of gawking at the radiator convinced us it would not be a bad idea to sit and wait for it to cool, which we did. There had been no opportunity to drive any distance on Gibraltar's limited roads, and breaking down so quickly now was not a good omen.

"Cripes! Look at the steam! The bloody radiator looks ruined. Haven't we got enough troubles?"

"Apparently not."

"Are you trying to be funny?"

"Nope."

"Did you fill the jerry cans with water, Bob?"

"What do you mean, did I fill them? That was your job, wasn't it?"

"Yeah? Who says it was my job?"

"Oh, shut up, both of you. I filled them."

Driving with two wheels on the gravel shoulder to keep out of the way of passing traffic, we limped the 12 kilometers back to town to find a repair shop.

"I wonder how much it's going to cost?"

"Probably a king's ransom."

"Yeah, these Arabs are notorious thieves."

"And con men."

"And swindlers."

"Can't we go a little bit faster?"

"Why?"

"Oh, I'm just getting a little tired of kids on bicycles going by us and laughing."

"Well then, I've got just the answer."

"Yeah, what?"

"Don't look at them."

Suspicious Minds

At the first dusty little workshop we came to on the outskirts of town, we turned in and armed ourselves with the French dictionary before getting out. With exaggerated expressions of woe, and after thumbing frantically through the little book, we outlined our misfortunes to the sweat-stained, T-shirted proprietor of "Alphonso's." We finally had to lead him to the vehicle and point out the felonious radiator; he brightened knowledgeably.

Nodding and smiling like a door-to-door salesman, Alphonso regretted he couldn't help us personally, but if we would go with him into town, he would take us to his friend, who was in the radiator business. Feeling dubious, we fell in behind the battered pickup and followed him through the streets.

"Where are we going?"

"He's taking us to a friend of his."

"What for?"

"Probably to share the pickings. You know, one fellow directs the suckers to the other, and afterwards, they divide the loot between them."

He stopped in front of a tiny shop with the word "RADIATORS" over the door, and jovially introduced us to his worried friend, Manuel.

"Who's that?"

"His partner in crime, I guess."

After the customary round of hand shaking, they jabbered together in Arabic for a few seconds.

"What's that they're saying?"

"They're deciding how much they can take us for. What do you think?"

Our misgivings were rising by the moment.

No Quick Solution

We were hoping for a quick and inexpensive repair job; perhaps a few seconds with an acetylene torch, and we would be on our way. Then again, we had had problems in the past with radiators—ruined ones that had to be replaced. This one appeared well beyond repair.

Alphonso left us in the hands of his partner in crime and disappeared with an uninspiring "Bon voyage!" Manuel said the radiator would have to come out, and when we had complied with the request, he proceeded to strip it down with astounding proficiency. This demonstrated beyond doubt that the radiator was indeed irreparable. It was rusted out and rotten to the core.

We stoically resigned ourselves to fate and the procuring of another radiator, a job that included a tour of three scrap yards and the critical inspection of five used radiators. After having examined the fourth and rejecting it, Manuel ceased to be looked upon as a Barbary pirate and was accorded instead the respect due a conscientious craftsman.

Our fears about being bilked turned out to be groundless. Manuel, finally satisfied with the fifth radiator, haggled the price down to half that originally demanded by the Arab in the scrap yard when he perceived the radiator was for tourists.

After four hours of searching, testing, welding, and checking for further defects, the bill came to $17; the radiator, now reinstalled in the Rover, was functioning perfectly. We gave Manuel $20 and many thanks, since the part alone cost $13. That sort of sincere honesty had to be encouraged.

One of the wonderful things you learn in life is that most people you meet are good, honest, and decent and mean well. It is the occasional negative or dishonest person who puts you on your guard with everyone.

The Road to Casablanca

It was sundown when we got out of Tangiers once more, after having cooked our supper on the sidewalk while the radiator cooled, much to the amusement of the passers-by. There was no need to stop before Casablanca; we had set ourselves a tentative schedule and were running half a day behind it.

It was 3 A.M. when we arrived outside Casablanca, blind and sleepy from the long day and night since Gibraltar. Fearful of cutthroats and thieves, with which the infamous city of intrigue and Casbah must surely be rife, we parked in the middle of a vast field, far from any buildings, and slept on and around our supplies rather than risk the ground outside.

Thus passed our first night in Africa. A small boy tending half a dozen sheep was the sole spectator to our emergence from the Rover the next morning. Rubbing half a dozen spots where the corners of the boxes had dug into us in the night, we stretched and yawned in the warm sunshine and unloaded a few cans of food for breakfast. After eating the beans and sausages, we drove into the busy city of modern skyscrapers and traffic jams, and within minutes got lost in the search for a place to buy discount petrol coupons.

On to Marrakech

By the time we extricated ourselves from the maze of crowded, cobbled streets, we had the coupons and were on the road to Marrakech.

The change in the people and the country from the day before in Gibraltar was profound. Gone were the trousers, shirts, and jackets of the European continent. In their places were the flowing robes and dark burnooses of Arabia, and the women with their faces covered, except for a tiny patch over one eye through which they peered at our passing.

The old men in the rocky fields, who tended sheep or hacked listlessly at stringy rows of corn, wore rolled headdresses that covered their ears and necks from the baking sun. These merged into loose folds of cloth that enveloped the body and legs to the ankles, where gnarled feet protruded into rugged rope or leather sandals.

The sun was hotter than it had been the day before. The fields, except those with primitive irrigation systems, were parched and yellow with thin, scrubby grass and the odd thorn tree. The occasional river was shallow and light brown with mud; the undrinkable water flowed languorously between dusty banks lined with tired cypress trees. The countryside—from the ancient stone houses and crumbling fences to the worn footpaths that wound from the road into the rocky, lifeless country beyond—gave the impression of uncaring timelessness.

Traveling Across a Poor Land

Here the bicycle and the burro were the common forms of transportation. Clay and sticks substituted for the bricks and mortar of Europe as the most popular building materials. Lassitude and passivity had settled over a land poor so long that the people accepted indigence and subsistence as a way of life, one not to be questioned in this world. It was easy to understand how the Muslim law of Kismet ("Everything is written and cannot be changed—unless Allah wills it.") had been received and embraced so unquestioningly by these people.

Spain had been poor, with its peasants and third-class trains, its dirty streets and blackened cities, but what we were seeing now was a poverty so deeply ingrained in the fiber and social structure of a land as to be ineradicable. The people looked as though they had lived with it for so long that any other way of life would be a step toward dissolution of their system. A change would not be progressive or even regressive, but just a removal of the condition of being poor, and expecting nothing more than a continuation of that condition.

Driving our Land Rover, we felt incomparably wealthy next to the citizens of the country, but it didn't seem to matter much to them. Ours wasn't an affluence to gloat over or talk about; it was rather something to know, have, and not make too much of.

Routes Across the Sahara

Our beautiful, detailed, and incredibly accurate Michelin map indicated three main routes across the Sahara. We decided to remain with our original plan—to cross Morocco to the Sahara, cross the Sahara through Spanish Morocco to Senegal, 1,800 miles beyond, and travel around the hump of Africa to Nigeria. This route went through almost every country in West Africa, over a distance of about 5,000 miles, and was, as far as we could discern, the most interesting and comprehensive of the three routes.

Our goal for the day was Agadir on the Atlantic coast in southern Morocco. It would be our jumping-off place for the Sahara and we thought getting there would be just a long, boring drive to be completed as quickly as possible.

In our urgent desire to make as many miles as possible each day, we drove steadily, stopping only for an hour at Marrakech to eat our supper and refuel from the jerry cans. We then drove on through the night into the Atlas Mountains.

Terrible Roads

The road leading into the Atlas Mountains is paved, as is the one leading to Tarroudant and Agadir from the other side. But the 60 kilometers in between were the worst we had ever driven; it took two hours of jolting, bone-rattling fighting with the wheel and gears to get over them. Three times the radiator had to be topped up with water from the jerry cans; however the Rover responded beautifully the whole way.

When we came back onto the paved road, shortly after midnight, it was with the beginning of a pride and affection for that vehicle that was to grow to an undying love. I look back on that Rover with lifelong affection, as an older man might remember a childhood sweetheart.

By that time, we were again wilting from fatigue, and could think of little beyond getting to Agadir and going to sleep. At 3 A.M. we drove through the dark, silent streets of the city to the sea, and then along the sea road until we found a cliff high above the crashing surf. There, in a rocky field, we threw our bags on the ground and slept like babies.

Further Repairs

The radiator had sprung a leak in the night and required a welding torch to seal, so that was the first business of the day. After breakfast in a goat-soiled alley, during which our two stoves blew up in flames, we sought out a workshop for the necessary repairs.

The French-Arab owner was very accommodating, and in addition to not charging us for the welding, he gave us some advice concerning our proposed route. The first, in which he was echoed by his partner, was that we should not attempt to cross the Sahara at that time of the year. It was too hot, they said. We would ruin our vehicle and have to leave it there. It was dangerous, as we knew nothing about desert traveling. And there was nothing to see in the desert anyway.

No Easy Way

We thanked him for his concern, but expressed a friendly disinterest in his gloomy predictions. We weren't going to spend any more time than was absolutely necessary in the desert, we told him amiably. We were going to drive straight across to get to Black Africa without further delay.

When he saw we had no intention of heeding his warnings, he gave us another tidbit to think about. The Moroccans and Algerians were embroiled in a border dispute in the area we'd be driving through that afternoon. Several soldiers had been killed in the past weeks. If we must go, we had better visit the military headquarters in town and get a *laissez-passer* (to allow to pass—a permit) to allow us through the lines. That piece of information interested us a lot.

The Border Dispute

We didn't know much about African politics, and had no desire to become involved with them. This expedition was purely a friendly one—a gesture of goodwill—and any way we could avoid involvement was good for us. We therefore drove straight from the workshop to army headquarters to get a pass to allow us through the disputed area.

We arrived just after midday on Saturday, but the offices were already closed and would stay shut until Monday. Since we couldn't proceed without the official authorization, we would have to wait until the offices reopened. That wasn't such an objectionable idea since many miles of sunny beaches stretched out around Agadir. However we were a bit perturbed at the delay and the mess it made of our schedule, which called for us to make 200 miles per day.

Almost Heaven

Ten miles up the coast from Agadir we found an uninhabited little cove with 100 yards of firm, clean sand that was sheltered from the wind and invisible from the main road. It was the type of place the holiday brochures describe to lure tourists to North Africa. The sun was warm and brightly beaming the whole day. And the privacy was above reproach. Except for an occasional passing Arab on his drowsy burro, we didn't see another person all weekend.

The water was lovely, like warm silk to swim in, and we forswore swimming trunks most of the time to cavort as close to nature as possible. In that place and time, it seemed no price was too much to pay to be world-beaters. It was letter perfect—except for one little detail—and that was the flies.

Flies Everywhere

From the first tinge of sun in the eastern sky to the last streak of crimson on the western horizon, the flies were everywhere. In the morning we woke with flies on our lips, around our eyes, and in our ears. We were beset by clouds of them at every meal and throughout the day—buzzing, crawling, and nibbling droves of irritating flies. Any activity that involved sitting in one place was undertaken with something to wave back and forth in front of the face to keep the flies away. Conversation, viewed from a distance, looked like a waving game.

Waving our hands like windshield wipers to keep the flies away soon became a part of life in North Africa, as normal as breathing. We became accustomed to the flies after a while, like one does to a plaster cast on a broken limb. We were always happy when the setting sun drew them away; they wouldn't be seen again until the crack of dawn the following morning, when they returned in endless numbers.

Life's Like That

The flies in North Africa, like the wind and rain in France and the cobblestones in Spain, were like metaphors for life. It seems that whenever you embark on any new endeavor, you are beset by countless little problems, details, and unexpected irritations, plus difficult and dishonest people of all kinds. They go with the territory. They are an unavoidable part of the price you have to pay to accomplish anything new or worthwhile. This is probably what William James of Harvard meant when he wrote, "What cannot be cured must be endured."

We were up with the sun—and flies—on Monday morning, eager to continue on our way into Africa. We took an invigorating swim to wake up, knowing it would be almost a week before we would reach the sea once more, below the Sahara, in Senegal, on the other side of the desert.

The Map, Radiator, and Warnings

Call it luck or fate or a manifestation of brotherly love—but so often the one thing you need the most at a particular moment is providentially provided to prepare you for the next stage. Without the Michelin map, and the early breakdown and repair of the radiator, we certainly would have perished in the Sahara Desert. Every experience, no matter how unexpected or frustrating, was teaching us something we would need to know to survive in the weeks and trials to come.

> "He who knows no hardships will know no hardihood. He who faces no calamity will need no courage. Mysterious though it is, the characteristics in human nature which we love best grow in a soil with a strong mix of troubles."
> —Harry Emerson Fosdick

CHAPTER 13

The Best-Laid Plans of Mice and Men

> "Each experience through which we pass operates ultimately for our good. This is the correct attitude to adopt, and we must see things in this light."
> —RAYMOND HOLLIWELL

AT 8 A.M. WE DROVE UP THE gravel driveway to the military administration building; we had our map and a French dictionary to explain what we wanted. It took a little sign language and word hunting to send the message to the unshaved Moroccan soldier on the front steps that we would like to see an official to procure a *laissez-passer* for the frontier. We were eventually ushered into a bare office with only a desk and two chairs for furniture. One of the chairs was stuffed with a large, fretful captain.

The answer we received was equally bare. The border was closed. Period. There was no possibility of our passing through the disputed zone. It was too dangerous. If the Moroccans didn't shoot us going, the Algerians would probably shoot us coming. He was polite, concise, and busy. We would have to find another route.

"Well, that was quick," said Bob. "What do we do now?"

"Like the man says, we have to find another route."

Back to the Drawing Boards

Alas! It was one of the ups and downs of world beating. But why did we seem to be getting all the *downs*? Huddled over the map in the Land Rover, having had six weeks of tentative planning dashed in six minutes of Moroccan officialdom, we glumly worked out another plan.

The second trans-Saharan route on our map was through Algeria, across the heart of the desert and into Mali, and continued along the Niger River into Dahomey, west to the Atlantic Ocean, and eventually into Nigeria. To intersect this route in the shortest distance, we would have to follow a series of ragged roads that ran 400 miles eastward, across the Moroccan hinterland to the border with Algeria and a town called Figuig. From there, we would turn south to cross the desert and be once more on our way toward Nigeria.

Two Steps Forward, One Back

Coming to Agadir had been a waste of four days, 600 miles worth of petrol, and one eighth of our supplies. To go back and toward the east involved a long, hard drive.

"It's sure as hell a long way to Tipperary," said Geoff, folding the map so our route was exposed.

"With our average speed, we can be in Algeria in 20 hours," I calculated. "The sooner we get started, the sooner we get finished."

"Oh crap!" said Bob. "That means we're going to have to drive all night again. What point is there in that?"

"We're behind schedule, Bob," said Geoff. "We've got to make up the time we've lost, and then we've got to make up the time we're losing while we're making up the time we've lost."

"Yeah, what could be simpler than that?"

Geoff eased out the clutch and steered the Rover back onto the main road. The sun was already beginning to beat down through the canvas top, making the inside of the vehicle stifling hot when it wasn't moving. It was, indeed, a long way to Tipperary.

One hour out of Agadir, we pulled off the road into an olive grove and ran the Rover into the shade to cool. The ignition was acting up due to what seemed to be a combination of poor contacts in the ignition system and overheating. We decided to cure both at the same time.

When the engine cooled we put in a set of heavy-duty points we had bought in Gibraltar. They were a special type we had never seen before and we never looked at them again. These amazing points lasted forever, reduced our gas consumption, gave us greater acceleration, and caused the vehicle to run cooler.

By now it was midday. The sun was so intense it broiled the air even in the shade and convinced us driving was not a good idea until later in the afternoon. This was our first exposure to the heat of the midday sun, something that each day would soon be designed around.

An Unexpected Meeting

Later in the afternoon, soon after we had started off again, we were passed by a large Land Rover. In it were the two English girls we had given a ride from the ferry in Tangiers four days previously.

Recognition was simultaneous, and we both stopped to exchange greetings. They were driving from the railhead in Agadir with a sturdy-looking English woman, and were on their way to Tarroudant, about 30 kilometers farther. There they would work with blind children for the summer. They asked if we would like to follow along and come in for a cup of tea.

Forty minutes later we entered the mud-walled city and followed the other vehicle closely through the narrow, shadowy streets. It stopped deep in the town at a large gate in the wall surrounding an old Moorish house. The gate was opened by an ancient Arab and closed behind us after we had entered the flag-stoned courtyard.

The house was built of mud bricks in a box shape around a small lawn fringed with flowers. It had high ceilings done in mosaic and was wonderfully cool inside. On either side of the courtyard were blooming orange trees in neat rows on a carpet of lush grass. I couldn't help but think it was a lovely place for a blind children's orphanage.

Let There Be Light

"Blindness," said Miss Walters, as she poured the mint tea into tiny cups, "is considered a curse, put on a family by Allah. If it has not cleared up by the time the child is five, they believe the only way to lift the curse is to do away with the child."

"You don't mean a family will actually kill its children, do you?"

"Yes," she replied. "It's quite common in Arab lands. However, often the child is taken into the country and abandoned, left to die of starvation and exposure."

"Surely there must be some law against that sort of thing," said Geoff. "Isn't there any way of stopping it?"

"Oh yes," she said, "the police watch out for it. Most of our children have been brought here at the insistence of the police, or after they have been found wandering around, or been terribly beaten and left for dead."

"Why don't the parents bring the children here?" Bob asked.

"We've been trying to encourage that for six years now," Miss Walters explained. "But they feel we are somehow contradicting their beliefs, and they rarely do."

At that moment the door opened from the courtyard, and a single line of young Arab children were shepherded patiently into the room by the old fellow who had opened the gate for us. Their clothes were old but neat and clean, and their little faces all brightened when Miss Walters called out to them in Arabic. They were both boys and girls, ranging in age from five to eleven, and their glassy, inconsistent stares made it immediately apparent they were all blind.

Beaming with Happiness

"This is Freddy," said Miss Walters, gathering one of the little boys into her arms. "He had a particularly bad time of it before we got to him, didn't you, Freddy?"

The little boy obviously didn't understand the words, but his face beamed a joyous grin toward the sound of the voice.

"His grandmother brought him to us after he'd been beaten terribly and left to the wild dogs outside the city gates. We didn't think he was going to live, but he fooled us."

Freddy came to the sound of our voices and shook hands with each of us in turn. His face was lined with scars from recently healed cuts, and one arm was encased in plaster. But even with the scars and the blank gaze, his face was beaming with happiness.

After the children were led into the garden to play on the grass before dinner, we rose and excused ourselves, thanking Miss Walters for the tea and an enlightening visit. We wished the girls a good summer and assured them we could find our way out of the city.

The Good that People Do

After leaving the orphanage we drove in silence until we were back on the road and heading away from Tarroudant.

"It would be interesting to know just how much goes on under the surface that you never even hear about," said Geoff, breaking the silence.

"Look at those girls back there," said Bob, "ready to spend the whole summer taking care of those kids, just for the sake of doing it. Makes a guy feel kind of useless."

"Yeah, and that's the kind of thing you never hear about young people doing. All you get in the papers are stories about protest marchers and gang wars."

"Yes, it's true," said Geoff. "Gives one something to think about, doesn't it?"

Later I realized that much good happens in this world that is never recognized, reported, or rewarded. And many of the true heroes and heroines are quiet men and women who serve others unselfishly, one day at a time. As Robert W. Service wrote, "To help folks along, with a hand and a song; why, there's the real joy of living!"

A Hard Day's Night

We turned off the paved road onto gravel just as the sun set. Two hours later it was dark and we were hopelessly lost in a maze of cart tracks, creek beds, and what appeared to be roads through the rocky brush land, but were in fact dead ends. The four-wheel drive of the Rover carried us across washouts as wide as 300 yards and up the far sides to continue along the footpaths and goat trails.

Shortly before 11 P.M., after going around in circles for hours, we straggled onto a well-graveled road and came upon a sign that informed us how far we hadn't come that evening. Half an hour later the right front tire went flat, and we lurched to a dull halt. It was turning out to be a crummy night all around.

Unprepared for the Inevitable

This presented us with a little problem. Because the cheapest tires in Gibraltar had been selling at eight pounds each, we had chosen to ignore the fact that only two of our tires were half decent. The four-pound price tag on the cheapest jack we had looked at discouraged us from adding that instrument to our toolbox before we left. We hadn't bought a wrench for the lug nuts either. Except for our spare tire, we couldn't have been less prepared for flats if we had made an effort.

But we weren't lacking in imagination. With a heave-ho and grunt, we lifted the front of the Rover onto three jerry cans to suspend the guilty wheel. While Bob unbolted the spare tire from the hood and Geoff prepared tea, I experimented with various methods of removing rusty lug nuts without the proper wrench. There aren't any, especially in the middle of nowhere, in the middle of the night.

The Code of the Road

We had to rely on the next motorist and the code of the road—the creed by which we traveled. It was a simple, unspoken, and reciprocal agreement that ruled the conduct of drivers in less populated areas. If we saw someone with difficulties, we stopped and did our best to help them; and in turn, we reaped the benefits of someone stopping for us when we had problems, as we did at that moment.

In the driving we had done in northern British Columbia and all across North America—especially in rural areas—we had come to accept this code as a responsibility of driving, just like the dimming of headlights in the face of oncoming traffic. In that lonely spot, we had no doubt this code would be honored; it was merely a question of when the next vehicle would come along and whether it would have the necessary tools. In our years of driving thousands of miles, we had joined a silent brotherhood of the road. Since we had always paid our dues, we had no fear of being ignored by one of the fraternal members.

A Friendly Bus Driver

The water for tea was beginning to steam when the first vehicle appeared in the distant blackness. It was a full 15 minutes before the vehicle—a bus—came over the rise and bore down upon us where we stood drinking tea.

The bus came to a smooth halt 20 feet from the rear of our Rover, where it held us with our teacups in its bright headlamps. I went to the door, explained our difficulty to the burly driver, and asked him if he might have the correct wrench. He nodded, assuring me that he had a large tool box, and cut the engine. Turning to the passengers, he said something in Arabic and chuckled, at which the passengers chuckled in agreement and started leaving their seats to get off the bus, for natural reasons.

The Proper Tool

As the driver and his assistant busied themselves with the toolbox, which was locked under the luggage compartment on the outside of the bus, the passengers—all men in various types of dress—filed off the bus to casually observe.

The driver found a T-bar tire wrench and went to the front of the Rover to try it. We followed behind to do the work if it was the correct tool. It was, but the driver of the bus and his helper refused to accept our offer, jokingly insisting that they take care of it. There was nothing to do under the circumstances but to pour another cup of tea.

In the glow of the lights from the tail lamps of the Rover and the parking globes of the bus, the passengers had gathered and now sat or stood conversing quietly or looking on with curious expressions. Several had squatted on their heels, and three or four sat cross-legged in their suits or robes.

Two old men, however, lay out on the ground with their hands on their chins, watching us interestedly and talking to each other in little whispers. These two looked exactly like grizzled old hounds curled before a fire. The soft sounds of the tire changing in the background created a rather eerie, though peaceful, atmosphere. Around the vehicles surged the silence and darkness of the balmy summer night, like a breathless sea hugging around a small island held in position by chains of warm velvet. Overhead, the sky was a sheet of tiny stars that sparkled faintly in the blackened heavens. It felt like a spell was cast over us in the stillness, hinting at eternity. We leaned on the Rover and sipped tea without speaking.

Time to Go

The spell was broken by the laughing of the driver at the jerry cans that were substituting for a jack. We put down our cups and took up positions along the bumper, lifting the Rover and dropping it squarely on the road. The driver and the passengers gave a delighted cheer and happily climbed back onboard the bus.

We offered the driver a cup of tea, but he just laughed, shook hands, and took his place behind the wheel. With a roar and beep-beep, the bus crept away, picked up speed, and lumbered smoothly down the road, gradually disappearing into the night.

The episode had taken less than ten minutes from start to finish. Once again we were alone with the still of the night, standing by the darkened tailgate with cups of tea in hand, a long, long way from home.

The Law of Reciprocity

You will find with experience that mutual reciprocity is one of the greatest of all principles for assuring success and happiness in life. This principle flows from the Law of Sowing and Reaping, which says, "Whatsoever a man soweth, that also shall he reap."

In day-to-day life, whatever you put in, you get out. Whatever you are reaping today is a result of what you have sown in the past. And there's no escaping.

Whatever you do for others will eventually be done for you, "pressed down, shaken, and overflowing." Whatever you do to others will come back to you as well, so always treat others the way you want to be treated.

The great law is: *The more of yourself and your resources you give away with no expectation of return, the more will come back to you from the most unexpected sources, and in the most remarkable ways.*

Always be looking for ways to give, to contribute to others. The rewards will flow back to you with the force and power of universal law. And in the long run, it never fails.

"For every force, there is a counter-force. For every negative, there is a positive. For every action, there is a reaction. For every cause, there is an effect."
—GRACE SPEAR

CHAPTER 14

A Change of Pace

> "Your chances of success in any undertaking can always be measured by your belief in yourself."
> —Robert Collier

THE DAWN FOUND US DRIVING steadily eastward through desolate land. We had crossed the Atlas Mountains again in the night and now they rose bare and forbidding, far to the north. To the east, south, and west the rolling terrain extended to the far horizon, unbroken by trees, hills, or salient objects of any kind. The entire landscape was covered with gray-black rocky gravel that settled close upon the earth and allowed only an occasional tuft of hardy grass through its roughened surface. The road was merely a well-marked track, scraped clear of loose stones to lessen the destructive force on the passing vehicles.

There was an aura of primitive beauty about it. Even though we were chilled by the cold of early morning and hungry and tired from the long night, we couldn't help but feel a trifle awed by the stark simplicity of that empty land.

The Edge of the Desert

"This is the northernmost reach of the Sahara," said Geoff, opening the map to its full length. "But we still have to go another 500 miles south before the real desert begins."

"If it's like this here," said Bob, "what will it be like in the middle of the desert?"

"It'll probably be the dullest land on earth," I said. "We'll get across it as quickly as we can, that's for sure."

"Yes," agreed Geoff. "We didn't come to this continent to see the Sahara—it's just something in the way. The sooner we get it behind us, the better."

"I wonder," muttered Bob, "just what we came to this continent to see."

"Black Africa, old buddy. That's what. And it won't be long now."

Except for the odd goat herders and their tiny flocks, which fed off God only knows what, the few inhabitants of that region lived in small towns that seemed older than history. These mud-bricked clusters of dwellings, often surrounded with high walls, were invariably built around an oasis that was visible from many miles away because of the bright green of the tall date palms.

The life-giving water came from wells dug deep in the clay beside parched creek beds, and was hauled by hand or treadmill and spilled carefully into the closely watched vegetable gardens. The hardness of the life was etched into the faces of the old men and women who raised their heads at the sound of our vehicle, and then returned to their endless toil. We were only a two-day drive from Europe, but it seemed we were in a land that time had forgotten.

Ksar-es-Souk

The first large oasis we reached that morning had one lonely petrol station where we had our tire repaired. Shortly before midday we passed through Ksar-es-Souk, the first town of any size. Ten kilometers later we were blessed with our second flat tire, and sat down to wait for the next motorist.

An Arab-driven, weather-beaten old dump truck came along the dirt road in half an hour and the smiling driver stopped and got out to see why we were waiting. He gladly loaned us the large wrench we needed and then drove off after we had changed the tire. Better safe than sorry, we figured, and returned to Ksar-es-Souk to have the flat repaired before continuing.

Compared to the relative bustle of the dusty little town an hour before, all was empty and silent when we drove up to the tire shop we had seen on the main square. The shops were closed and shuttered, as was the tire shop, so we parked the Rover and sat in the shade of a small café to wait. It was obviously lunchtime, and we assumed the stores would be open in another few minutes.

The Afternoon Sun

The cold Coca-Cola advertised in the cracked window of the single café turned out to be warm, but the proprietor was a friendly fellow so we didn't complain. My knowledge of French had progressed to the stage of being able to ask simple questions and understand simpler answers; I asked the fellow just when the shops would reopen.

"Oh," he said, "not long."

"About what time, exactly?"

"Oh, perhaps 4 P.M., perhaps 5 P.M."

It was then just after 1 P.M.

"All stores are closed in the afternoons," he said.

Well, that was just dandy. We would have to revel in the joys of sitting and waiting for the next few hours.

We had been driving more or less steadily across country and away from towns in our first five days in Morocco. This was our first exposure to the profound change in the way of life necessitated by the extreme heat of the desert regions. We were to find that throughout North Africa and the Sahara, during the hours when the sun is at its zenith, all work and most activity comes to a standstill. To compensate for this, the working day begins early, at 6 or 7 A.M., and continues from reopening time, usually 4 P.M., until 7 or 8 P.M.

The four or five hours in the middle of the day are spent in noisy cafés that blare Arab music, in bed sleeping, or in some other pursuit requiring a minimum of effort. Rarely will one see a vehicle on the road during the searing heat of midday because of the danger of blown head gaskets or the oil in the crankcase thinning to the point where it no longer provides sufficient lubrication. That causes the engine to seize up and the car never runs again. Many people had perished that way. It began to dawn on us that there was going to be a lot more to this Sahara crossing than rough roads and passport stamps.

Attitudes Toward Time

It took us a long time to get over the hurry-up, right-now attitude we had brought with us from Europe and North America. In fact, we never did completely shake off the sense of urgency that accompanied everything we attempted. We did eventually adapt, however—to an amazing degree—to the unhurried pace of life around us.

But at that moment we were fresh from 20 years of "not now, but right now!" We couldn't help but become impatient when we were delayed for any reason. No one seemed to understand we were in a hurry. We had a schedule to make, places to go, things to do. To us, procrastination was an evil. But to the world we now found ourselves in, it was as natural as the midday heat.

Waiting three hours in Ksar-es-Souk to have a tire repaired was the beginning of a gradual realization of what we had bitten off in coming to Africa; in the long run, it made everything just a little bit easier to chew.

Pace Yourself

Successful people tend to be action-oriented. They have a sense of urgency. They want to get on with the job, finish it, and move on to the next thing. For them, time is precious.

But the majority of people move at a much slower pace. They see little need for speed. They take their time and work at their own pace.

One of the basic general rules in life is that, "People don't change." Part of being flexible and adaptive is for you to pace yourself as well. Slow down when you have to. Don't allow yourself to become tense or anxious, especially when you are at the mercy of the schedules of others.

As the Bible says, "There is a time for every purpose under heaven." Sometimes the smartest thing you can do is to just "go with the flow."

> "There are many truths of which the full meaning cannot be realized until personal experience has brought it home."
> —JOHN STUART MILL

CHAPTER 15

You Will Die in the Desert

> "The longer I live, the more I am certain that the great difference between men, between the feeble and the powerful, between the great and the insignificant, is energy—invincible determination—a purpose once fixed and then death or victory."
>
> —Sir Thomas Fowell Buxton

At this point we began to have an experience that was repeated in different ways throughout the trip. One of the Arabs at the tire shop asked where we were going. We told him we were going across the Sahara and south into Africa.

He immediately said, "Oh no, you can't do that. You'll die in the desert." He said it with such conviction and finality that I wasn't sure I had understood the French words.

I asked him to repeat them. He said, *Vous allez mourir dans le désert.* I looked it up word for word so I was clear about what he had said. When I double-checked the meaning with him, he nodded and smiled. I had it right. We smiled as well, and assumed he was just joking, or perhaps this was a common way of greeting desert travelers.

Later, however, he brought over a couple of Arab friends and introduced us as the young men who were going off to "die in the desert." They seemed quite cheerful about it, as if we had said we were going to Disneyland, but we were a bit irritated. This was not what we wanted to hear.

A Common Refrain

From that day forward, whenever we told someone we were crossing the Sahara, they would immediately respond, *Non, non. C'est pas possible. Vous allez mourir dans le désert.*

And by the way, these were not just city Arabs or town dwellers. They were often Taureq or Bedouin, people whose ancestors had lived in the Sahara for 1,000 years. They were in a position to know.

I learned that whenever you decide to break out of the mold and try something new, different, or unusual, people will line up to tell you you can't do it, you'll fail, or you'll lose your money, time, or investment—"you will die in the desert."

To succeed at anything, you have to learn to ignore the naysayers or negative people, many of whom should know better. You must have the courage to step out in faith, with no guarantees of success, and rise above all resistance and press on regardless.

Changing Terrain

The country we passed through in the morning had gradually changed from stony terrain to scrub brush and rocky waste. After we left Ksar-es-Souk, with the repaired tire firmly bolted to the hood, the country changed again, becoming more rugged and overgrown with heavier sagebrush.

In the late afternoon, we crossed two shallow rivers; the roadway was marked by boulders spaced a few feet apart in the water. The deepest part was just over two feet, but the Land Rover waded through it like a sturdy little freight boat as water gurgled through the doors onto the floor. There didn't seem to be anywhere that vehicle couldn't go.

Sick as a Dog

After Boudenib, 60 kilometers east of Ksar-es-Souk, the country flattened out again and the bad road became even worse. We were continually pounded by the jolting of the washboard roads. The constant wind made cooking our repetitive supper almost impossible. On top of these little joys of traveling in the outback, Bob had become violently ill. His stomach had started to bother him after supper the evening before and he had been unable to do more than pick at breakfast. Geoff and I didn't think too much about it, except to observe that if Bob didn't eat his share, there was more food for us.

The long day from Agadir, the rough night on the broken roads, and the long hot day that was just ending had destroyed Bob's body's resistance to illness. His whole system seemed to be out of kilter—head, stomach, and bowels. He was bringing up everything he ate or drank, even water, and was afflicted with dysentery so persistent and painful that we were stopping every few minutes to let him out of the Rover. He fumbled frantically at his pants as he dashed to the side of the road. He was dizzy, his head pounded, and his face was white and filmed with cold perspiration. Whatever he had, he had it in a bad way, and there was nothing we could do about it except drive on.

Unprepared for Illness

Aside from a few bandages and a box of aspirin, we had no medical supplies whatsoever; we were too healthy to worry about disease, dysentery, diarrhea, or even severe pain. Geoff and I had taken first-aid courses and passed at the top of the class, but we were not prepared for something like this. The only answer was to get to Figuig as fast as possible and hope to find a doctor or someone who could prescribe a medicine for Bob.

Figuig was still many hours away, and we couldn't continue in our exhausted condition without eating something. We tried to keep our kerosene burner lit by placing it in a gully, but the wind gusted nastily from all angles, carrying sand and grit into the food and blowing out the flame so often that we finally gave up and ate the slop cold. Exhausted and caked with sweat and dirt from the road, with the cold supper still gritty in our mouths, Geoff and I made a place for Bob to lie in the back of the Rover and continued on.

Traveling at Night

That was a bad night. It started off with Bob sick and all of us dead tired, and got worse as the road deteriorated to a broken track within a couple of hours. It seemed as though the blackened country was crisscrossed with tracks that confused us and left us hopelessly lost, time after time.

Having no idea where we were on the map, we resorted to using our compass, as well as a couple of stars, to keep going in the general direction of east. We hoped to eventually cross the north-south track to Figuig and get our bearings once more. But the impassability of the rocky terrain kept turning us around and sending us off on diverse tangents, while the broken ground underneath threatened to shake the laboring vehicle and us into pieces. Fighting the road, wheel, and gears was a Herculean effort that forced us to change drivers every half hour.

Our speed was never more than 25 or 30 miles per hour, but hitting a washout or small crevice, even at that low speed, would cause the vehicle to bounce off the ground and come hammering back down. This brought moans and curses from the suffering Bob in the back, and took our taut nerves to the snapping point. We'd slow down at every hard bump and proceed more carefully, hunched forward tensely in anticipation of the next jolt.

From Bad to Worse

The headlights played tricks on us repeatedly, hiding large ruts in shadows and making smooth stretches appear dangerous. We'd been driving for six jarring hours and struggling to focus our bleary eyes on the ground ahead when we suddenly came over a rise and discovered the road was gone!

I desperately slammed on the brakes but it was too late. We plunged off a riverbank and crashed into the opposite bank before coming to a sudden halt. Bob was hurled from out of the back of the Rover right onto our heads. For a second we just sat there, all tangled up in each other and lacking the energy to move. We were sure the whole front end of our vehicle was ruined.

Geoff and I untangled ourselves from the moaning Bob, and crawled out to take a look at the situation. Bob leaned his head out the door from where he lay and retched hollowly, gagging from the emptiness of his stomach. The headlights were still on and murky against the dust rising from the collision with the bank. The only sound was the wind whistling through the dry sagebrush that bordered the gully in which we had landed.

Single Unit Construction

Thank God for small favors and single-unit construction, we muttered. The heavy steel bumper was solidly into the clay bank, but there wasn't a scratch on the vehicle. Bob climbed shakily into the back of the Rover again while I tried the motor. It started with a hollow pop and ran smoothly. Shoving it into four-wheel drive, I backed it out of the dirt and then followed Geoff's flashlight to get out of the gully. Geoff clambered wearily into the Rover and slouched back, watching the illuminated road ahead.

"You know something," he sighed. "We've let ourselves in for far more than we realized with this Africa idea."

"What do you mean, Geoff?" I let out the clutch and we started slowly forward. "Well, just look at us in comparison to a year ago," he said. "Here we are in the middle of nowhere, lost and beat as hell, with Bob sick as a dog, and 8,000 miles to go. And we've only really been in Africa for a week. Where's it going to lead to?"

"It'll be interesting to find out. I don't even want to take a guess, except South Africa."

"Yeah," he said. "That's something, anyway."

The Road to Figuig

We drove cautiously for the next hour and finally intersected the long-sought road to Figuig. According to the map, there was only one road so we had to be on it. We turned left in the direction of the North Star. At the most, Figuig could only be a couple of hours farther, but we were dead tired. Bob had finally fallen asleep, and there was no reason to go on anymore. I coasted the vehicle off the road into the brush and cut the engine.

"We're home," I said, but Geoff was already dragging his sleeping bag out of the back. Within a minute, we were sprawled in our bags on the sandy ground and fast asleep.

Our Last Day in Morocco

It was 9 A.M. when we stirred from our beds on the dirt, awakened by the passing of a truck full of Arab workers all shouting at us. Bob had improved considerably with sleep, but still couldn't look at breakfast. He was a bit shaky on his feet and very pale, like a man who had been terribly frightened and hadn't quite regained his composure.

Owing to our loss of direction in the night, we had come on to the gravel road much farther from Figuig than we had calculated—twice as far in fact. It was shortly after 1 P.M. when we arrived in the little, unpaved border town and drove up to the old building with the Moroccan flag in front. We were informed that we had to be checked out of Morocco before entering Algeria, and the man in charge would not be back until 3 P.M. We got out the makings for tea and Geoff set to it.

A Cheap and Lousy Stove

At first we tried to keep the stove going on the tailgate of the Rover, but there was too much wind. We then set the cheap contraption on the ground-level porch of the customs building, lit it, and put the kettle on to boil. Several curious Arabs who had been lounging around the building gathered to stare at us and observe the tea-making operation, as simple as it was. The decrepit stove picked this particular occasion to put on a show.

We had leaned the wooden top from a packing crate against the stove from one side to stop the wind, and the seam on that side burst and ignited from the pressure of burning gasoline dribbling down the side. In seconds, the ground around and under the wooden crate was aflame, with black smoke billowing up around the kettle. As more gasoline leaked out and stoked the fire, the smoke increased in density, enveloped the stove, and sent the flames up two feet.

The Arabs became quite concerned and pointed to the stove and jabbered excitedly, offering advice on how to extinguish the little inferno that had now obscured the stove and kettle and was filling the verandah with oily smoke.

Then suddenly the bottom of the stove and remaining petrol went up with an ominous whoosh that caused the onlooking Arabs to jump back in fright. The smoke filled the little porch even thicker than before, and swirled in the gusty breeze and poured over the brick wall next to it.

A Cup of Tea

Geoff had by now completed the laying out of the cups, teapot, sugar, and can of evaporated milk on the tailgate. With a nonchalant smile at the Arabs, he strolled into the blazing cloud and plucked the blackened kettle from the flames. Just as casually, he strolled back and made the tea, with a bored look at the astonished locals. I yawned and turned a nearby hose on the fire, dousing it and cooling the misshapen lump of metal that had been the stove. Then, picking it up as though it were a valuable instrument, I wiped it off a bit with a piece of paper and set it back in the Rover. Bob was sitting in the front seat, engrossed in Scaramouch, and didn't even bother looking up.

We managed to convey to the Arabs that this was our normal way of making tea—you had to *smoke* it. From their huddled chatter and bewildered expressions, we got the impression it was not done that way very often in Figuig.

Another Wrong Turn

The captain in charge of Moroccan customs arrived at 3:30 P.M. and examined all our papers before stamping us out of the country. After the handshaking routine with the entire office staff and about six of them telling us we would die in the desert, we were directed toward the east end of town and told that Algeria was *thataway.*

There were two roads leading in the general direction of east, and with that unerring sense of path finding—inherent in us pioneers from the West—we took the wrong one.

Stuck in Morocco

The street soon became too tight for us to turn around; it narrowed to a passage just wide enough for the Rover, and then turned sharply down a steep slope.

In an attempt to turn the Rover around in the narrow street, we became stuck. The engine stalled and wouldn't restart. We got out and tried pushing the vehicle back and forward, but to no avail. We were stuck fast.

Almost immediately, the street filled with curious young men and boys, dressed much alike in baggy pantaloons and worn, buttonless shirts. (Aha! The necessary labor force is at hand.)

"What are they staring at?"

"Why don't they offer to push? "

"How do you say, 'push' in Arabic?"

"Maybe they need a little encouragement."

"Yeah, let's set them a good example."

With dumb smiles, we gave the Rover a couple of useless shoves, laughing foolishly and motioning to everyone that they could play too. They thought it was a splendid idea, and the entire crowd—about 20 men in all—clustered around the vehicle and started pushing in all directions. We laughed and waved them to the front end, chanting in French, "un, deux, trois—and shove, un, deux, trois—and shove."

A Team Sport

Everyone picked up the chant, and the street soon filled with cheering and grunting. They dislodged the Rover on the third heave. During the round of applause and congratulations the men gave each other, we fiddled with the electric fuel pump and got the engine started again. There was a sigh of relief.

We had to back all the way up the street we'd come down, beeping the horn and waving to the gang chasing along in front. They wanted to play "Push the Happy Green Land Rover" again. This time we took the right road, which ended at the edge of town and a few minutes later came to the guarded frontier of Algeria. Our Morocco days were at an end.

Patience Is a Virtue

There is a time for urgency and aggressive action, and there is a time for patience. It is essential for you to be able to decide which is which, and act accordingly.

Many of your decisions will turn out to be wrong. The smartest thing you can do in many cases is to stop and reconsider. Slow down. Think it through. Develop alternatives.

Then, take a deep breath, smile, relax, and be patient with the fact that not everything happens at the time and speed you desire.

Henry Ford once said, "Patience and foresight are vital for success, and the man who lacks patience is not cut out for responsibilities in business."

Be cool. Go slow. Take it easy. Everything is probably unfolding as it should, in its right time.

> "Life is a series of experiences, each one of which makes us bigger, even though sometimes it is to realize this. For the world was built to develop character and we must learn that the setbacks and griefs which we endure help us in our marching onward."
> —Henry Ford

CHAPTER 16

Algeria and the Sahara

> "It is in the compelling zest of high adventure and of victory, and in creative action, that man finds his supreme joys."
> —Antoine de Saint-Exupéry

THE BARBED WIRE OF THE disputed border blocked off any thought of entering Algeria at this point. It was about 50 yards deep and ran in both directions a far as we could see. It was grim looking and impressive; we had not seen anything like it before.

The first ten yards were a mass of barbed, coiled loops about ten feet high, with three barbed-wire fences running parallel through them about six feet apart. Then came a cleared space, 30 yards in width, with a single 12-foot high, electrified fence running down the center on heavy cement posts. The other side of this no-man's-land was bordered with another mass of the terrible-looking strands. At intervals of 200 yards, on the other side of the wire frontier, the ugly faces of concrete pillboxes glared at the palm trees of Morocco.

A Gap in the Wire

Although there was no road leading up to a passage through the wire, our map indicated there was a way somewhere, and since one direction was as good as another, we turned right and followed the wire south. It was a good guess; three kilometers further we came to a road in a channel leading through the wire and up to an electrified gate.

Two dirty soldiers pointed machine pistols at us, while a third swung the gate open and motioned for us to enter. Once we were inside the canyon of barbed wire, the two soldiers flanked our vehicle, weapons drawn, while we drove at a walking speed along the narrow alley to the next gate. We had no inclination to drive any faster than they wanted us to.

Our First Impression of Algeria

On the far side of the second gate, two more Algerians waited with machine pistols to make sure we didn't overrun their country. We were ordered out of the Rover while they briefly inspected it for contraband Moroccans; they then ordered us to follow another car to their headquarters, about three blocks into town. With all that hardware around, they didn't need to order. The slightest suggestion would have been quite sufficient.

With the aid of our map, we answered all their questions concerning our route and destination. The answers were obviously to their satisfaction, for we were soon allowed to proceed. We were told, however, that we would have to obtain Algerian visas immediately upon arrival in Colomb-Béchar, the next town south. We assured them we would be there within two hours and would most certainly comply with the request. After pumping up one of our tires at the air hose outside, we drove south from Beni-Ounif on the first paved road we'd seen since Tarroudant, three days before.

Damage to the Rover

The paved road also confirmed a suspicion we had formed regarding our front end being damaged from the riverbank we'd hit in Morocco the night before. The steering wheel had become more difficult to handle. Halfway to Béchar, we stopped to check a grinding sound coming from the front tires, and were chagrined to find that the rubber was scraping off at an alarming rate. In fact, there was no tread left, and it was obvious at once that the wheels were toeing in due to something being broken or bent in the front suspension. We drove slowly the remainder of the way.

The Need for Visas

A well-dressed Algerian flagged us down as we approached Colomb-Béchar and explained he was from the police and had been informed from Beni-Ounif of our arrival. He led us into town to the police station, took our passports, and told us to return the next morning with 14 dinars each (about $3) for our visas.

We were to learn later that visas were a serious business. They are not required to pass from one country to another in Europe. But once you get into Africa, you cannot travel between countries without them. The correct visa, stamped into your passport, makes the difference between entry and rejection. The absence of a visa can lead to arrest or detention, as we were to learn later.

In life, there are critical skills and information that are like visas. They make the difference between success and failure. If you lack them, you cannot proceed or get ahead. Ignorance of them does not excuse you from the consequences of their absence.

Unable to Continue

Since our two front tires were now completely bald, we could not avoid the glaring reality that we needed four good tires and a spare if we were going to continue into the desert. That meant procuring two more tires immediately, if not sooner. It was late afternoon, and all the shops in the small town were open. But neither of the two tire shops in Béchar had used tires for Land Rovers, and the price they were asking for new ones was a whopping $42 each. Each shop had one tire that fit our vehicle, and we decided to have one installed before driving out of town to make camp for the night. We had a lot of discussing to do.

Sitting by the Rover in a small grove of palm trees, we worked out our position on paper as of that moment. The situation was definitely not good. We were almost out of money. The ferry had cost $50, the insurance another $48, and the food $100. After buying gasoline and oil for 1,200 miles in Morocco, and paying for another stove, tire repairs, and the radiator, we were down to $150 when we reached Béchar. The $42 for the tire had dropped the total to $108, and the bad news was just beginning.

Bob Bails Out, for Good

The following morning, we would have to pay $9 for visas and another $42 for the second tire. If we forswore the needed repairs and took a chance on the tires lasting, we would have just over $60. We needed a wrench for the wheel nuts and enough gasoline for 2,200 miles—the distance to Lagos. The gasoline alone in Morocco and Algeria cost more than $1 a gallon. Even if we averaged 25 miles to the gallon, we would need a minimum of $100 to reach Lagos. There was simply no way it could be done.

"Well," said Bob. "That is the end of that."

"What are you talking about?"

"We've had it; that's all," he replied. "The whole thing's been an abortion from start to finish—and the end is now."

"Just because we're a little low on money? We're not broke yet, you know."

"No, we're not broke," he sniffed. "We've got enough to get back to Gibraltar and sell the Land Rover, and we've got no other choice. I say we leave first thing in the morning."

"Bob, old buddy, this is a discussion to find a way to go on, not back. We've come too far to go back."

"The hell we have!" he replied. "It's on paper in front of you. We can't go on."

"What's your opinion on this, Geoff?"

"Now there's a question," he said, picking up the poetry book beside him. "Would you like to hear a poem?"

"What kind of a poem?" I already knew.

Ignoring the question, he began to read from "Carry On" by Robert W. Service:

It's easy to fight when everything's right,
When you're mad with the thrill and glory.
It's easy to cheer when victory is near
And wallow in fields that are gory.
It's a different song when everything's wrong,
When you're feeling infernally mortal.
When it's ten against one and hope there is none,
Buck up little soldier and chortle,
Carry on, carry on! There isn't much punch in your blow
You're glaring and staring and hitting out blind,
You're muddy and bloody but never you mind,
Carry on, carry on. You haven't the ghost of a show.
It's looking like death, but while you've a breath,
Carry on, my son, carry on!

The Resolve to Carry On

Geoff closed the book with deliberation and spoke to Bob.

"That's how I feel, Bob. For the first time in my life, I've really got a little despair and defeat to contend with. We didn't expect this trip to be easy. If we'd thought it would be easy, we would not have come. And if we quit now, not only do we let ourselves down, but we also let Jack Turing down, and that I won't do. There has to be a way to get to Johannesburg, and no matter what challenge we face, that's where I'm going."

Geoff and I agreed that Johannesburg was our goal, regardless of the difficulties that cropped up on the way. "Surely, if we're determined enough, we'll find a way," I said.

"Do you know something?" Bob spoke slowly and distinctly. "You're both crazy. You read a stupid poem, and you're too blind to admit you're beaten. I'm not interested in this idiotic idea anymore. When you stop fooling yourselves, you'll see that I'm right. But I've had enough; I'm leaving for Gibraltar tomorrow morning."

Try as we may, this time we couldn't change his mind.

Heading Back

After cashing the rest of the traveler's checks at the bank the next morning, we left the Rover to have the second tire fitted and walked over to the police station to retrieve our passports. On the way back to the vehicle, we stopped and bought a wrench to fit the wheel nuts. We were probably going to need it.

While we waited for the tire, Bob resolutely packed his rucksack with his belongings and one week's worth of tinned food. Geoff gave him $9 in Moroccan and Algerian money; it was all we were willing to spare and left us with exactly $50.

Bob refused to change his mind. The bout with dysentery had taken the spirit out of him, and he wanted nothing more than to get back to England and forget this trip had ever happened. Geoff and I were sorry to see the end of such a long friendship, yet glad to be rid of the voice of dissent and pessimism. It was a mixed emotion that actually left us feeling neutral about his decision. We were thinking more of the road ahead, and what we would have to do to keep from returning to Gibraltar as well.

Saying Farewell

There being no other mode of travel, Bob had decided to hitchhike back to Gibraltar. We therefore drove him to the main highway on the outskirts of town and let him off with his heavy pack.

"You sure you won't change your mind, Bob?"

"You should change yours," he said.

"Bob, old friend, do you really think that we won't make it? Do you think we could ever quit without making it?"

He looked at us carefully for a few seconds. "Ah, you'll make it, all right. I know you'll make it, somehow. But I'm just not interested anymore."

"So long, Bob. Say hello to Gibraltar for us."

We made a U-turn on the empty highway and drove back into town. Our friendship of many years had come to an end, at least for the foreseeable future.

Reviewing the Situation Once More

After receiving the money from Jack Turing and before leaving Gibraltar, we had rewritten to three or four people, affirming our requests for loans and asking that they send them to us in care of Barclays Bank, Lagos. We also left the address of poste restaunte, Lagos, at the bank and post office in Gibraltar so that any mail to arrive after our departure would be forwarded.

We still had a lot of faith in our friends and were sure that once we reached Lagos, we would have ample funds to complete the trip to South Africa. There now remained the small matter of getting to Lagos—across 1,000 miles of desert and three more countries.

We knew we couldn't possibly drive all the way on our limited finances; however if we could reach Gao on the Niger River, 1,200 miles south on the other side of the Sahara, we could leave the Rover with the police and hitchhike to Lagos, and return with enough money to carry on from there. It seemed to be a reasonable plan, and we were quite confident it would succeed.

Parting of the Ways

Few relationships in life are permanent. Many are functional, formed to achieve a certain purpose by combining certain strengths until the goal is attained, after which they no longer serve the best interests of either party.

When goals or circumstances change, the players often change as well. New players come on the stage with new roles, and other players leave the stage, to be seen no more.

> "No man ever achieved worthwhile success who did not, at one time or other, find himself with at least one foot hanging over the brink of failure."
> —Napoleon Hill

How many relationships in your life have reached the point where it is time for you, and the other person, to move on?

People are who they are. They are going to do what they are going to do. Each person has his or her own agenda, and you can't change it. Sometimes the best thing you can do is to accept the situation the way it is and let them go. Get on with your own life.

SECTION V

Never Give Up

> "Austere perseverance, harsh and continuous, rarely fails of its purpose, for its silent power grows irresistibly greater with time."
> —JOHANN WOLFGANG VON GOETHE

"IF AT FIRST YOU DON'T SUCCEED, try, try again." This approach to life has been responsible for the success of many men and women struggling against apparently insurmountable obstacles.

Sometimes your greatest asset can be your ability to persist longer than the other person. Your willingness to continue, even when you feel like quitting, will often win you the day.

Between where you are and your goal, there are a number of hurdles or "tests" that you must successfully pass to succeed. And you never know how many there are. You only know the number is limited and that at any time you might be just one step away from great achievement.

Expect to meet many obstacles, difficulties, and temporary failures on the way to your goal. They are essential to your eventual success. You need them. They are each sent to teach you something vital that will help you in the future.

You can never tell how close you are to your goal, right now.

> "There is no failure except in no longer trying. There is no defeat except from within, no really insurmountable barrier save our own inherent weakness of purpose."
>
> —Elbert Hubbard

CHAPTER 17

Sahara Crossing: The First Attempt

> "Developing the plan is actually laying out the sequence of events that have to occur for you to achieve your goal."
> —George Morrisey

After leaving Bob at the highway, we returned to town and spent the remainder of the morning rotating our tires; we put the two worst ones on the defective front end. In the heat of midday, we washed all our clothes in the dwindling river, bathed ourselves, and put our things in order for the big push. When the petrol station reopened at 4 P.M., we filled the tank and three jerry cans, and started out on the long haul south.

Welcome to the Sahara

Two hours and 90 kilometers later and only a short distance before Abadla, the first town after Colomb-Béchar, we ran into a sandstorm.

Although it was still a full hour before sundown, the light began to fade rapidly, and the sky became overcast. Then, off to the east about five miles, we saw it. Like a huge, thousand foot high dirty cloud, a wall of murky gray was moving across the land like a monstrous dark wall, enveloping everything in its path. We were driving parallel with its front, and from the wind rattling the plastic windows, we immediately recognized what it was.

No Escape

The sandstorm seemed to be moving quite slowly and we thought perhaps we'd be able to outrun it. However, its speed was deceptive, and it rolled over us as we reached Abadla. The few people still outside were running for cover, clutching clothes and headdresses over their faces. We didn't stop at all, but continued through the howling, dry blizzard to get out from underneath it. The windows and the air vents of the Rover were shut tight, but it made little difference. The fine sand poured in everywhere, and into everything and forced us to pull our shirts up over our noses to reduce the dust we were inhaling.

The storm was like a dirty blizzard and so thick it obscured the road. Geoff had to peer intently through the dusty window to keep us from lurching off into the sagebrush. The angry wind pummeled at the canvas top and shook the doors, whistling, gusting, and hitting us from one side and then the other. Then it shifted again, rose, and came straight down the road, shaking the Rover like a small boat on a choppy sea.

This Too Shall Pass

Then, just as suddenly, we were out of it and driving in the quiet sunshine of early evening. The whole countryside behind us was blotted out in a whirling mass of gray, while ahead the road flowed on peacefully across the empty landscape. A few kilometers farther we stopped, wiped the grit from our faces and ears, and dusted off the windows; the distant roar of the storm could still be heard coming through the air. This was our first welcome to the Sahara.

Later I found that the storms of life—the unexpected crises—come suddenly and wreak their havoc, causing damage and endangering lives. But because you usually can't anticipate or avoid them, you must respond to them effectively and hope for the best. Once the storm is past, you pull yourself together and carry on with your life and journey as best as you can.

Into the Night

The sun sat on the horizon like a burnished ball of gold when we came out of the sandstorm. As it gradually fell below the horizon, it looked like a knife-edge of flame. Then it was gone. The darkness fell and then lifted with the twinkling of a million stars.

The country had begun to flatten after Abadla, and the occasional mesas that had dwarfed the sagebrush-covered desert, at heights just under 1,000 feet, ceased to be a feature of the landscape. The headlights sucked in the flowing ribbon of tarmac, to the accompanying purr of the tight little engine and ominous growl of tires scraping on the front. The miles fell behind into the darkness with easy regularity. We drove in silence broken only by the odd comment on how lucky we were that, after all the floundering that had marked our first six weeks on the road, the way ahead at last seemed clear and largely uncomplicated.

Fellow Travelers

There was no traffic in either direction for a long time after dark. The first headlights that appeared on the road ahead aroused little interest until we passed the car and saw that it was on the shoulder and quite stationary. Stopping immediately to investigate, we found a 1955 Ford packed with seven Arabs sitting among baskets, bedding, and one dog. The driver, a bedraggled Algerian in a dirty shirt, got out as we approached and began jabbering too rapidly for us to understand.

We answered him in English and got the desired reaction—he shut up. Then, by speaking slowly and distinctly in French, we gleaned that he had stopped for some reason, after which the car had refused to start again. We got the flashlight from the Rover, lifted the hood, and exposed a filthy engine with jumbles of loose wires and broken fittings—a real mechanic's nightmare. With a pair of pliers and a screwdriver, we tightened everything that had any thread left and told him to give it a try. It made no difference; the engine turned over but would not fire.

Get It Running

There was no question about leaving these people. The code of the road in that empty country required that we either send them on their way or take them. I brought the Rover around behind the old car and Geoff, over the protests of the Arab, took the wheel of the Ford while I pushed the old wreck down the highway. After a quarter of a mile, it finally caught with a roar, sputtering and coughing.

Shouting over the noise of the engine, we told the driver to keep the revs up and, no matter what, not to stop before Abadla. We waited until the rumble of the old Ford had faded into the distance before continuing. It had been our first opportunity to reciprocate for the assistance we had received, and we were glad of it.

Never a Dull Moment

Half an hour later we came upon another vehicle and were met with a strange scene. A half-ton Citroën pickup truck, piled high with baskets and blankets, was parked by the road; behind 16 Arabs squatted peacefully around a little fire. Stopping the Rover where we could watch it, we approached and asked the man who rose to greet us if he needed anything.

Oh yes, he said cheerfully, he was out of petrol and would be most pleased to buy a little from us provided we had enough to spare. But first, he said, we must have a cup of tea. Always suspicious of smiling foreigners, especially in the middle of the night, we declined the tea but poured ten liters of petrol into his tank and charged him what it had cost us in Colomb-Béchar. However, he was not to be put off, and insisted we come and sit by the fire.

A Roadside Tea Party

An old Arab was feeding pieces of broken brushwood into the little blaze under a blackened pot. Everyone seemed quite relaxed about being stuck in the middle of nowhere, 40 miles from the nearest town. The driver produced a package of cigarettes and we squatted with the fellows to join the party. When the tea was ready, we relaxed a little and became a part of the gang.

The tea was poured into thick, little clay cups, and was sweet, minty, and very hot. Soon we were chatting away jovially. But for us the complete nonchalance of the strange group toward their circumstances was slightly unfathomable. We were enjoying the tea and chatter but were becoming uncomfortable about the time we were losing; they didn't seem to care at all.

Finally, the tea was finished and the party broke up. All 16 of the long-robed Arabs arose to shake our hands—some twice—with cheery smiles and vigorous head nodding. As we approached our vehicle they began to reload into the pickup, until it was a heavy mass of humanity and the rear end almost touched the ground. We waited until they continued on their way before driving on. We were behind on our schedule, and hoped our services wouldn't be required anymore that night.

Ruined Tires

About 20 minutes later our left front tire went flat with a dull plop. In the 135 kilometers from Béchar, the half-worn tire had been ground right down to the tube and ruined completely. The other front tire was only slightly better.

We realized we faced a major mechanical problem, and although we had a spare tire of sorts, it would be folly to continue. Not only was the vehicle not capable of being driven, but we were also too tired. We drove the Rover 20 yards off the road, parked it, and went to sleep on the sand nearby.

We had left civilization behind, but not the flies. More dependable than an alarm clock, they drove us out of our bags at half past sunrise, buzzing delightedly at the two guests who had stopped during the night.

A sober inspection of the Rover showed it would have to be partially repaired before we moved; otherwise the other tires were likely to be ground to the inner tubes and we'd be left stranded. Mounting the front bumper on the jerry cans as before, we used machetes to dig out under the wheels and then removed them for inspection. All we could see however was the other side of the front wheels. We decided against dismantling anything before having a qualified opinion on the cause of the trouble. We needed to have a mechanic give us an opinion. I left half an hour later to hitchhike to Béchar.

Hitchhiking in the Desert

It was one hour before a northbound car came along the lonely road, another hour before I reached Abadla, and three hours before I was dropped off in Béchar. In the meantime, the sun had burned off the coolness of the morning and set in like a bake oven, making me thankful I'd thought to bring a canteen. The lack of passing motorists had turned an 80-mile trip into a five-hour ordeal in the hot, empty land.

At the main garage in Béchar, I tried to explain our problem. They told me they would have to see the vehicle before passing judgment. Next I tried the Foreign Legion post on the edge of town, but they wouldn't let me in the gate to speak to a mechanic. The guard, however, told me to ask at the Highway Department building, a mile down the road.

The Highway Department

The girl at the desk in the entrance hall ushered me into the unadorned office of Monsieur Leroux. He was the type of man who can be found occasionally in obscure places, seemingly for the set purpose of restoring one's faith in human nature. He was husky and had a long face and an ability to grasp the essentials of a situation, no matter how confused its presentation; and my presentation was surely confused.

As soon as I had outlined the problem and showed him approximately where the vehicle was on the large wall map, he told me to go back to the Rover. He would radio to his garage in Beni-Abbes, 40 kilometers past the spot where the Rover was stranded, and have someone sent out to take a look at it. There was no question of payment or mention of the fact that it wasn't his responsibility to help itinerant travelers, nor would he accept any thanks. Only ten minutes after entering the building, I was back on the road and waiting for the next car south.

The Return Trip

Four hours later, I finally grinned down a truck that got me back to Abadla, where I waited another two hours for a second ride in another truck. I arrived back at the Land Rover just before sunset.

It was like coming home after a weekend out of town. Geoff had passed the day reading and waving to the few motorists, all of whom had stopped to offer assistance, food, and water. Two hours previously, he said, a light truck had come from the south, and the two Arabs inside had stopped to inspect the Land Rover and said something about tomorrow morning before disappearing back down the road.

I explained what had taken place in Béchar with Monsieur Leroux, and we reasoned he had sent the two fellows and they would return in the morning to repair the defect. We were there for another night.

Time for a Council Meeting

It was time for another war council to decide how to proceed. The mechanical difficulties were only part of the problem facing us; now we needed a minimum of two new tires before we could continue toward Lagos. The repairs were expected to be expensive, and due to our financial situation we couldn't have them done and also continue with the Rover. Since turning back like Bob was unthinkable, we would have to find another solution.

There was only one alternative—hitchhike to Lagos, pick up the money we assumed would be there waiting for us, and then hitchhike back to Algeria for the vehicle. It would be extremely difficult, but it was our only choice. We certainly could not quit, not at that stage of the game.

We could leave our Land Rover at the Highway Department in Colomb-Béchar, load up with enough food for two weeks, and hope for the best. Once over the Sahara, which seemed to be our growing stumbling block, we would be in more heavily populated countries and surely get along somehow. Realizing that any more discussion was worse than fruitless, we turned in early to be well rested for the coming day.

No Good News

At 7 A.M. the light truck from the previous afternoon reappeared, and the two Arabs examined the Rover once more. The driver of the vehicle shrugged and said there was nothing he could do, but he would escort us back to the workshop in Abadla where perhaps it could be repaired.

We put the old spare on in place of the ruined tire and followed him slowly. The mechanic at Abadla hemmed and hawed for the entire morning before informing us he knew nothing about Land Rovers and we would have to go to Béchar to find someone who did. He had held back that little tidbit of information until it was too hot to drive, forcing us to wait the afternoon in a little mud-walled café, listening to the wailing of Arab music coming from the speaker above the door.

Back Again

The return to Béchar took four hours of 15-mile-per-hour driving. The grinding sound of our tires made us cringe, and it was with great relief that we made it back to the riverbank outside of town to spend another night. It was a bit like the battle of Dunquerque, in that we had made a successful retreat, but weren't any closer to winning the war.

We woke in the morning amid a herd of goats bleating, their bells tinkling merrily. The old gaffer steering them along the riverbank just gave us a toothless grin and plodded on swinging his staff. Fortunately, the goats avoided stepping on us directly, and we withdrew into our sleeping bags to avoid any low-flying hooves until they were past. It was impossible to sleep after that, even though the flies weren't there to remind us it was time to be up and out hitchhiking.

Our patron saint of Colomb-Béchar, Monsieur Leroux, readily agreed to our leaving the vehicle in the Highway Department compound, where it could be watched during the day. We thanked him again profusely, and then pulled on our loaded rucksacks and hiked out to the main highway to hitchhike 2,000 miles to Lagos, Nigeria.

Attacking to the Rear

Sometimes a tactical retreat, allowing time to reassess and reconsolidate, can save the entire situation. There is a time to advance boldly, and a time to back off and reconsider.

The person on the wrong road who is going back the fastest is often the one going forward the fastest in the long run, especially if he is on the wrong road.

It is essential to conserve your resources. Don' t risk everything at once. There are some decisions you cannot afford to make. The cost of being wrong is too high.

Look at your life today. Where do you experience the most stress? In what areas would it be a good idea for you to reassess, withdraw, and regroup?

Taking time to rethink and reevaluate your situation can enable you to see it in a much better light. Always be prepared to admit you could be on the wrong track and trying to do the wrong thing—or the right thing in the wrong way.

> "To decide, to be at the level of choice, is to take responsibility for your life and to be in control of your life."
> —Arbie M. Dale

CHAPTER 18

Sahara Crossing: The Second Attempt

> "The greatest thing a man can do in this world is to make the most possible out of the stuff that has been given him. This is success, and there is no other."
> —ORISON SWETT MARDEN

THIS PLAN, TO HITCHHIKE ACROSS the heart of the Sahara Desert to Lagos and then return, as though going to the corner store to pick up some groceries, surely ranks as one of the dumbest decisions of my life.

Looking back at it with a shudder, I can think of no pastime more unrewarding and fraught with disappointment than that of a hitchhiker in the deserts of Algeria. A more miserable, wretched, and soul-searching way of traveling surely cannot exist. Temperatures that climb during the day to over 120 degrees Fahrenheit, not a breath of wind stirring, distances between towns of 50 miles or more, and virtually no traffic on roads except for brief periods each morning and afternoon, all make traveling by thumb the lowest form of mobility.

Broiling Under the Desert Sun

We got our first ride just after 10 A.M., which seemed like a good start. But ten minutes later it ended at a small village on the outskirts of town. And there we sat, waiting for a ride, for five broiling hours in the raging sun. The urchins from the nearby village laughed and threw stones at us for a while. However, we tired of the game before they did and our aim was better, so they eventually left us alone to fry in peace. Our real enemy was the sun—that merciless ball of flame that produced a heat we didn't think possible, coming as we did from the cool mountain country of British Columbia.

Not only was such heat possible, it was also very real, and in our circumstances, unavoidable. There was little traffic on the road, so we couldn't seek shade without risking missing a possible ride. Although we weren't having much luck with our schedules, we were still determined to reach our destination as quickly as possible, in spite of the difficulties it entailed. The heat, as terrible as it was, we accepted as an occupational hazard, to be endured since it seemed to be an unavoidable part of the job of world beating.

Our Second Ride

At 4 P.M., after waiting all day, we finally got our second ride, in the back of a vegetable truck loaded with onions, oranges, and Arabs. We were so pleased to be under way again that we would have ridden in a garbage truck.

When the Arabs started singing a native refrain, we joined in and howled along. While they laughed at us among themselves, we stole all the oranges we could without being seen, stuffing them into our already-fat rucksacks. The driver turned off in Abadla, stopping to let us climb out. But as we started hiking away, he suddenly called us back. Going to the rear of the truck, he pulled out a sack and gave us each four oranges, smiling and wishing us "Bon voyage" at the same time. We thanked him and walked away sheepishly, feeling like ingrates for stealing a few oranges earlier.

We lugged our heavy rucksacks, full of canned food from Gibraltar, to the dry riverbed on the far side of Abadla. Once more we sat and waited for hours by the roadside. It was dusk before a Frenchman stopped and took us another five kilometers, turning off on a small dirt road and leaving us far from any human habitation just as night fell.

Any Port in a Storm

Hours later another car came out of the darkness and stopped. The Arab driving the small, overloaded Citroën station wagon insisted he had plenty of room for us. We didn't need much encouragement, but he was wrong about having "plenty of room." Including the family, baskets, and bundles, he did not have room for us. Nonetheless, we squeezed in, and in return for the ride, he talked at us incessantly.

During the next two hours, from our cramped positions in the rear seat, we vigorously agreed with him that Arabic was the most important language in the world; his skinny daughter had a beautiful voice; and everyone should see Algeria before they die.

At midnight he let us off at the turning point to Beni-Abbes. A tiny two-room house stood at the lonely crossroads, and for some reason, the Algerian police were checking identification papers there by lantern light. We had to stand for half an hour with several truck drivers before showing our passports to the bored policeman. We then shouldered our packs and walked down the road for 15 minutes under the silent, star-riddled desert sky. By the quiet roadside, we spread our bags and drifted gratefully off to sleep.

We had been on the road for 14 hours, covering the impressive distance of 140 miles, and the traffic was diminishing with every mile we proceeded south into the desert. At the rate we were going, it would be a long, long way to Tipperary.

No Rides to be Had

The decrease in vegetation was the first thing we noticed in the morning, after the flies had arrived to tell us that the sun was up. The ground was bare, rocky gravel and flat and unbroken for miles, and the road stretched across it north to south, from horizon to horizon. The tiny building at the crossroads looked like a toy block that had been left behind when the desert floor was swept clean, and we felt like ants in a huge, empty ballroom.

In the five hours between our waking that morning and the sun reaching its zenith, only three trucks passed on the road south. Each driver stopped and inquired about our destination, but since they were not going too far, they all told us to wait for another truck.

It was even hotter than the day before and by 11 A.M. the heat was too intense for us to sit unprotected any longer. Since there had been no traffic for the last two hours, we donned our packs and hiked back to the little white building to stay until the sun abated somewhat. The hike was only about one mile, but it felt like five miles. We were sweating and puffing with the effort when we flopped down on the bench on the cement verandah.

The Midday Heat Once More

The building turned out to be a café of sorts, selling as its sole product warm orange soda to passing drivers. The owner was definitely not in the business to get rich.

By noon several Arabs—two boys, four young men, and three grizzled older fellows—wandered in from somewhere to sit out the heat.

They were soon joined by a young, clear-eyed Algerian who parked his truck by the road and lazily sat down with a magazine at the one table on the porch. We were there for the afternoon with nothing to do, so we eventually started chatting with the amiable driver, who immediately offered us a ride back north to Colomb-Béchar if we were going that way.

We declined, but as the sun burned hotter and hotter, we began to rethink the whole idea of hitchhiking.

"Geoff, this is the stupidest thing we've ever done," I said.

Outside the building, the rising heat waves were so heavy they blurred everything over a distance of 100 yards. Even in the shade we were breathing laboriously, the salty perspiration dripping off our chins and soaking through our clothes. The air was heavy with the drone of the ever-present flies.

"What else can we do?" he replied after a while.

"I don't know, but there has to be another solution. It's so stinking hot here that you could can the heat and take it home."

"In the last two days we have traveled only 140 miles. Do you know how many days we could be stuck in the desert?"

We sat musing quietly for a few minutes.

"We need more money; we'll have to borrow some more. Is there a Canadian embassy in Algiers?"

"There's only one way to find out. You speak better French than I do. Tell your friend we accept his offer for a ride."

A New Strategy

That afternoon in the oppressive heat, we worked out a new strategy, rationalizing away the idea of hitchhiking with reasons that were as good as they were obvious. The energy-sapping, 120-degree heat was making itself felt, and it was difficult to envision glorious sagas of winning in the face of great odds when we were feeling like boiled dishrags. There comes a point when stubborn resolve gives over to simple reasoning, and we were there.

We needed our vehicle to make the trip, and we needed a way to get our vehicle repaired and running properly. We decided to return to Béchar that night with the truck driver. Tomorrow Geoff would leave for Algiers with a hard-luck story to deliver to the Canadian embassy, about how we had mailed most of our money to Lagos, and due to unforeseen difficulties, needed a small loan to get us there. We would promise to repay the Canadian representative immediately upon our arrival.

In the meantime, I would remain in Colomb-Béchar to sell our extra groceries, raise some money, and get the necessary repairs. It seemed a good plan, and much more logical than this heartbreaking, death defying, and botched effort at hitchhiking.

Lunch for Everyone

Borrowing the proprietor's stove about 3 P.M., we got out a can of beans and started preparing a late lunch, with every Arab eye on the porch following our movements. Up to then, they had been sitting quietly in various positions of lassitude on the floor and along the bench at the end of the porch, saying and doing nothing. None of them had anything to eat, and from the ragged clothes that hung on them—young and old alike—the reason was obvious. Missing a meal wasn't going to be a new experience for them.

"Geoff, I can think of a better idea than dragging all this food back to Béchar," I said, referring to the bulky packs.

He looked at the blank stares coming from the hungry Arabs, and then back at our packs.

"Yeah," he said. "These are the only people I know who are worse off than we are."

Borrowing a large pot from the wall of the café, we emptied ten cans of beans and spaghetti into it. The unkempt proprietor, who lived in one room and sold his wares from the other, watched us thoughtfully for a while; he knew what we were doing. He had been ignoring the presence of the ragged crew on the porch, preferring to do what little business he could with his only cash customers—the truck driver, Geoff, and me. Now he felt he had better get into the act; perhaps he feared he would lose face if foreigners fed his people.

As the stew began to steam and boil, he produced a huge loaf of bread and a few tin plates, which he laid out on the slatted table. He helped ladle the stew and pass the plates to everyone. The gang squatted on their haunches, eating two to a plate and slurping the food down and jabbering happily in Arabic the whole time. The proprietor didn't partake, but brought us another bottle of orange soda—a gift this time—and sat watching interestedly while we ate. Because of the language barrier, the preparation and serving had been done with a minimum of conversation, but the communication seemed to be quite good for all that.

In life you will regret many things, but you'll never regret being too kind or too fair, too helpful or too generous. From those to whom much is given, much is expected. Never be reluctant to give of yourself and your substance. It always comes back to you.

Back to Béchar

The ride back to Béchar was broken at Abadla (a town we were rather sick of seeing) while the driver chatted with a couple of his friends. We sat muttering in the truck the whole time, but knew we were better off waiting impatiently there than warily along that empty highway. At sunset back in Colomb-Béchar, we straggled up the stony riverbed to the palm grove to spend our sixth night in Algeria. Except that the riverbed was now dry, things were pretty much the same as they had been the evening of our arrival a few days ago.

The two days of exposure to the unmitigated heat exacted their toll that night. Geoff was lucky—he paid only in physical exhaustion and was unconscious shortly after dark, sleeping through the night without stirring. I know he didn't stir because I was awake with stomach cramps and dysentery until the early hours of the morning.

For the rest of the time we traveled in Africa, the dysentery (otherwise referred to as the Algerian runs, the Nigerian trots, tummy palaver, rumbling guts) was a part of life. It was brought on by the weather, water, insects, or local foods, but it was ever-present. Constipation is a word that does not exist and is not understood in Africa above the tropic of Capricorn—or below, for that matter.

Money and Repairs

With four cans of spaghetti, two cans of beans, and ten dinars in his pocket, Geoff left for Algiers the next morning and took all the papers he would need to prove his story to the consulate. He expected to be back within three days. I wished him luck and waved him good-bye. He was on his way to do his job, and I was hiking back to the Highway Department to start mine.

In the rear of the little Highway Department bungalow were a bath and two small bedrooms, one of which the radio operators offered me as a place to stay until Geoff returned. The offer was accepted immediately. I had already been wondering how I was going to keep our things safe while the vehicle was being repaired.

Off to the Market

After moving our things into the room, I sorted out enough food for 12 days including six cans of beans and spaghetti, and then took the remainder into town to sell.

Scanning the shelves of the little store for the prices on items similar to mine, I added the sum, tacked on 20 percent, and started the bartering. The Arab storekeeper was not a beginner at this game. He also worked out the value of my things—mostly peas, condensed milk, beans, and spaghetti—added it up on a piece of paper and made me a "final" offer. Twenty minutes of final offers and ultimatums later, we came to a compromise of about 60 percent of the retail value—104 dinars, or about $24—which was approximately what we had paid for the items in Gibraltar.

Repairing the Rover

The finances replenished somewhat, I then took the Rover into the main garage in Béchar, where I explained our hitting the bump to the jovial manager in the service department. He told me he would have to take it apart and look at it. "Come back tomorrow after lunch," he said.

We seemed to be making a little progress, I thought. I certainly hoped it wouldn't cost more than the $40 that represented our total savings. There was no telling how successful Geoff would be with his story in Algiers, and it would be a tragic thing for him to come back broke, and find me also broke and the Land Rover in the shop with an account against it.

Two days later the Rover was finally returned to me. One steering rod had been bent, shortening the distance between the forward edges of the front tires and causing the excessive wear. After discovering the fault, the mechanics took it out, heated it with an acetylene torch, tapped it straight, and reinstalled it. From beginning to end, once they got at it, the job took half an hour, involved no new parts, and cost a total of 12 dinars, or about $2.50.

Little Things Mean a Lot

For the two days I had been waiting, nervously fingering the 180 dinars in my pocket, I had been trying to think of something else to sell just in case I didn't have enough money. We had ruined three tires, been set back ten days, lost a childhood friend, and suffered through two days of heat in the open—all for a lousy 12-dinar repair job. Driving the snug-steering vehicle back to the radio shack, I was trying to decide whether I was mad, glad, or sad—or a bit of all three.

Again I learned that often the most important thing you can do when faced with a new problem or situation is to stop and think for a while. Don't rely on your own limited knowledge. Ask someone for input, advice, or guidance. Sometimes a few words or instructions from an experienced person can save you huge expenditures of time or money. If we had gone to a garage immediately upon arrival in Béchar, we might have saved ourselves a lot of time and trouble.

New Tires

The next problem on the agenda was tires. Although the garage had no new tires for a Land Rover, it had one good used tire, which I bought for 50 dinars. A search of the junkyards around Béchar turned up nothing, but in back of the Highway Department, half buried in the sand, was the remains of a Land Rover that had been demolished in a collision. The tires had blown out on impact, but except for tears in the sidewalls, two of them were almost new.

The garage's parts department denied having what I needed, but the thin-faced, harried Arab agreed to look in the back anyway, and he found them—large rubber patches made for repairing the inside of tires. These patches are frowned upon universally by companies dealing in tires, for obvious reasons. But I had once had occasion to use them on a car when I was in school, and knew they had amazing potential.

After three hours of scraping, sanding, and shaping—and buying two new, heavy-duty tubes—I now had four good tires and a spare, and the Land Rover was ready to roll once more.

The Kindness of Strangers

Adding to the delight of having the Rover repaired and ready at such a low cost, a Frenchman, with whom I had chatted at the garage, came by at that moment and said that he had a sixth tire if I wanted it. I followed him to his house where he rolled the tire out of his carport and showed me that it was ripped on one side, but if I could use it, I could have it. You bet I could!

From several truck drivers in Béchar, as well as the garage owner and the friendly Frenchman, I learned that there was an 800-mile stretch in the desert where it would be impossible to get petrol or any repairs. The trucks that went across every two weeks or so in convoys carried half a dozen spare tires, parts to overhaul their entire vehicles, and enough petrol for the round trip. They said the desert was dotted with the abandoned vehicles of travelers who had not been properly equipped. This "simple" matter of a long, hot drive was turning out to be a complex affair.

The evening after settling the tire problem, I removed a 16-gallon tank from a ruined truck and mounted it on blocks in the back of the Rover. That tank, along with the three five-gallon jerry cans, gave us a fuel capacity of 39 gallons. I figured that at 25 miles per gallon, this was seven gallons more than we would need for the long stretch. With the addition of a jack, we were as prepared as we could possibly be for the crossing. All I needed now was Geoff and a little bit of money. But Geoff was already one day overdue.

The Familiar Work of Waiting

Geoff had reckoned on covering the 500 miles to Algiers in one day, and had allotted one day to obtain the money and one more day for the trip back. He had hoped to arrive in Béchar the night of the third day, or at the latest, the morning of the fourth.

Before being given the place to stay at the Highway Department, I had assured him I would camp by the riverbed on the edge of town and be waiting for him when he returned. Now that the vehicle was road ready, I started making regular pilgrimages to the riverbank, where I sat and read Paris Match, looking up the new French words to pass the time.

The Time Drags By

The time began to drag after the fourth day and the fifth, and the sixth came and went with no sign of him. I read or wrote poetry, and went for walks. I gave the young radio operator a couple of driving lessons, and started going into town with him at lunchtime to eat Arab food. I did calisthenics to keep fit. I wandered around the town. I wrote in my journal and translated bits of French. But still the time dragged and I began to worry.

What if Geoff had been hurt or fallen sick and was unable to remember that I was back in Béchar? He had the passports and all the papers from the Rover so I couldn't leave and go looking for him without being arrested for lack of identification.

I checked at the post office to see if he'd written, but there was nothing. On the morning of the seventh day, I drove to the riverbank again and waited until noon; however there was still no sign of him. More than impatient, I was genuinely concerned, nervous, and worried.

A Foolish Error

That afternoon, when the traffic on the roads had stopped for the midday heat, I did a very foolish thing. Thinking perhaps that a bit of strenuous exercise would relieve the tension, I went for a long walk in the open country west of town. I was bareheaded, and it was in the very heat of the day.

Half an hour of walking in the broiling sun brought me to a place where thousands of empty bottles had been dumped in piles over an area of several acres. Setting a long row of bottles on a ridge, I walked back a few yards and hurled rocks at them until my arm was sore. Feeling a bit giddy from the 120-degree heat, I walked back to my "home" an hour later.

The radio operator on duty, an ex-soldier, looked up when I came in and commented that it was not a good idea to walk around without a hat in the sun. I laughed and told him Canadians were hardy—we didn't worry too much about such things. He left at 6 P.M. as usual, and after one more visit to the riverbank, I crawled onto my canvas mat and went to sleep. For some reason, I was feeling especially tired.

Sunstroke Can Be Deadly

The next morning I couldn't get up. The noise of the radio operators arriving in the room outside the door woke me, as it had for the previous week, but my body failed to respond when I tried to stand. "Perhaps I need more sleep," I thought, and closed my eyes once more.

It seemed only a moment later that I reopened them, but the sun was leaking in the window from high in the sky. My watch said 11:30, which make it a total of 15 hours since I had laid down the night before.

"This is ridiculous," I mused. "No one needs that much sleep." With a deep breath and a shove, I got to my feet. That did it. A searing pain shot through my head and down the length of my body, like a tongue of flame, and everything went black, with flashing lights dancing and screaming through my eyeballs. Lurching against the wall, I stood shaking in agony, my limbs trembling and heart pounding. "What the hell is wrong with me?" I thought, as the pain lashed across the nerve endings. I'd never believed such suffering to be possible.

A Near Death Experience

For five minutes I remained perfectly still, and gradually the room came back into focus and the roar of blood in my temples abated. I had to get to the bathroom outside the door, I thought. I must have been poisoned from the food I'd been eating. That's why my abdomen felt like a knife was being twisted into the muscle. Moving very slowly, I aimed a foot in the direction of the door six feet away, and pushed gently from the wall. The agonizing pain crashed back, worse than before, leaving me gripping the door handle from the floor and holding on for dear life while the cold sweat poured down my face.

It was another five minutes before the furious pounding diminished again, and 20 before I was able to crawl to the bathroom and get back to the canvas mat on the floor. I collapsed, unconscious, thoroughly spent with exertion, and confirmed in the belief that I could soon be dead. I think I might have been looking forward to the relief of it.

Two Days in a Haze

I spent the next two days in a state of semiconsciousness. My existence consisted of trips to the bathroom, aspirins washed down with water from the canteen, and dazed slumber. I found if I didn't move a muscle, my head remained clear. The Arab radio operators in the next room accepted that I was sick and paid no more attention to me, except for the young fellow, who plagued me continually with questions and requests for driving lessons, to which I was barely able to reply.

Slowly, very slowly, like a tide going out, the pain began to abate. Once it appeared I would live after all, I discarded the idea of seeking medical attention because of the possible cost. We simply couldn't afford doctors if we were going to have enough money to get to Lagos.

By the afternoon of the third day I was finally able to get up and move around, and though still weak, drove out to the riverbank to check for Geoff. That evening, I drank a little tea with plenty of milk and once more collapsed to sleep for 12 hours. What I had was a "minor" case of sunstroke. This bit of bad luck I experienced, through foolishness and ignorance, serves as an excellent example of just how hot it really is in that country. And we still had several hundred miles to go before arriving in the hottest part.

Never Assume Anything

One of your greatest enemies—or weaknesses—can be complacency. Never take an important situation for granted. Don't assume things will be all right whether you do anything or not. Prepare for any evenuality. Be careful.

On the fourth day of my illness, the pain and constriction in my stomach were replaced by a nagging hunger, reminding me that it had been a long time since I'd eaten. After checking once more to see if Geoff had returned, I bought six eggs in town and took them back to the radio shack to scramble. The eggs were just beginning to steam when the stillness was shattered by a loud whoop coming from a dirty, unshaved fellow toting a rucksack and wearing a battered old straw hat.

Back in Business

It was Geoff in all his glory. He was weather-beaten, dusty, and eight days late, but from the smile on his face, I knew right away that he had the money. I was sure glad to see him.

It had not been easy to hitchhike to Algiers. Rides on the main road north, had been fairly easy to come by, but there had not been a lot of traffic going long distances. Geoff had spent two days and take eight rides to get to Algiers. He had gone the wrong way once and gotten lost twice, and arrived late in the afternoon of the second day. By the time he made his way to the part of town housing the foreign embassies, they were all closed; there was also no Canadian delegation to be found.

Sitting down on the curb opposite the heavily guarded palace of President Ben Bella with a can of beans, Geoff pried it open with a screwdriver and used the bent tin lid as a spoon to wolf down the contents. He was debating where to sleep the night when a muscled, sharply-dressed Algerian in tight black pants and a purple T-shirt walked past him on the sidewalk, stopped, and then turned around and came back.

A Place to Sleep

Curious but friendly, the Algerian asked Geoff where he was from and where he was going with a rucksack on his back. Hunched over the can of beans, Geoff replied that he had just arrived from Colomb-Béchar, and was going to visit his embassy in the morning. When asked where he was staying in Algiers, Geoff said a temporary lack of funds was limiting his choices; he was going to sleep in a park. The good-looking Algerian laughed and said Geoff could sleep in his nearby apartment if he wished. A bit suspicious but game for anything, Geoff thanked the Algerian for the offer and accompanied him to his home.

The apartment wasn't large but it was in a new building and quite luxuriously furnished, with a balcony overlooking a nearby hospital. Once inside, the Algerian poured them both drinks from a small bar and later fried a couple of steaks in the kitchenette while keeping up a steady stream of questions and jokes. Geoff was becoming sleepier as the evening progressed and was a bit uncomfortable after noticing there didn't seem to be a bed let alone two beds in the apartment.

Just after 10 P.M. the friendly Algerian indicated it was late and time for Geoff to sleep. Turning a handle on one of the walls, he pulled down a well-concealed double bed and told Geoff to make himself comfortable.

"No," said Geoff, "you sleep here; I'll sleep on the floor."

"No, no," said the Algerian, smiling. "You must sleep in the bed."

"No thank you," said Geoff, also smiling. "The floor would be just fine; I much prefer sleeping on floors anyway."

The Algerian insisted and Geoff resisted; he was beginning to think he'd better go and find a park after all.

The Algerian looked at Geoff and was obviously a bit perplexed. Suddenly he broke into a big grin of understanding. Motioning for him to follow, he led him to the balcony and pointed to the hospital below. "That is where I work," he said, "and I am leaving for work now. I won't be back until the morning."

Geoff would be alone in the apartment and was free to sleep wherever he chose. He was already in the bed when the fellow left ten minutes later.

Show Me the Money

Early the next morning, Geoff put on his clean shirt, carried from Béchar in a plastic bag, and went off to peddle his story. The chosen victim for his tale of woe was the British consul on the third floor of an office building downtown.

The consul was singularly unmoved by the unfolding tragedy in the desert, and the array of papers proving the existence of a vehicle and a destitute friend had no effect on him. Every summer, he said, people like Geoff came there looking for handouts or passage money home. "We are not authorized to supply funds, except in the case of emergency or theft," he went on, explaining that even then it was only the necessary amount to fly the destitute traveler back to England. "Haven't you got any relatives to whom you can wire for money?" he asked.

Geoff replied that he could ask his parents, but couldn't afford a cable (all the money was in Lagos, you see). "Well, old boy," the consul replied brightly, "you can use our wire service and pay for it when the money comes." He wrote out a request for $150, which the consul sent that morning. Geoff wrote a letter explaining the circumstances behind the request, sent it, and then shouldered his rucksack and wandered into the streets to begin the wait.

Hurry Up and Wait

After two days of sleeping in a urine-stained alley while the rats nibbled at his ankles and ate the bits of bread in his rucksack, Geoff thought there had to be a better place to sleep. An undersecretary at the consulate, where he hung around most of the day waiting for a reply to his cable, told him of an old hotel on the waterfront run by an Englishman for seamen and expatriates. The manager of the Republican Hotel listened to his tale of desert tragedy and said he could sleep in the broom closet if he wished. After the alley, the broom closet was just dandy.

For the next five days, Geoff haunted the British consulate, stopping to inquire every two hours. The rest of the time he spent reading old periodicals and anything available concerning the country through which we would be passing. He learned many interesting details that were to become very important later.

I wasn't exactly enjoying my sojourn in Béchar, and Geoff was a long way from delighting in the excitement of Algiers either. He had no way of knowing how I was faring and felt obligated to keep expenses down to a minimum. So he refused the consul's offer of a small loan and instead lived for the entire ten days on his limited supply of canned food and the ten dinars he had taken with him.

The Parents Come Through

Finally, on the morning of the ninth day after leaving Béchar, a bank draft came through the consulate in the name of Geoffrey E. Laundy for the grand sum of $150. Half an hour after receiving the money, Geoff was on the southbound road out of town. He was estatic! Once more, we had been saved, and could continue on our journey.

A good night's sleep in a culvert did him no harm, and neither did a ride straight through to Béchar early the next morning. When there was no sign of me at the riverbank, except for a lot of tracks, Geoff went to the only other place he could think of me being—the Highway Department. And there I was.

Ready to Go at Last

That afternoon, when the petrol station reopened, we filled the tank and jerry cans and once more drove out of Béchar toward the south. After 17 days in, out, and around that town, we never wanted to see it again. But without those 17 days and the repairs and equipping of the vehicle and replenishing of our finances, there are many things we might never have seen again, if at all.

Thank Your Lucky Stars

These were the worst of times, and the best of times. We were frustrated and stymied at every turn, making mistakes and doing incredibly dumb things. But unbeknownst to us, we were learning at a rapid rate. We were inadvertently becoming the kind of people we would need to be for the crossing ahead.

We learned one of the most important of all success principles through these setbacks and difficulties. Every experience in your life seems to be part of a grand plan to teach you something essential you need to know to move forward. When you are in the midst of a crisis, you often can't make out the lesson. But it's there nonetheless.

Give thanks for all the good things in your life. Actively seek out the blessings in the most difficult of circumstances, and the good in the most aggravating of people.

The more you give thanks for what you have, the more things you will have to be thankful for. It's a universal law.

> "The very greatest things—great thoughts, discoveries, inventions—have usually been nurtured in hardship, pondered over in sorrow, and at length established with difficulty."
> —Samuel Smiles

CHAPTER 19

Third Time Lucky

> "Troubles are often the tools by which God fashions us for better things."
> —HENRY WARD BEECHER

WE WERE IN NO REAL HURRY that evening, all the desire to rush having drained away in the aftermath of almost three weeks of going nowhere, except perhaps to being a bit older and wiser. We had both had time to think about what we were doing and examine the idea as a whole. We chatted quietly and philosophically as the miles rolled steadily by, to the comforting hum of good tires on good road.

Geoff had brought an article from a *Life* magazine on existentialism, which he read as we drove. After he had folded and put it away, we discussed the theory of "engagement," the coming to grips with your environment, which precedes "essence," the maximum enjoyment and satisfaction possible in life.

We agreed that since we left Vancouver, we had been more involved with the business of actually asserting ourselves in our environment than ever before in our lives—increasingly so since we left London seven weeks earlier. It had been damn difficult much of the time, but we couldn't think of anything we'd rather be doing than driving that little green Land Rover down that quiet road, toward the heart of the greatest wasteland on earth, with the stars twinkling overhead and a song in our hearts. If that was existentialism, we believed in it.

Rolling Along

Once more, we drove through Abadla and across the dry riverbed, down past where we had come to an inglorious halt 17 days before, through the crossroads at Beni-Abbes, which had been our farthest point south, and on into the night. We kept going for miles, not stopping until we were far beyond the spots in the unfeeling desert that had marked our defeats.

Our destination was Adrar, a tiny dot 376 miles south of Colomb-Béchar. From there it was 86 miles to Reggane, an even smaller dot, and then came the 800-mile stretch to Gao. At midnight we stopped for our meatballs and spaghetti, washed down with black coffee to clear the drowsiness for the all-night drive.

The Sahara Escarpment

The map indicated the paved road ended about 100 miles north of Adrar; when we reached that point, there was no need to check to be sure. In the dark night, the Rover left the pavement, lurched at an angle, straightened, slammed into a series of ruts that almost tore the wheel out of my hands, bounced crazily, and shook to a halt with my foot hard on the brake.

A brief inspection showed we were still on the road, what there was of it, and that we would have no choice but to creep along at ten miles per hour for the next five hours, until the sun came up the next morning. But with the rise of the orange-gold ball far to the east, it was not the road that arrested our attention.

We were atop the last rise in a series of low rocky hills overlooking the desert floor, which stretched away forever. The distant horizon was obscured by a pink haze. Silently—almost reverently—Geoff stopped the vehicle. We climbed onto a jagged shelf to take a good look, gazing in quiet amazement.

The Face of Death

Before us flowed a ragged landscape, silent as a graveyard, with little more than a few tufts of withered grass. The Sahara seemed to be lying dangerously in wait, without a sound or the slightest trace of movement; it was like a monstrous trap for us to step into. We stood staring, completely awed, at the immensity of what we had dared to challenge in a half-broken vehicle with three bald tires and enough gasoline to get halfway across.

The lifeless enormity of the desert, and the terrible ignorance with which we had considered it "just something in the way," gave me a feeling of looking into the face of death.

We realized with great clarity that if we had not had every difficulty of the past 17 days and learned the appropriate lessons that went with each one, we would certainly have "died in the desert."

Sleeping Out the Heat

About 30 miles before Adrar, when the sun was high in the sky and the midday heat was building up, we stopped by the track to sleep the day in a conical mud hut. It was deserted and had been for some time, judging by the amount of sand that had drifted into it. It was ideal for our purposes.

The flies made sound sleep impossible, but we managed to doze comfortably until 3 P.M., when we ate "breakfast" and refilled the tank from the jerry cans before continuing on into town. We had finally gotten over our tendency to rush things, and amidst the timelessness of that huge wasteland, we would have felt a little foolish going any faster than was absolutely necessary.

A Town in the Desert

The drab brown buildings of the spread-out Arab town of Adrar began emerging from the haze of dust and heat about 15 minutes before we arrived. The town was supposed to have 1,000 inhabitants, but it was sprawled over several miles with no main center of population. A huge empty lot, probably once a parade ground for the French army, marked the point from which the wide, dusty streets meandered in all directions toward the outskirts.

The one trace of "the good life" facing this square was an old hotel, for which we aimed. One day in the heat of the desert, as well as the lingering evening heat, makes a person rather favorably inclined toward something cold to drink when the opportunity presents itself—and that hotel reeked of opportunity.

News of a Convoy

Just as we got out of the vehicle, a European with short khaki pants, thin white legs, knobby knees, bald head, red face, and sunburned arms approached and asked in heavily accented English if we were also going with the convoy. "What convoy?" we asked.

We knew of the occasional truck convoys formed for mutual security on the journey to Mali, the first country below the Sahara, but they were largely suspended during the summer months because of the incredible heat. He accompanied us into the hotel and explained.

This was a late convoy, the last of the season. It had been forming for ten days and now consisted of almost 30 trucks. They would be leaving the next day—or at the latest, the day after—a rare stroke of luck for us.

Now that we were getting into this desert-crossing business, the prospect of 800 miles alone was not a joyous one; the unexpected existence of the convoy, which we had not suspected, was a fact we viewed with no little relief. The alternative, which we felt had been forced upon us by circumstances, was to cross by ourselves—one vehicle and two young men against the desert.

Strength in Numbers

A great life lesson is that there can be strength in numbers—as long as all the players are unified behind a common vision and goal and everyone is committed to pulling their own weight. Real strength lies in unity.

The fellow who told us about the convoy was named Hermann. He was a German from Hamburg and a minister with a degree in theology. He told us he was on a leave of absence from his parish, hitchhiking down through Africa to study the need of the black people for Christianity and write a thesis to be applied toward his doctorate. He spoke French as well as English, and we were rather impressed. We even stopped swearing for a few minutes.

Hermann had arranged a ride with some other Germans as far as Gao, 800 miles south. He had met them three days previously, and they were also awaiting the convoy.

Our Social Director

With the vague air of a social director under whose auspices we had fallen, and as though he greeted and invited thousands of Canadian travelers to Adrar to cross with the convoy every day, Hermann assured us he had a place we could stay and would soon introduce us to the others with whom we would be making the journey. We smiled and accepted his casual patronage; there was nothing to lose.

Through some process we didn't question, he had acquired squatter's rights to an empty house on the outskirts of town where we drove after leaving the hotel. Facing a large square, the old dwelling was rundown, deserted, and only accessible by a small gate in the high wall around the half-acre of dusty yard in the rear. There was, however, a tap in the back, which could be manipulated to produce a tired dribble of clear water—our most important item once we had everything else we needed. For a brief camping spot, it was quite satisfactory.

Hermann himself was no longer staying at the house, choosing rather to keep close to his countrymen and future ride, a sentiment we well appreciated. After a brief inspection of the place, we gave him a ride to an open-air workshop on the far side of town to meet the other Germans.

New Traveling Companions

By this time Geoff and I were three weeks into Africa and brown from the sun, with black stubble surrounding dry, cracked lips that marked our weather-burned faces. Our hair fell uncontrollably in two or three directions, our clothes were well lived in, and we were a good deal leaner than we had been in Gibraltar days. I suppose we looked something like desert travelers, and the Germans were our identical counterparts.

When we rolled up with Hermann, they were sitting around a small stove waiting for a pot of water to boil; except for a seemingly disenchanted glance at our companion, they continued watching the pot. I sensed immediately that we were not the first people Hermann had introduced to them, and that he was not as well thought of as he had led us to believe.

The shop was half-covered by a tin roof, the rest being open to the air, and the whole area was surrounded by a high wall topped with broken glass. A Volkswagen minibus, obviously belonging to the Germans, was propped up on two bricks, and an Arab was working on one of the rear wheels. Camping gear lay on the ground on all sides, evidence that they had not just arrived for repairs that day.

Hands Across the Sea

Taking the initiative from Hermann, I said "good evening" in German, one of about three expressions I remembered from a year of studying that language in high school. One of the fellows, Hans, got up to acknowledge the greeting and shake hands; the others remained seated disinterestedly around the blackened pot, which was just beginning to steam. From this simple meeting was born a most extraordinary friendship.

Hans was clearly the leader of the group. He looked like a young lion—fit, tanned, and blue-eyed. He was well muscled, though not tall, and had an air of authority about him. He was the kind of person who could take in all the details of a situation quickly, make a decision, and then act.

Hermann stepped forward to explain what they were doing in Adrar and where they were going, which immediately put us on a common footing. Josef, the tallest of the group, invited us to join them for coffee. With a jumble of French, English, German, and Spanish, plus Hermann translating occasionally, we soon became quite friendly, joking about the various incidents that had preceded our separate arrivals in that little town.

Traveling Tales

They had left Munich in southern Germany the same day we had left Gibraltar and had experienced as many problems as we had. Their most recent difficulty was a back wheel that had bogged down in the sand outside Adrar. The torque in the sand had caused the spline to shear off on the inside of the wheel drum.

They had been camped at the blacksmith-type garage for three days while the Arab mechanics fiddled with various ways of repairing the wheel; none had yet been discovered. We left one hour later after a good deal of laughter, and assured them we would come by in the morning to see how they were getting along. The seeds of friendship were beginning to grow.

Missing Objects

Prudently moving everything that could be stolen inside the gate, we set up camp that night in the yard under the stars, preferring the ground to the dirty cement floor inside the house. In the morning we cooked breakfast, visited the little marketplace off the main square to see if there were any vegetables for sale, and then returned to shave and wash our clothes.

Like fools we had left our belongings in the yard, and much to our chagrin, our one camera and an alarm clock had vanished. Considering that we would likely never have another chance to take photographs of the desert ahead, the loss of the camera was a minor disaster.

Mad as hatters, we drove straight to the old police station and raised a fuss, committing the police chief to do everything in his power to recover the items. He climbed into his official black Citroën and followed us back to the house. The speedy arrival of the two vehicles scattered a band of ragged children playing near the gate.

The chief shouted harshly at them to come back, which they did, terrified and skulking like whipped puppies. Two of the brats were trembling so much they could barely speak, but all denied any knowledge of the theft. The Arab police chief rubbed his swarthy mustache and shrugged, insisting that such a thing never happened in Adrar and promising further inquiries. We never saw the camera or alarm clock again.

We relearned an important lesson: never become too complacent or overconfident. Be on your guard. The most successful people are invariably those who are the most fastidious about the critical details of their work. They don't take things for granted or trust to chance. They know it's the details that will get you every single time.

A Snail's Pace

Back at the shop, the repair job was proceeding at a snail's pace. This was making the Germans nervous about being ready in time to leave with the convoy. Just to double-check, Hans, the leader of the group, came with us to confirm the departure date with the truck drivers camped on the edge of town.

There was no need to be concerned, they assured us. They weren't leaving until the next day, or maybe the day after. We returned to the garage to urge the Arab mechanic to hurry. He merely gave us a bored shrug. There wasn't enough "get up and go" in that garage to fill a teacup.

Swimming in the Desert

We sat in the shade pondering how to pass the time. After a couple of minutes, Hans brightened. "Would you like to go swimming?" he asked. He had to be joking; we hadn't seen enough water since arriving in Algeria to even take a bath. But Hans insisted he knew of a place if we could go in our Land Rover.

With the seven of us jammed into the vehicle, Geoff followed Hans' directions out of town. The midmorning sun was almost overhead and the dashboard thermometer reading 110 degrees. Only five kilometers out of Adrar, a slash of bright green slowly emerged through the dancing heat waves.

Another two kilometers brought us to a large vegetable farm surrounded by a hedge; above it turned a steel windmill. Still following Hans' eager directions, we circled the perimeter to the far side and stopped at a gap in the thorn bushes. Quickly doffing our clothes for bathing trunks, we followed the four Germans through the hedge and across the cultivated rows.

There amid the melon plants and citrus trees was a large reservoir, 50 yards square and five feet deep. Its brilliant algae-green water shone like a huge emerald. With a yell and whoop, we were all in the water, splashing, diving, and cavorting like exuberant porpoises. For two hours we stayed and played in the cool water, bothered by no one except an old Arab who shouted at us for a while and then stalked away muttering.

Teaming Up with the Germans

On the way back to Adrar, everyone laughing in high spirits, we made a critical decision. We told the Germans not to be too concerned about their Volkswagen bus. If the trucks left before it was repaired, we could form a convoy of two and make the crossing together. The pact made, we left them at the workshop, where a young Arab was slowly filing away at their wheel drum, and went "home" to sleep through the heat.

The Weather in the Desert

We had arrived in Gibraltar on April 20, and it was now May 30. Except for an increase in the temperature as we moved further south, the weather never varied. The sun rose clean and fresh about 5:30 A.M., climbed to its maximum height and intensity by 1 P.M., cooled by 6 P.M., and set shortly after 8 P.M. There were never any clouds, and there was no mist, little dew, and always a scarlet-red sunset to finish the day. Occasionally there was wind, but by and large the weather was consistently beautiful and completely dependable.

The mornings were fine and cool and early rising was a pleasure. The evenings were warm but not hot and the air was dry, causing perspiration to evaporate rapidly. The gentle evening breezes came like soft caresses through our hair and into our open shirts and made idle contemplation a pleasurable pastime.

Ready for the Crossing

We had arrived in Gibraltar a full five pounds heavier than we'd left London, thanks to all the exercise and eating we had done on the way. Since arriving in Tangiers, we'd both lost ten pounds and felt none the worse for it. We weren't eating much, and according to the books, we weren't eating well, but we were physically sound. We were sleeping better, though lighter, waking quickly and completely at the slightest noise. Our senses of hearing and sight were sharper, our reflexes were faster, and our mental grasp of situations, as well as our adaptability to them, was much quicker. Even our ability to see the humor in a difficult situation was improved, though we had never been overly beset with pessimism.

In short, we felt more genuinely alive, mentally and physically, than we could ever remember being and we seemed to have a confident glow. We felt ready for anything—to sing a song, write a book, cross a desert, love a woman. It was a good feeling. We were looking forward to the future.

At Peace with the World

In both Béchar and Adrar the vast quietude of the Sahara Desert seemed to work in a strange manner on us during those days of forced waiting for the next segment of the journey. It gradually drove the impatience and insistence out of us, and replaced it with a calm acceptance of a slower pace of life to which we simply had to adjust.

Instead of increasing the need and desire for human companionship, that great empty land had the opposite effect. The feeling of solitude and the joy of being quietly alone with our thoughts became very precious, more so than they had ever been in the city. Geoff and I found we derived a great deal of pleasure from hours spent reading, writing, or staring at the flickering embers of the tiny campfire, with scarcely more than a word passing between us.

Even when we sat around in the evenings with the Germans, it was much the same. And yet, without words, the bond joining the six of us set, hardened, and bound our lives together in the course of three short days.

Fish or Cut Bait

The next morning was Wednesday, and the Arab at the garage was still avoiding any serious work on the Germans' wheel drum. "Why don't you tell him to get a move on?" I asked Hans. He answered that none of them spoke French except Hermann, whose meek inquiries the Arabs just ignored. The whole idea of poking around at such a small job for five days was nonsense, and now that we had agreed to cross with the Germans, the minibus was partially our problem as well.

I decided to assert myself and get the minibus back on the road. Picking up the wheel drum, I took it to the Arab in charge of the workshop. Politely, in slow French, I told him that if the Volksbus wasn't ready to leave that evening with the convoy, not only would we finish the job ourselves, but he wasn't going to be paid one dinar for the five days he had already wasted.

With great indignation, he launched into a long story about how hard he'd been working on it, and how much work he had to do in the garage. He said he didn't realize the convoy was leaving so soon, and didn't think it mattered how long the job took because we were waiting for the convoy anyway.

Money Talks

Carefully avoiding being outright rude, I repeated that the car must be ready by that night at the latest, or he wouldn't be paid. I thrust the wheel rim into his hand and gave him a big grin, then turned and went back to where the Germans were sitting and watching. They hadn't understood anything except the object of the exchange.

The Arab examined the wheel drum for a second, and then shouted at two of his assistants, who came running. Waving the drum in their faces, he berated them for their laziness, pointed vigorously at the crippled Volksbus, and relayed the urgency of getting the job done by that evening. They all glared at me as if I were some kind of traitor.

With the mechanics finally making progress on the repair of the wheel drum, we left the Germans to begin repacking their vehicle.

When I returned to the shop in the late afternoon, I was told the repair had been simple—a matter of welding new spline onto the sheared drums. It was the filing of those new splines to make them fit on the axle that was taking so long. The man in charge insisted, however, that the job was almost finished.

The Germans were all packed to leave, and we agreed to meet at our "house" the next morning to cross with the convoy.

The Issue of Traveling Companions

Choose your friends and associates carefully. Work only with people you respect and whom you can count on. Take your time in assessing new people. Until they are tested "under fire," it is hard to assess their true character.

Your choice of the people you surround yourself with in life can affect your success more than any other factor. The people with whom you most identify have an inordinate influence on how you think, feel, talk, and behave.

Your choice of traveling companions in life can determine the success or failure of the entire journey.

> "There are powers inside of you which, if you could discover and use, would make of you everything you ever dreamed or imagined you could become."
>
> —Orison Swett Marden

SECTION VI

The Greatest Desert on Earth

"All great masters are chiefly distinguished by the power of adding a second, a third, and perhaps a fourth step in a continuous line. Many a man has taken the first step. With every additional step, you enhance immensely the value of your first."
—RALPH WALDO EMERSON

WHATEVER YOUR GOAL, you can achieve it by taking one step at a time. This is one of the greatest of all success principles. "By the yard it's hard; but inch by inch, anything's a cinch!"

Do you want to be financially independent? The achievement of personal wealth begins with you saving your first dollar, and then adding one dollar at a time. Do you want to be thin, fit, and healthy? Superb physical health simply requires that you eat a little less and exercise a little more each day.

If one of your goals is to be among the top people in your field, you can achieve it by getting better little by little. You can practice and develop one skill at a time. You can learn and grow each day.

Take your biggest goal and break it down into daily, even hourly, activities. Then discipline yourself to take the first step, and then the next step, and then the one after that, until you finally arrive.

Remember, *happiness* is the progressive, step-by-step realization of a worthy goal or ideal. And whatever someone else has done, you can probably do as well. The goals others achieve are also possible for you, if you just take the first step.

"Nothing splendid has ever been achieved except by those who dared believe that something inside of them was superior to circumstance."
—Bruce Barton

CHAPTER 20

The Convoy

> "Help thy brother's boat across, and lo! Thine own has reached the shore"
> —Hindu Proverb

We had just finished packing our things carefully back into the Rover the next morning, Thursday, when Hans and Helmut came roaring up in their Volksbus. It was fully repaired and they cheered jubilantly and blasted the horn. Their joy was infectious, and we were all excited at the thought of being on the road again. Geoff and I leaped into the Rover and raced pell-mell, bumper to bumper, back into town with the Germans.

The convoy had left at dawn, but planned to stop for the night at Reggane, 80 miles south, so we weren't pressed for time. After stocking up with gasoline and water, we checked the oil and water in the vehicles, as well as the tires, declared ourselves road ready, and set out to catch the trucks. We'd been four days in Adrar and were glad to see the last of it.

The Algerian government stamps your passport in Adrar, 500 miles north of the border; as far as they're concerned, you no longer exist. If something happens to you in the desert, you're on your own.

The Truckers to Africa

The Arab truck drivers on the run from Oran and Algiers into central Africa are a lazy lot. They carry bales of cheap textiles, tin pots and pans, canned fish and tomato paste, and other cheap, high-profit goods to be sold in the bazaars of sub-Saharan Africa. They are in no hurry and often stop on the trip south for days at a time to visit friends and family. When they do drive, it is only for two or three hours in the morning and perhaps the same in the evening.

They rarely drive at night, the time we preferred to travel, and the 2,000-mile trip to Gao from Algiers, or the 2,500 miles to Niamey, in Niger, usually takes them four weeks. The financial benefits of making better time don't weigh too heavily on them.

Waiting Out the Heat

It was therefore not surprising when only two hours out of Adrar, we came upon three of the trucks that had left that morning stopped next to the "piste" (the track) for the midday heat. Since it was just 11 A.M. and the sun was becoming fierce, we waved to the Germans to stop and turn off and parked in the shade of one of the trucks.

There was only a slight draft of hot air coming through the open doors of the vehicle, and the heat was terrible. The difference in the intensity of the sun between three weeks earlier and 400 miles north, and now on the outskirts of Adrar, was astonishing. The temperature rose to 125 degrees in the meager shade of the vehicle. Struggling for breath in the searing heat, with sweat pouring off us in sticky rivulets, we drank and drank and drank and consumed five gallons of water between us in that five-hour period.

Sleeping was out of the question, and eating virtually impossible. We didn't even have enough energy to talk much. Instead each of us thought miserably to ourselves, "If it's like this here, what will it be like when we get into the middle of the desert?"

Nonetheless, for the sake of the vehicles, we disciplined ourselves to stay until 4 P.M., when it had "cooled" to 100 degrees. Then we left the lumbering trucks and continued to Reggane.

The Jumping Off Point

Reggane is the last town in Algeria, although the frontier was 500 miles farther south on the other side of the desert. There was one lonely petrol pump about 200 yards from a cluster of brown buildings, several of which were deserted and already beginning to fill with sand in the doorways. There had once been a Foreign Legion post at Reggane, but now it stood away from the houses, windblown and uninhabited.

It was just before sunset that Thursday when we arrived, and the funereal atmosphere of the lifeless, darkened doorways made us willing to drive right on through. However, we had to refuel and refill our water cans for the last time.

We stopped the two vehicles by the lone gas pump and waited for someone to come and unlock it. When five minutes passed with no one in sight, Hermann said he would seek information about the convoy.

Before leaving Adrar, we hadn't seen too much of Hermann. He hadn't accompanied us swimming, but was always in town chatting with storekeepers, police, and anyone else he could find. He was about 35 years old, and not our type of friend, so his little side trips didn't cause too much concern. Besides, he was constantly returning with gems of information about the area and desert.

A young Arab eventually came running with the key to the pump and we topped off our tanks. After filling the water containers at a nearby well, we followed the dirt road around and to one side of the settlement and there met Hermann. He had found the main convoy and learned that they weren't leaving until the next day—or perhaps the day after. He suggested we camp somewhere nearby until they were ready to go.

Going It Alone

With this latest news of further delays, we decided to hold a council to determine our next course of action. We had all had enough of the convoy's procrastination. The Germans were just as anxious as Geoff and I to cross the desert. The breakdowns, holdups, retracing of steps, expenditures, heat, and local mentality—all had worn our patience thin.

We discussed our options by the Rover's headlamps while Helmut and Kurt made a large pot of coffee. The only reason we had waited for the convoy was for added insurance against a breakdown in the desert. But two vehicles, we reasoned, were enough insurance to get us over the last lap, especially since the convoy would be coming behind us.

There was a waterhole marked on our map 450 miles south, at a place called Bordji-Perez. If something happened to one of the vehicles, we could drive back to Reggane or to the waterhole in the other one , or just sit tight until the convoy came along. Hans was in complete accord with us and the other Germans didn't argue with what he said. The only dissenter was Hermann.

A Dissenting Voice

Hermann now gave his opinion as if he were dealing with people in complete ignorance of a field in which he specialized. Having spent so much time gathering bits of information, he had apparently lost sight of the fact that we had all crossed the same rugged country to arrive in Reggane and were equally aware of what lay ahead.

He nonetheless delivered his opinion confidently, pointing out that if both vehicles broke down, we could die before the slow-moving convoy came up. He went on to say that the only way to cross the Sahara was with a large group for mutual protection. It was better to go slower and be assured of success than take the chance of going alone. He ended by saying he knew of a great place for us to camp while we waited, as if that ended the discussion.

As it happened, Hermann was correct. But because we didn't like him, we rejected his ideas and input and refused to consider their possible validity. We made the mistake of focusing more on "who" was right rather than "what" was right.

A Time to Choose

The Germans, with the exception of Hans, seemed hesitant. Geoff just looked at Hermann as though he had said something foolish, and then walked away. I finally told Hans that Geoff and I were leaving that night, convoy or no convoy. They must make up their own minds.

Hans looked me in the eyes for a few seconds in silence, and then—his mind suddenly made up—turned to Hermann and told him we were all leaving in half an hour. Hermann could come or stay as he chose. Then we all sat down and drank the coffee.

Hans was clearly the leader of the group. Not only did he accept complete responsibility for every detail, but he never shrank from making a decision and taking action. He was as solid as a rock.

How Leaders Lead

Leaders lead by example. They demonstrate the qualities of courage, vision, and foresight. Above all, they step up to make decisions and take command.

Leaders accept a high level of responsibility for results. They take initiative and are action-oriented. They don't wait for things to happen; they make them happen.

Each person can be a leader by deciding to act like one whenever the situation calls for it.

We have never been more in need of leaders—at every level of our society—than we are today.

> "When you take charge of your life, there is no longer need to ask permission of other people or society at large. When you ask permission, you give someone else veto power over your life."
>
> —GEOFFREY F. ABERT

CHAPTER 21

The Crossing

> "The one thing over which you have complete control is your own thoughts. It is this that puts you in a position to control your own destiny."
>
> —Paul G. Thomas

THE COFFEE WAS FINISHED when Hermann finally decided to come with us, but he didn't pretend to be pleased at having his advice ignored. His know-all attitude was beginning to grate on Geoff and me, and we were glad he was riding in the other vehicle. At 8 P.M., with the Volksbus leading, we pulled out of Reggane and drove into the dark toward the Tenezrouft—the heart of the Sahara.

According to the map the road ran almost due south across the desert and deep into Mali. The first place we could get water was a dot called Bordji-Perez at the 450-mile mark. The route was broken at two places—Poste Weygand and Bidon Cinque-Poste Maurice Courtier—between Reggane and Bordji-Perez. Geoff had learned a little about these places when he was waiting in Algiers.

The Desert Outposts

When the French controlled the Sahara, there was a steady stream of traffic across the desert into the colonies below. The two way stations were built by the Foreign Legion to allow travelers to break their journeys, make repairs, and restock with petrol and water. All travelers had to register at Reggane and deposit the equivalent of $300 per vehicle before starting across. The time of departure was noted and radioed to the next post, and a set time was allowed for the traveler to report before vehicles were dispatched from either end to find it. The $300 was to cover any expenses incurred by the French government on behalf of the traveler, and was returned in Gao upon arrival.

There were several facts that necessitated these precautions. Since the late 19th century when the Sahara officially became French territory, over 2,000 people had perished there. Many more were never found and presumed dead. The incredible heat is the fiercest on earth. A lightly dressed man who collapsed in the open sun at 1 P.M. would be dead of dehydration within 20 minutes. A person without a hat could suffer sunstroke, irreparable brain damage, or even death after only one hour at midday. Each traveler was expected to carry five gallons of water per day. Crossing the Sahara was rightfully made out to be serious business.

On Your Own

When the French withdrew from their colonies in Africa, the new government of Algeria abandoned the desert outposts and lifted all restrictions on travel. We had been officially stamped out of Algeria in Adrar and were on our own. We were crossing at our own risk and there would be no inquiry if we never came out. With full confidence in our vehicle we were not frightened at the prospect; however like soldiers before a battle, we certainly had something to think about.

Clear Goal, Hard Going

Our goal for the first night was the second of the abandoned way stations, Poste Maurice Cortier, which was two thirds of the distance across, or about 300 miles. If we could get there before the sun caught us, we would have shelter and only 150 miles to go to the well at Bordji-Perez the next night. The difficult part of the crossing would then be behind us.

The *piste* (track) was immediately terrible. Fifty years of heavy traffic and several of neglect had left it a mess of ruts, holes, and bumps. The drifting sand had covered the road in countless places with a layer of fine powder, often to a depth of 18 inches—and in stretches of as much as 200 feet. It was in one of these dry swamps that our troubles began.

The Troubles Begin

We were perhaps 20 miles along. Geoff was driving and the Land Rover was about one quarter mile in front of the minibus. Hitting the soft sand felt as if all four tires were dropping simultaneously to half pressure. Geoff shifted from fourth to third and then to second to get more torque; he then tried four-wheel drive. With the motor screaming and front tires digging in, we slowly moved out of the patch onto the firmer road ahead.

"Guess we'd better wait and see if they get through," said Geoff, as he pulled to the side and shifted the transmission into neutral. We got out and watched the approaching headlamps from opposite sides of the vehicle. As the roaring Volksbus hit the silt, the sand rose in a spray like splashing water and the vehicle careened from side to side. It continued slower and slower until it came at last to a tired halt. As it stopped, the dust billowed past it and across the headlamps in thick rolls. Hans was already out and inspecting the sunken back end.

Pulling and Dragging

Without a word, Geoff got into the Rover and started backing it up. I walked over to the vehicle and asked Hermann if they had a towrope. They did, and while Helmut dug for it, everyone gathered around and looked at the wheels. They were buried in the sand to the frame and barely visible.

Even with the Rover pulling, the Volksbus refused to budge. We put our backs into it and tried again. It moved a little and then once more bogged down. We would have to dig it out and try pulling with the wheels clear.

While Geoff maneuvered the Rover forward and back so he could pull from an angle on undisturbed sand, Hans and I started digging underneath the bus' rear wheels with machetes; Josef and Helmut worked on the other side and Kurt helped Geoff with the rope.

There was nothing casual about our attitude toward the job. We scrambled frantically to get the bus out and going again. We dreaded being caught by the sun without protection, and had a long way to go to reach that protection. Yet as fast as we dug, the sand ran back in. Soon we were all dripping with perspiration, including Geoff and Kurt, who had started digging with pots at the front tires.

Hapless Hermann

The last one to descend from the bus had been Hermann, and he stood back and like an interested spectator to watch us work. After a couple of minutes, he came over and said we must get all the sand out from around the wheels—as if we weren't already trying to do just that. We had better not drive anymore in the dark, he added, then climbed back into the vehicle and lay down. We were concentrating too hard on the digging to pay attention to him.

In another five minutes, we had the wheels as clear as they were going to get and with the Land Rover pulling, the wheels of the Volksbus spinning, and the four of us pushing and straining every sinew, the bus slowly began to move—10 feet, 20 feet, 40 feet—and then it stopped. We stopped too, lungs and legs burning from the exertion.

Geoff had just come back to see how it was going when Hermann stuck his head out the window to inspect the proceedings. That was too much, even if he was a minister. Puffing and wiping the salty sweat from my nose, I walked around the bus and yanked the side door open.

"Get out!" I panted. "You can damn well get out and work with the rest of us."

"I thought the work was all finished," he replied in an offended tone as he climbed out onto the sand.

"Well, the work is not all finished," I said, and pointing to the rear of the bus, added, "You can push from there until the bloody thing is out."

"You take a turn at driving," Geoff said quietly. "I'll kick him in the ass if he looks like he's slacking off."

Hermann petulantly took up a pushing position against the back of the Volksbus, and Hans changed with Helmut as driver. I got back into the Rover, gave a blast on the horn, and let out the clutch full throttle, slowly inching forward until the vehicle was on solid roadbed. We were out.

Everyone Doing his Share

Everyone on small teams must do their fair share. Each person has to pitch in to get the job done. Everyone is responsible for the end result. No one can stand aside and expect someone else to do more while he or she does less. Unfortunately, there are always slackers and free riders, people who try to get by doing the very least, even though they expect to be rewarded at the same level as the hard workers.

As Hans untied the rope, we all cheered, laughed, and climbed back into our respective vehicles. Even Hermann—his face dripping from effort—looked pleased, though guilty. We pushed on, relieved and eager to make up the lost time and delighted at having met an obstacle and surmounted it as a team, but hoping that the necessity would not arise again.

Our relief was short-lived. Ten minutes later the Rover piled into another drift. We just managed to get clear when the Volksbus came in behind us and bogged down again. This time Hans didn't spin the back wheels—a frantic effort that only dug the minibus in deeper. We leaped out of the vehicles before the dust had settled and muscled the van out with brute strength.

Not stopping to rest in our urgency, we yelled and cheered each other on, chanting and straining on every third count until it came clear. This time we were too out of breath to rejoice. We just climbed back in and drove on.

It Gets Continually Worse

For the next five hours, the pattern of the Volksbus bogging down, and we muscling it out repeated itself over and over again, until we were ready to collapse from exhaustion. Sometimes we could use the Land Rover to pull or push, but most of the time we had to push it out by hand with our lungs screaming and every muscle painfully straining.

But no one was complaining, and after the incident with Hermann, no one shirked. Everyone gave the best they had to give, every time they had to, no matter how tired they were. It never occurred to Geoff and me that we were breaking our backs for a vehicle that wasn't ours but was owned by fellows we'd never met until a few days ago and would probably never see again after the crossing. We were in this together, 100 percent.

A Silent Pact

We had formed an unbreakable pact, not in words but by implication. When we first said we'd wait for the Germans if the convoy left before their vehicle was repaired, the fabric binding our seven lives together began to interweave and entangle. We were caught up in it and carried forward—inextricably and powerfully—and felt the strength of the bond growing over the miles.

There in the desert we were the only people on earth. Every bit of our separate lives, every laugh, tear, success, and failure, had played its part to bring us together in the middle of that wasteland.

We were channeled by fate into one small struggling mass of humanity pitted against the desert. When we heaved together in the powder-fine sands to extricate the Volksbus, it was not their Volksbus but *the* Volksbus, and it was pulled out by *the* Land Rover. We succeeded or failed together, as one indivisible entity. And the strength of the bond lay in the strength of the individuals who formed that bond. No one could give any less than his best, for our entire beings—our very lives—depended on defeating 450 miles of unfeeling sand.

The Invisible Bond

There was little conversation as discussion was irrelevant. In a way not fully understood by us, we were caught up in something that transcended words and philosophy, something strong and that couldn't be clearly examined until the journey was finished. And it couldn't be finished unless and until we reached the water at Bordji-Perez.

What often kills a marriage, merger, or partnership is the notion of his or hers, mine and yours, ours and theirs. When you're in the Sahara—or facing any significant challenge—such distinctions can be fatal. You must believe and act as if "we're all in this together."

From Rough to Smooth

By 2 A.M. we had been clear of heavy sand for almost an hour, but the going was still rough on the vehicles—and on us—so we signaled a stop and suggested a 20-minute coffee break. The fatigue from the long day before and five hours of steady exertion that had marked most of the time since leaving Reggane was making itself felt on all of us.

While the water boiled on the Germans' little stove, and with the vehicles positioned so that the headlights of each fell on the other, we hauled out our petrol containers and refilled the tanks. The miles of strain and high revs in getting in and out of the sand had consumed too much of the precious amber fluid. Something was also wrong with the carburetor on the Volksbus, causing it to use too many liters of petrol for too few kilometers. Hans and Geoff took the carburetor apart and cleaned it while drinking coffee, then reassembled it carefully. Then we continued onward.

Thinking Out of the Box

The track was still shaking the Rover violently and without a moon the endless country beyond the range of the lights appeared dark and forbidding. But a thought occurred to me. The reason we were staying on the rough piste was that, if we strayed off it and couldn't find it again, we would be lost in the desert. However, since the road ran straight north and south, we could *deliberately* drive off it to the west and know the road was to the east. The open desert was probably a lot smoother than the worn track, and we couldn't possibly get lost as long as we kept the road on our left.

Swinging the Rover up over the sandy ridge bordering the track, I drove an eighth of a mile straight west and told Geoff what I had in mind. As we leveled off and drove parallel to the piste it was obvious we'd made a useful discovery. The open country stretched flat and unbroken to the farthest reaches of the headlamps. The bouncing and rattling that had kept us peering ahead for deep ruts was gone. We were free to swing to the right or left or drive in circles if we wanted. From a narrow broken track ten yards wide, we had come upon a sand-gravel highway that covered the length and breadth of the Sahara between the piste and the Atlantic Ocean, 1,800 miles to the west.

Resistance to New Ideas

Excited about our discovery, I swerved back over to the piste to stop and let the Germans catch up with us. I then explained the idea to Hermann so he could translate it to the others. But he balked. It was too risky, he said. The piste was the only safe place to travel if we didn't want to get lost in the night, and besides, we shouldn't be driving at night anyway.

I patiently asked if he could explain the idea to Hans and Helmut, the drivers, and let them decide. He explained it in a discouraging tone of voice. They began arguing among themselves in German; Hermann was adamant that they not leave the security of the broken track. We got back into the Rover and left them to work it out for themselves, driving along parallel with them on the smooth desert floor for a few minutes and varying the distance from a hundred yards to a quarter mile.

Give It a Try

Hermann had obviously made a fuss about our idea to get back at us for having made him sweat a little; the Volksbus lurched along the uneven piste for several more kilometers. Then all at once it swerved and lurched over the sand ridge, off the piste, and came straight for us. Just before reaching us it swung parallel and we drove along side by side, laughing and honking at the newfound sensation of freedom.

I don't know what was said between the fellows and Hermann in that brief interim, but after that incident, he didn't have so many suggestions to make—and no one paid much attention to him when he did make them.

We stayed off the piste for the remainder of the night, always keeping it fairly close on the left. We had a wonderful feeling of freedom driving that way, sometimes close enough to touch the other vehicle, other times swerving far out, cutting in on each other, andturning just in time to avoid a collision. Most of the time, though, we drove about 100 yards apart with one or the other a little ahead, boring our way through the night with the stabbing headlights.

This was another valuable lesson. It is normal and natural for us to get into a comfort zone, or rut, and then resist every suggestion to get out of it—even if we're not happy with it. We must continually be asking, Could there be a better way? We must deliberately force ourselves to try something new or different if the old way is no longer working.

Absolute Nothingness

Even with the windows open to let in the cool air as we drove, we were having real difficulties staying awake in the early hours of the morning. The first edge of light in the east somehow lifted the dull fatigue a little, and soon we could see the terrain. At the first clear view of it, I snapped wide-awake and nudged Geoff who was dozing on the seat beside me.

"Look at that, Geoff! Just open your eyes and take a good look!" Geoff shook his head numbly and leaned close to the windshield. His eyes widened and his jaw went slack. Then he sat back in his seat and just stared. We had come to the end of the earth. It was a land where the nothingness was absolute. We had never seen or imagined anything like it.

The barren terrain had begun in Morocco. As we had driven south, the land had weakened; the pulse had faded and diminished. The silent rattle of its last breath had touched us in the dark. Now, at last, the land was dead.

The Volksbus had fallen behind in the predawn hours, and we were alone, pressed between the sky and the yellow sands, in lifeless void with only the sound of the engine to break the eternal stillness.

Flat as a Tabletop

Before us lay a flat, unbroken, and yellow expanse that flowed endlessly away on all sides to the horizons. Further north there had been tufts of scraggly grass and a bit of rugged sagebrush fighting for survival. Now there was only lifeless sand. Before there had been a slight roll to the arid terrain that broke the monotony of the desert; now it was perfectly flat. Where once there had been a glimmer of hope that nature had not turned her back on the Sahara, now there was nothing.

The brilliant blue of the sky joined the dirty yellow of the desert floor in a perfect circle; we were the precise center and remained so as we moved. The flaming gold of the sun, climbing high in the sky, was the one thing nature had bestowed on the last of the lands. We felt as if we had come in on the middle of a colossal joke being told by the sun to the unhearing sands; its punch line was death.

We slowed to let the Volksbus catch up with us and resolved not to lose sight of it again. When it appeared about ten minutes later, we increased our speed and stayed even with it. There were no more cheery grins and waves. The long, trouble-filled night had set us back too far on our proposed schedule. With the sun sitting on the horizon like an evil yellow cat waiting to pounce on two silly mice a long way from their holes, the only thing that mattered now was mileage.

Crossing Your Sahara

The keys to great success have always been *focus and concentration.* There are critical times when you must throw your whole heart—mind and body—into what you're doing in order to succeed. As Peter Drucker wrote, "Whenever you find something getting done, you find a monomaniac with a mission."

Once you begin you must devote your entire time and attention to the task or goal. Throw your whole heart into it. Never let up. Keep pushing until the objective is reached. Resolve to press forward until the goal is 100 percent complete. This is the ultimate test.

> "It is the constant and determined effort that breaks down all resistance, sweeps aside all obstacles."
>
> —Claude M. Bristol

CHAPTER 22

One Oil Barrel at a Time

> "Nature can not be tricked or cheated. She will give up to you the object of your struggles only after you have paid her price."
> —NAPOLEON HILL

IT'S IMPOSSIBLE TO GET LOST DRIVING in the Sahara in the daytime. The piste is marked with black 55-gallon oil drums at five-kilometer intervals, exactly where the road follows the curvature of the earth. No matter where you are on the piste you can always see two oil drums, one behind and one ahead.

As you reach one drum, the next one—five kilometers ahead—pops up on the horizon and the one five kilometers behind falls off, as if it had been shot in a shooting gallery.

All you have to do to cross the biggest desert in the world is to take it "one oil barrel at a time." The rule is that, if you go as far as you can see to go at the moment, you will be able to see far enough to go one step further. You can accomplish even the greatest goals "one oil barrel at a time."

Poste Weygand

At 6:30 A.M. a small blot appeared on the horizon ahead. In a while we came to Poste Weygand, the 160-mile mark; it had taken 11 hours of solid going. The site consisted of three decrepit Quonset huts and a large frame building, possibly an old barracks. Ghostlike and deserted, with doors half ajar and windows broken, the buildings sat like tombstones, alone and abandoned.

We didn't stop and only slowed 100 yards up the track to read the blackened sign. White letters under a skull and crossbones on a charred background stated in French, *Do not leave the piste beyond this point.* Ten minutes later we passed another blackened sign that stated simply, "Tropic of Cancer."

Our Enemy, the Sun

Now the sun became the true enemy. It had first appeared in the east as a golden sliver of light along the horizon. Then the first roundness peeked over the horizon, as though looking for a victim. Slowly the entire sun rose into the sky where it lingered on the horizon before beginning its inexorable climb toward midday.

Geoff and I entertained each other by quoting verses from "Carry On":

And so in the strife of the battle of life
It's easy to fight when you're winning;
It's easy to slave, and starve and be brave,
When the dawn of success is beginning.

But the man who can meet despair and defeat
With a cheer, there's a man of God's choosing;
The man who can fight to Heaven's own height
Is the man who can fight when he's losing.

Carry on, carry on. Things never were looming so black;
But show that you haven't a cowardly streak,
And though you're unlucky, you never are weak.
Carry on! Brace up for another attack.
It's looking like hell, but you never can tell.
Carry on, old man! Carry on!

The Race Was On

The race for Bodin Cinque (Poste Maurice Courtier), the second abandoned army post, was on in earnest. However, we knew it was impossible to cover 170 miles before the sun reached its fiery zenith. We had lost too much time in the struggles of the previous night. It was now a matter of how close we could get to that landmark.

The Land Rover was running beautifully. Throughout the strenuous night it had never coughed, sputtered, or failed to respond to the continuous demands of pushing, pulling, and dragging through the clinging sands. The hum of the 96-horsepower engine transmitted its confidence through our weariness and let us feel that, whatever difficulties lay ahead, our vehicle would remain one constant dependable factor.

The Volksbus however, was having troubles. The battered machine gave the impression it was going along with this mad idea, but did definitely not approve. It began to protest as soon as it was driven off the paved roads. Each time it went over a hard bump a tire would blow out. If driven in heavy sand, it would bog down and refuse to budge.

Now that it had been tricked into coming so far into the desert, it refused to run properly and devoured petrol. Several times in the night we had stopped and adjusted the carburetor in vain efforts to cut down on its gluttonous consumption. As the heat increased that morning, the Volksbus ran even worse, forcing us to go slower.

Victims of the Desert Sun

The Rover's ideal cruising speed was about 35 miles per hour. With the firm unbroken terrain, we should have been driving at maximum speed the whole time; however, we were lucky to drive at 25 miles per hour without leaving the Volksbus behind. Meanwhile, the sun continued its relentless climb and burned away the early morning chill by the time Poste Weygand had fallen off the horizon behind us.

We began to pass the remains of vehicles that had not survived the crossing. Most were shapeless masses of colorless scrap—all their usable parts having been stripped off by other travelers. However, on three occasions the automobiles were in good condition, complete with tires, seats, and windows. They were locked tightly, as though their owners had parked them minutes before and then vanished. Just after 10:30 we came to one of these cars, a Renault-Dauphine, sitting a few yards off the barely discernible piste.

Stopping to scavenge anything of possible use, we soon saw there was nothing of value left in or on it except the tires, and we were too exhausted to consider taking them off. We climbed back into our vehicles to escape the blistering rays of the overhead sun and pressed on. Then minutes later the Volksbus developed a vapor lock and came to a halt. The fuel pump on the Rover was also acting up with the heat and the engine quit as we approached the van. We had no choice. We were there for the day.

Stuck in the Open

At 11 A.M. the thermometer read 110 degrees and the air was already stiflingly. Geoff dragged a full jerry can of water out of the back of the Rover and onto the seat between us. Now that the vehicle was no longer moving, the relief from the heat afforded by the air currents had ceased.

Breathing became laborious and conversation was an effort best avoided. Trickles of sweat began to flow down our faces to mingle with the soaked stench of our shapeless T-shirts and drip onto the seats where we sprawled, drained of strength after 30 hard hours without sleep. Outside the noiseless inferno of golden rage pounded down in merciless fury on the two little vehicles that represented the only life in the heart of hell.

The mercury began to spike inside the glass tube of the thermometer. By noon the temperature was 120 degrees and rising, as though to mock the inert figures in the soundless vehicles. The only motion was the slow tilting of water bottles to quench an insatiable thirst that parched the throat and swelled the tongue, which remained thick and rubbery no matter how much we drank.

The sole noise in the scorching stillness was the steady gasping that never quite filled the straining lungs. We were all exhausted and semiconscious, but sleep was impossible. Motion was unthinkable. Just to breathe and drink took every bit of strength we had. And still the temperature climbed.

At 1:20 P.M. the red line had stopped rising at 130 degrees of searing, broiling, terrible heat. The yellow sands had turned a dazzling, blinding white, reflecting the glare at us from all directions. The only relief was in the blank, listless staring at the brown canvas top, with heads lolled back like those of rag dolls. The minutes never passed and the hours lasted forever. The thirst was unquenchable; a quart of water disappeared in three spasmodic swallows and minutes later our throats were so dry, it took a choking effort to swallow. The intensity of the bake-oven temperature was unbelievable, unbearable, and inescapable. It was an incredible feeling to be held in one spot, immovable and suffering, in the middle of nothing, with only the sun above and the sand disappearing into the distance on all sides.

The Agony Recedes

Finally the worst passed. By 2 P.M. the mercury had begun its slow descent, and by 4:30 it had sunk below 110 degrees for the first time in almost seven hours. We were utterly debilitated and felt only a vague wonderment that the ordeal was finally over.

Our 40 liters of water had dwindled to ten, and the Germans' supply wasn't much better. Everyone looked haggard and a bit stunned as we adjusted ourselves in our seats, started the vehicles, and continued on. We were just halfway to Bordji-Perez and way behind schedule. We knew we'd be in serious trouble if we didn't get there before the heat of the next day.

Our Spirits Revive

The exhausted semiconscious state we were in before the heat stopped us had changed very little; however, with the motion of the vehicle and the decline in temperature of the dwindling day, our rundown feeling gradually gave way to a tired patience. Spirits had also risen among our comrades. When the Volksbus pulled level with us, Josef and Hans were sitting on the roof wearing old pith helmets and looking for all the world like two hardy explorers who'd lost their camels.

Hans had a pair of binoculars and was scanning the horizon when he took them from his eyes and pointed to a dot far ahead, indicating that we should stop there. The dot slowly took form and became a Taurus van—similar to the Volksbus—sitting perfectly intact a quarter mile off the piste.

We coasted to a stop next to it. The Germans were out and all over it before the engines had died, forcing open the locked doors and hood to get at the seats and motor. They would have made great car thieves.

With a dexterity that amazed and delighted Geoff and me, they stripped every spare part and accessory—the radiator, the fuel pump, the carburetor, the distributor, all the spark plugs, and most of the loose wiring—and stored it away in the Volksbus. The two front tires found their way off the vehicle and onto the roof rack, leaving the previously intact Taurus van a half-wrecked hull in a matter of minutes. I sure hoped no one was coming back for it.

Food and Repairs

Since we had eaten nothing that day and were stopped anyway, we decided to rejuvenate our flagging constitutions with a little nourishment. Besides, there was work to be done on the Volksbus if it was going to reach Bordji-Perez. The sun was low in the west by this time and the terrible heat was gone for another day. But a soft breeze came up, making it difficult to operate the stove. The Sahara was not about to forgive us easily for coming so far. The inside of the van provided some shelter, and the beans and sausage were soon steaming in the pan.

We were eating more from necessity than hunger—the sun and the fatigue destroyed our appetites. The food tasted like chalk in our still-swollen mouths. We gave up the idea of eating after a few laborious mouthfuls, but could still drink. Geoff soon had a pot of tea brewed, into which he sliced one of our three lemons and added half a cup of sugar.

That was the most delicious drink I had ever tasted in my life. I had partaken of lemon tea many times over the years, as had Geoff. However, until we drank that steaming, sweet, and tangy liquid in the middle of the Sahara it seemed we had never been thirsty before, and never quenched a thirst in so regal a manner.

We made pot after pot, gulping it down and letting its warmth flow and sing through our tired limbs and erase the day's hardships and the night's apprehension. There was nothing special about the ingredients, nor anything unusual about the taste as lemon tea goes, but in that place and at that time it was nectar such as the gods on Olympus had never tasted.

An Unexpected Delay

When we were at last satiated and the dishes were stored back in the Rover, we joined the Germans at the rear of their vehicle to see how the repairs were coming along. They had adjusted the carburetor and changed the points and were trying to start the engine. For some reason it refused to fire. Geoff started the Rover and we gave the minibus a push in a circle that brought it back to where we had started. It still showed no sign of life. After changing the points again, we pushed the bus faster in a larger circle but got no response from the engine.

This was serious. A car that wouldn't start in these conditions, with our water supply almost depleted and the next well almost 200 miles away, must be repaired quickly or abandoned, and we all knew it. Hans, Geoff, and I worked impatiently by the powerful beams of the Rover's headlamps to find the fault. The other three fellows stood by, unable to help, while Hermann lay prostrate and snoring on the sand nearby.

Try and Try Again

Nothing we tried made any difference; there was no spark in the electrical system to fire the plugs. Our frustration at the unsolvable riddle grew by the minute and our tired hands and weary minds refused to function properly, causing us to drop tools and come up with confusing and unworkable solutions. We snapped at each other from frayed nerves and exhausted irritation as nothing was accomplished. I finally dropped the screwdriver I'd been working with, walked back to the Rover, reached in, and switched off the lights.

Geoff stood up and glared at me. "What the hell do you think you're doing? How do you expect us to see?"

"Enough is enough," I said. "We're calling a halt. We're just too washed out to think clearly, let alone find out what ails the bloody thing. I vote we all lay down for an hour and then try it again."

Hans was standing by Geoff, eyes blazing at the interruption in the light. When I explained to him what I told Geoff, he wearily nodded in agreement. "You're right about us being wiped out," sighed Geoff. "We're getting nowhere this way."

A Brief Respite

Like seven corpses, we all stretched full length on the sand around the silent vehicles and dozed for an hour. No one slept; our nerves were too taut for that. But by 10 P.M. our heads were a little clearer and we went back to work on the carburetor while Helmut and Kurt boiled water for coffee. Hermann hadn't moved.

As we worked away on the ignition, we agreed that, if the minibus wasn't started by midnight, we would have to leave it. With what water we had left, we couldn't possibly survive another day in the sun.

Then it dawned on Hans what was wrong. He unscrewed the two bolts anchoring the distributor, removed it, and held it in the light. Dismantling it to expose the condenser, which he also unscrewed he peered at the tiny wire inside and broke into a triumphant grin. The wire had worn through without breaking, making it impossible to see until it was removed and examined at a certain angle under the light. Excited with relief, we quickly replaced the condenser with a new one from the well-equipped spares kit on the roof rack. Reassembled and fastened tight, the engine caught with an angry snort and ran perfectly. It was 11:50 P.M.

We gulped down the coffee and were immediately on our way. Barring any unforeseen incident, we now had enough time to make it to Bordji-Perez by the next day.

The Second Way Station

We passed through Bidon Cinque two and a half hours later with both vehicles running smoothly—the Volksbus at a good speed for the first time and keeping up with—even ahead of—the Rover the whole way.

The second way station was much larger than Poste Weygand and in much worse condition. Walls were caved in, windows were broken, and all the wooden buildings had been gutted by fire. The desert was well on its way to reclaiming and blotting it out, the sands having filled the Quonset huts to a depth of three feet. There was a haunted, lifeless shroud of stillness hanging over the post and after a quick inspection, we were glad to get away from it.

Only 80 Miles to Go

At 2:30 that morning we figured we had eight hours to travel the 80 miles to Bordji-Perez. It seemed the difficulties were all behind us and we were on the downhill side of the slope at last. Then we made the mistake that nature never lets pass: we became overconfident and complacent about our inevitable success and sped up to hurry the process along. That was when the real problems began.

Just 30 minutes outside Bidon Cinque the Volksbus came to a sand-spraying, lurching halt; the left rear wheel falling off and the axle was buried deep in the ground. I swung the Rover around and came up with the lights so we could view the bus clearly. It was worse than bad. The wheel had shaken loose, shearing its nut and cotter pin, and instead of falling off and rolling clear, it had jammed under the fender as the vehicle dug into the sand. Before it could even be examined properly, it had to be dug out, jacked up, and braced. The splash of dust hadn't yet settled when Hans was out and digging with both hands.

Back to Work

There was little room to work, and it was slow, painstaking labor. We spent about 40 minutes of precious time digging, jacking, bracing, re-jacking, rebracing, and prying before the wheel came out and the truth was known. The only question we had was, Can we fix it, or do we leave it? Considering how tight we were with the Germans, the answer was as important to us as it was to them.

We mutually determined the wheel could be fixed, at least temporarily. Only the spline on the wheelnut and drum had sheared, not the one on the axle. We hammered the wheel back on and secured it with another nut, finishing the job by jamming a thin screwdriver through the axle in place of a cotter pin.

Slow Going

It was 4 A.M. when our "convoy" moved out again. We knew the wheel wouldn't hold long, but then it didn't need to. Hans was taking no chances. He drove as though he had a cargo of eggs on board. We followed slowly behind to watch for any sign of wobble in the crippled wheel.

All went well for the next hour. Hans avoided any swerving or speed increases that might antagonize the shaky wheel. With only 45 miles separating us from water, and the dawn just beginning to glow in the eastern horizon, it looked as though we would make it after all. Again we became overconfident, and again the wheel wobbled, came loose, jammed under the fender, and ground the Volksbus to a sickly halt.

The Situation Worsens

The silent work began anew. It was exactly the same as the first time—the jacking and bracing, the division of labor, the slow, sweating process. Hermann was asleep on the sand as the sun came up and the wheel came off once more.

The drum was worse this time, and our alternatives were limited to one—the same as before. As long as there was the slightest chance we could get the Volksbus to Bordji-Perez, we entertained no thought of leaving it. Hans hammered the wheel back on, forced the half-stripped nut onto the axle, and banged a new screwdriver into the hole to hold it a little longer.

The Enemy Returns

The sun sat on the eastern horizon for a few minutes, as if to mock our efforts, then began to move slowly and ominously up the sky. We watched its relentless progress through weary eyes as we nursed the tired Volksbus along. The fiery orb had watched and waited; now it was coming in for the kill.

With 30 miles to go, the wheel fell off again. It was the same process—digging, jacking, repair job, new screwdriver for the axle, wake Hermann, and carry on.

At 9:30 A.M. the wheel fell off again; this time it was buried deeper and took 45 minutes to dig out and hammer back on. Still, we were not worried, as it was only 19 miles to Bordji-Perez.

But now the desert was beginning to bake. For the fourth time, the shaky wheel sheared and fell off. Hans dragged the worn jack to the wheel and mutely began to dig. Tapping him on the shoulder gently, I pointed to the sun ablaze in the sky and shook my head; it was no use. We were out of screwdrivers, out of water, out of patience, and out of time.

Geoff was already undoing the back of the Land Rover and we unloaded everything onto the ground except the two sleeping bags. The Germans hauled themselves inside, bringing some food and two empty water containers. We left everything else where it lay and, hoping the map was right about the water, drove on down the track.

Dealing with Adversity

Adversity often brings out the best in you. It can show you what you are really made of, and make you even better. When you embark on any new venture, you will have an unending series of obstacles and difficulties you could never have foreseen. But this is the "testing time" where you show your true character—and everyone is watching.

> "Adversity does not make the man; it simply reveals him to himself."
> —Epictetus

CHAPTER 23

Bordji-Perez

> "Within you right now is the power to do things you never thought possible. This power becomes available to you as soon as you can change your beliefs."
>
> —MAXWELL MALTZ

WE HAD BEEN DRIVING SLOWLY for 20 minutes so as not to overheat the vehicle, when the antennas atop the military post of Bordji-Perez appeared above a small rise far off to the left. Leaving the piste, we drove straight over the rise toward the first sign of life we'd seen in what felt like two months.

The final outpost consisted of a group of featureless mud buildings, completely encircled by a loose array of barbed wire. In front of the buildings was a large open area that was also enclosed in barbed wire; however, the wire had two wide gaps, obviously for access to the post from the road. Against a small clump of dark green bushes on the side of the open space near the buildings, we could make out one lone water pipe with a tap on the end. We headed straight for it.

It was 11:15 and the blistering heat was rising. In the packed Land Rover, we were already sweating profusely. Our water was now gone and the only thing on our minds was the quenching of the growing thirst that had already dried our mouths and parched our throats. Without slowing, I drove the vehicle through the first gap in the wire and stopped at the tap.

We had made it. Haggard, dirty, exhausted, and thirsty, we had nonetheless reached water. We had beaten the desert, after a hard battle, and the spoils were ours. We piled out of the Rover and converged on the tap.

The Politics of Water

Geoff was just about to turn on the water when he was suddenly stopped by an angry, incomprehensible shout. Led by an unshaven army sergeant in a dirty undershirt, six ragged Algerian soldiers hurried from the nearest building with rifles pointed at us as they waved us away from the tap.

"What are you doing here?" demanded the Arab sergeant in French as he came up and stood between us and the water pipe. The rag-tag collection of soldiers following him got into line and brandished their ancient weapons.

"We need a little water," I told him.

"Where have you come from?" he demanded, folding his arms across his flabby chest. "Why are you here? Why have you driven up to my fort? Where are your papers?"

He turned to the soldiers to see that they were taking it all in and had their weapons fixed on us. Then he turned back arrogantly and sneered, waiting for answers.

We were taken completely off guard by this barrage of questions and had no idea why he was carrying on in such a manner. We were tired and dirty, not in the least bit offensive, and obviously unarmed. We didn't even know there was a military post at Bordji-Perez. I tried to explain our position.

"We came from Reggane. We've been in the desert for two days and one of our vehicles broke down. We had to leave it. We need water and shelter from the sun, that's all."

"Where are your papers? Where is the other vehicle? I demand to see the other vehicle! Why have you entered the fort without permission? Give me your papers immediately!" He kept looking back at the others for approval.

Desert Diplomacy

Geoff got our passports from under the seat and gave them to him, but with the exception of Hermann, the Germans had left theirs in the Volksbus. The sergeant glared at the passports and demanded in a louder voice, "Where are the other passports? I want to see the others!"

"The others are in the broken vehicle about ten kilometers from here," I tried to explain. "We need water and protection from the sun until evening. We can bring the other passports to you then."

The sun was now pounding down on our bare heads from directly overhead and we were getting thirstier by the minute; our mouths were too dry to lick our cracked lips. And this idiot seemed to think he was some sort of god.

"Who is German?" he demanded, waving Hermann's passport. "I know German from the war. I speak good German. Who is German?"

Hermann stepped forward and spoke to him in German, trying to explain again what happened and that we needed water. It was obvious the man could barely understand the German he was supposed to speak so well. However, when Hermann switched into French, the man irately silenced him and demanded that he continue in German while looking cockily over his shoulder at his men. Finally, he seemed to figure out what we were saying and nodded with a know-it-all smirk, as though it were a pack of lies.

Desert Etiquette

The gate we had entered to approach the water pipe lay 200 yards away at one end of the rectangular parade yard. Opposite the front of the "fort" where we were standing and about 20 yards away, was another gap in the wire. From the worn look of the ground, it appeared to be the main gate to the fort. The man pointed to the nearby gap in the wire and said, "That is the water gate. You must come through that gate for water." We had entered through the wrong gate, and he would not give us any water until we came through the correct one.

"Oh, for hell's sake, let's go through the right stinking gate and get something to drink," snapped Geoff. "I'm dying of bloody thirst."

We were all tense with anger and exhaustion when we got back in the Land Rover. Helmut and Josef started to walk to the gate rather than ride the short distance, but were stopped at gunpoint. They must also go in the vehicle. Everyone must do the same thing.

I started driving toward the water gate, seething with anger at the unbelievable stupidity of the whole situation. But the power hungry soldier started shouting and waving again. I quickly halted the Rover.

"You cannot drive straight to the water gate," he stated indignantly. "You must go back the same way you came in and drive to the outside of the water gate."

It was utterly ridiculous. We were ten yards from the gate and the other one was 200 yards behind us. Speechless, with teeth gritted to keep from swearing at him, I swung the Rover around and headed back the way we had come, out the gate, along the perimeter of the wire, across the front of the fort, and back to the water gate; it was almost a quarter of a mile to go ten yards. And the farce was not over yet.

An Exercise in Exasperation

The loud-mouthed soldier had put on a dirty shirt and was waiting for us with eight soldiers. He shouted again and ordered us out and away from the vehicle. It had to be searched before we could have any water.

These men could not have looked stupider or behaved in a more idiotic manner if they had rehearsed it. The vehicle—with the exception of the sleeping bags, food, and water containers—was quite empty. Yet each soldier fell out of line and took a turn coming over and poking his rifle in and then his head in to look around.

Meanwhile, the mouthy soldier in the undershirt declared that he was keeping our passports until he had not only the others but also the broken-down vehicle for inspection to verify that we had not sold it to someone in the desert.

"Fine, fine," we agreed. "Now can we have a little water, and for the love of God, some shade from the sun?"

But no, this was forbidden as well. We couldn't come near the fort to sit in the shade. Instead, there was a stone hut about a quarter of a mile away where we must go to get out of the sun. As for water, we would have to come two at a time to the front gate and ask the guard on duty for permission to fill the containers. With that, he strutted into the fort like a bantam rooster, clutching our passports in his dirty hand.

A Terrible Urge

We were so angry that if we'd had weapons or any chance of success with our bare hands, we would have stormed that post and murdered every man in the place. We were all pent up with a hate that was only a few degrees short of uncontrollable. I'd never felt that way in my life, nor had I ever thought myself capable of such an emotion. Our eyes were slits and our jaws rigid to contain our burning rage as we drove to the hut. Even Hermann was gripped with the intensity of the sudden lust to kill.

Abigail Adams once wrote, "All men would be tyrants if they could." Some people, given a little authority, will often abuse their power for no other reason than to prove to others that they have it. These people can be dangerous.

A Little Water, at Last

The small hut was occupied by two Taureq holy men engaged in prayer when we walked in. There was a large earthen pot of cool water in one corner and we immediately grabbed and passed it around until it was empty. As the praying continued, we brought in our few possessions from the Rover and laid out our sleeping bags on the dirt floor. Somewhat cooled—temperamentally and physically—and paying no more attention to the Tauregs than if they had been fence posts, we sprawled out on the open bags and dozed off.

We couldn't sleep long or well. The tin-roofed hut was cooler than outside but soon turned into a sweatbox, and the flies descended upon us in swarms. After a couple of hours it was too uncomfortable to sleep and we were too tired to care, so with a few scraps of wood plus the loan of a blackened pot from our coinhabitants, we cooked up a stew of noodles and gravy that we devoured to the last morsel.

The Water Brigade

Hermann and Kurt were the first to make the trek for water, then Hans and Josef, then Geoff and I. Each time the containers were brought back they were immediately emptied and taken by the next two. On each visit we approached the guard and asked him politely if we could have a little water.

Following the playground rules, he then went to the post and returned a minute later to tell us our request had been granted, but we must hurry. The droopy-faced little soldier, his oversized trousers dragging in the dust, sloughed behind us to the tap and stood about ten feet off. After washing our faces and arms, we filled the containers and walked back out the gate.

The Germans Call it Quits

We had not known what to expect at Bordji-Perez and had vaguely hoped there would be some place for mechanical repairs. Since the fort and hut were all there was, the Germans decided to throw in the towel.

Without new parts, the Volksbus was beyond hope. They decided they would sort out what they needed and could carry, give us the remainder, and wait for the convoy to arrive. They could continue south with it to the first major city.

It was a wise decision and the best one under the circumstances, but Geoff and I were sad they'd failed, especially after all the hardship and bad luck they had experienced. We reluctantly agreed to take Hermann with us to Mali, where he would write or wire the families of the four fellows and tell them what had happened.

That afternoon Hans and I drove back to the Volksbus to bring it in. While he hammered the damaged wheel back on, I loaded everything of ours and most of the heavy things from the Volksbus into the Rover. We left the spare tires from the roof rack, as well as a complete spare engine lying on the sand. We then hitched the two vehicles together with the towrope and started back to the post just as the sun was setting.

Further Delay

When we towed the Volksbus up to the front gate, the man in charge came out and glanced at it disdainfully. He snatched the proffered passports from Hans and counted them. We told him three of us were leaving for Mali in a few minutes and needed our passports returned right away.

He looked at me up and down and sneered. They wouldn't be ready until 10 P.M., he sniffed. We would have to come back then. This time he strutted away without looking back. It didn't take much to work up a real hate for that fellow.

An Unexpected Windfall

If the end of the Germans' vehicle had been a tragedy for them, it was certainly nothing of the sort for us. Our petrol supply had been three-quarters consumed by the time we reached Bordji-Perez, and without the 15 extra gallons we inherited there would have been no possibility of reaching Gao. The Germans also gave us a large box with two hydraulic jacks, a tent, and some food and medicines, including the first malaria pills we'd seen. The addition of these articles made us fully equipped for Africa for the first time—except for visas, of course, and this was about to become our next big problem.

No Travel without Visas

Until we entered Algeria at Beni-Ounif, we knew nothing about the need for visas to visit foreign countries. The very word "visa" implied to us some special circumstance or reason for entering a country that went beyond the simple motive of ordinary traveling. Our passports had allowed us into England, France, Spain, Gibraltar, and Morocco without questions. We considered paying 14 dinars for visas when we arrived in Algeria to be an inconvenience more than anything else. After all, we were just tourists.

While some African nations were starting to encourage tourism, Mali was apparently not one of them. When Geoff inquired into Mali visas during his wait in Algiers he was told that not only were Canadians barred from Mali without visas, but the necessary ones would cost $40 each, a small fortune in our circumstances. Even worse, to get a Mali visa you had to send your passport to the Mali Embassy in Paris and wait four to six weeks, something that was clearly impossible for us.

Serious Consequences

Geoff was also told of four travelers who had crossed the Sahara with a convoy and then been refused admittance despite their willingness to pay anything to be allowed to continue. They had to wait at Bordji-Perez for a week before a northbound convoy came through with enough petrol to get them back to Reggane.

Despite this story, Geoff had decided that the visas were beyond our means and had returned without them. We had not been aware of a country named Mali before arriving in Gibraltar and besides, $80 was too much to pay to cross a geographical entity we had no interest in seeing. We decided to play the cards as they were dealt and work something out when the time came. Well, the time had now arrived.

The Personality for Success

Perhaps the most important and respected quality in people is "social" or "emotional" intelligence. It is the ability to read other people in a complex situation and then speak and act effectively.

Political savvy requires that you understand the dynamics of power and influence among people, and then decide how to respond appropriately to gain maximum advantage.

Of course the time when political skill is most required is often when you are angry, excited, or confused and least likely to have your wits about you. This is when you must remain calm and cool if you are to make the right decisions.

Your ability to think, plan, and act effectively in stressful situations will determine your success as much as any other factor.

> "Luck often means simply taking advantage of a situation at the right moment. It is possible to make your 'luck' by being always prepared."
>
> —MICHAEL KORDA

CHAPTER 24

Running the Border

> "The beauty of the soul shines out when a man bears with composure one heavy mischance after another, not because he does not feel them, but because he is a man of high and heroic temper."
> —ARISTOTLE

LATE THAT AFTERNOON, a truck from Mali came by and stopped at the hut for the night. The driver was as interested in our story and the ruined Volksbus as we were interested in what he could tell us concerning the road ahead.

He said the road was quite bad and confirmed that if we didn't have visas we would not be allowed through. We asked him if there were any more checkpoints past the border where visas would have to be produced.

There were. On the 350-mile stretch between Bordji-Perez and Gao there were three towns and each had a police post to check traffic. He showed us his passport and the stamps from each post to lend credibility to his story; he also assured us it was impossible to pass without our passports, insurance, and visa registration in order. We listened intently to everything he told us, but laughed off his pessimism.

No Turning Back

We were becoming reconciled to the sad fact that nothing in this trip was going to come easy. If it wasn't the Rover, it was the police, dysentery, heat, or insects. There was always going to be something to make it rough until we got to Lagos. As usual, there was no question of turning back. It was onward or nothing. We would just have to run the border, go around the checkpoints, and somehow get to Gao to secure enough petrol to get into the next country of Niger.

As foolish as it was, we appreciated the hazards of such a procedure. If we were caught in the country illegally, we could be imprisoned indefinitely and have all our belongings confiscated. It was not a pleasant prospect, but going back was worse. We would have to try it and hope for the best.

Saying Farewell

There remained nothing more to be said. We took down our German friends' addresses and shook hands all around, wishing each other good luck and promising to get in touch should we ever be in the other's respective country. We had converged and merged, and were now diverging on separate roads once more. Perhaps someday our paths would cross again.

At 10 P.M. we drove back to the main gate of the darkened fort to ask for our passports and fill our water containers. After 45 minutes and much confusion, we received our passports and water and left immediately for the frontier town of Tessalit in Mali, 75 miles to the south.

The Terrain Changes Once More

Even in the dark driving toward Mali we could see and feel that the barren desert wasteland was falling behind us. There had been tufts of withered grass and small clumps of sagebrush in the rocky country around Bordji-Perez. Now the lights of the Rover began to pick up stunted trees spaced haphazardly along the piste.

The reappearance of the sparse vegetation was comforting in a way. It seemed to stand as an assurance that nature, though not softening, would be willing to accede her position as our main antagonist. That would leave the physical and political factors as our major difficulties to overcome—the next price we must pay for entering Africa unprepared.

We had never been so completely cut off from everything in our lives. We had 1,000 miles of desert behind us, 1,000 miles of unknown country ahead, $50 in our pockets, and no clear reason why we were there to begin with. This insecurity generated a strange feeling of reckless determination; there was only one concrete objective to cling to and strive for—reaching Lagos, Nigeria. We proceeded toward that town like the Wise Men following the star of Bethlehem.

The Daring Plan

Hermann rode between us, straddling the floor shift on the raised transmission. Since he had a Mali visa he was coming only as far as the frontier, where he would wait until he could get another ride south in a day or two. Traffic on that stretch of road was not too dependable.

Geoff and I had little patience for Hermann. He had been nothing but self-righteous, meddlesome, lazy, and irritating. We were glad we wouldn't have to share his company any farther than Tessalit. He knew we would leave him by the road if he started in on his holier-than-thou advice. He sat quietly as we discussed our plans to run the border and debated what to do in case of this or that eventuality. Our first move was to be fairly straightforward.

We would drive straight to Tessalit, deposit Hermann, and take a look at the lay of the land. We would then return in the direction of Bordji-Perez without even inquiring into entering without visas. Hermann would tell the police, who would undoubtedly be suspicious, that we were going to wait for the convoy and make the trip to Gao with the trucks from Bordji-Perez. He would say he had been in a hurry and had paid us to bring him to Tessalit, where he hoped to find another ride. The story was flimsy but would serve the occasion.

After depositing Hermann, we would return along the road until out of sight of the frontier post, then turn west into the open country and begin an arc that would bring us around the border station and back to the piste about a mile beyond Tessalit. The road still ran more or less due south and with our compass to ascertain direction, we couldn't possibly get lost.

The Roads Get Worse

The truck driver had been right about the bad road. According to the map, it ran along the edge of a range of low rocky hills for the next 250 miles. Although it was still very much the Sahara, the level sand had been replaced by a stony, broken terrain through which a track had been scraped, obviously at great cost in time and labor.

No attempt had been made to keep the road in a reasonable state for the infrequent traffic. It was a mess of gouges and potholes and narrowed to a few yards in many places, making any speed over 20 miles per hour dangerous and rough on a vehicle. Realizing there was no margin for error, we kept our speed down. If anything happened to the Rover now, the jig was up.

No Comparisons

No one can appreciate the meaning of a hard drive until they have driven for many hours over treacherous road. In our previous long distance trips across Canada and the United States, Geoff and I had been at the wheel for as long as two days straight. Once I even drove alone over 3,000 miles from Niagara Falls in the East to Vancouver in the West in 65 hours nonstop. It took me 19 hours of solid sleep to get back on my feet after that trip. I was sure *nothing* could be rougher than that.

But I was wrong. Negotiating this buckled road late on a moonless night and hundreds of miles from civilization, while going into the fourth consecutive day without any sleep and having no idea what to expect ahead was a "hard drive" beyond my wildest imaginings.

Never Relax

Driving the Land Rover on this road meant constant maneuvering to avoid ruts and potholes and took intense conentration on the bit of road just inside the sweep of headlights. The eyes of the driver could never leave the road without the danger of an accident. Braking, shifting, and accelerating with hands locked on either side of the wheel and shoulders hunched forward to absorb the crashing, pitching motion, and peering intently through strained fuzzy eyeballs—that was a picture of the driver, hour after hour.

We were all were straining forward, with elbows on our knees and eyes fixed on the road to anticipate and prepare for the next jolt. We were sweating from taut nerves and gulping aspirins to relieve the splitting headaches that were our legacy from the heat and sleeplessness.

The only sensible thing to do was to stop for the night, rest our weary bodies, and continue in the morning when we had a little energy and could see the piste clearly. But we couldn't stop. It was now *Sunday* morning.

This was a critical factor by our reckoning. The chances were good that the Mali police would be less vigilant on a Sunday, and if we were grasping at straws in our attempt to run the border, the tiniest straw had to be utilized.

Four Trouble Spots

This was our plan. To reach Gao without being stopped, we had to pass police posts and roadblocks at Tessalit, then Aguelhok, Anefis, and Bourem. These four trouble spots were spaced so that we could just make it provided our luck held out.

We would circumvent Tessalit in the dark of early morning while everyone was asleep. We would drive around the town of Aquelhok just after dawn and before anyone was up. We would slip past Anefis in the midday heat when everyone was asleep. And we would get by Bourem just after nightfall.

With this strategy, we would run the least possible risk of detection by those police still working on Sunday. There was also the advantage of being able to see clearly where we were going once we passed Tessalit and were driving in day light. It wasn't much as plans go, but it was all we had.

The Border Running Begins

The half-obscured road markers kept us informed of our proximity to Tessalit, and as the distance diminished, the tension built. At 3 A.M. we passed several stone huts off to one side of the road and seconds later came to a road barrier and sign saying, "TEESALIT-ARRET POUR DOUANE" (Tessalit—Stop for Customs).

The road was clear on one side of the barrier; without thinking I swung the wheel over and drove past it before stopping, dousing the lights, and cutting the engine. The silence of the dark night fell over us.

The police post about 20 yards to our right was completely still. There was no sign of life anywhere.

"They must all be asleep," whispered Geoff nervously.

"Are you getting out or are you coming with us?" I asked Hermann in a low voice.

"Make up your mind," urged Geoff. "We're not staying here all bloody night."

The night was suddenly pierced by the angry barking of a dog, coming from the same direction as the police building.

"I will come! I will come!" sputtered Hermann anxiously.

I punched the starting button and released the clutch in the same motion, which sent the darkened Rover tearing down the uneven road. After 100 yards of near-blind driving, I switched on the lights and put the gas pedal to the floor. It was five kilometers before I cut the engine and lights once more and coasted to a stop.

Geoff was already out and in back of the Rover when it stopped, and I joined him there, standing without a sound and staring into the dark toward Tessalit for any sign of pursuit. Five minutes of listening for any sound satisfied us that our passing had gone unnoticed. Cursing that damn dog, we started the engine again. The illegal crossing of Mali had begun.

Washboard Roads

Imagine a road constructed entirely of eight-inch diameter logs packed closely together; now picture the same road with countless logs removed and others spread out and broken irregularly. If you can imagine driving over this surface in a light vehicle with a solid steel frame, and the bone-jarring, teeth-rattling effect of it, you can have some idea of what it was like being a traveler in northern Mali. Add a dash of numbness, a touch of fear, two cups of exhaustion, a layer of tension, sprinkled with dust and grime, and you get the glorious sensation of traveling without visas in sub-Saharan Africa.

By dawn we were bumping through a broken, jagged country strewn with black boulders. It looked like an abandoned devil's graveyard. Bits of scraggly sagebrush attested to the cruel landscape's ability to sustain only the barest forms of life. There was an air of silent foreboding hanging in the stillness, the rocky piste being the only sign that men had claimed a partial victory from the land. This track was the only route a vehicle could possibly take, and according to the map, it led straight into Aguelhok.

Aguelhok at Sunrise

Our first glimpse of Aguelhok was from a small hillock by the piste four kilometers out 5:50 A.M. half an hour after sunrise. It was a cluster of stone buildings facing what hundreds or even thousands of years before had been a large lake. Now there was only a flat expanse of white sand bordered by small dunes, sparsely dotted with stunted, scrawny trees.

Each of us took a turn examining the entire area with binoculars from atop a boulder. Our only way around the town was along the far perimeter of the old lakebed. We would be over a mile away but still in sight of the buildings; we hoped that since it was early morning no one would be looking.

This was our best bet. Geoff shifted into four-wheel drive and steered the Rover along the lake edge, keeping as far from the quiet village as possible without getting into the powdery sand around the dunes. We were over halfway through the wide arc that would take us back to the road when the firm, flat sand ran out. To follow the perimeter any farther would take us back toward town, so we took a chance in the silt.

The wheels started to spin and churn immediately, clawing for traction yet finding none and slowing our forward motion to a crawl. The

Rover slowly began to sink. Hermann and I leaped out and put our backs into shoving while Geoff kept the wheels turning slowly. Thank heavens that was all it took. In another 50 yards of arduous straining, we were through the dunes and curving back toward the piste, out of sight of the town.

We had no way of knowing if we'd been seen, so once we'd regained the road we drove for another five kilometers, then pulled off to listen and wait. Again we had been lucky. There was no sound of a pursuing vehicle from Aguelhok and after ten minutes, we backed onto the piste again and set out for Anefis, 193 kilometers farther south.

The Desert Wadis

The road still ran through parched country and although the dry, cracked ground was rocky, signs of life in the form of ragged trees and bushes were increasing with the miles. The sparse areas of greenery and trees were centered in the arid basins, or wadis, which are unique to the lower Sahara regions. A wadi is a shallow depression, like a huge dinner plate, usually several miles across and so gradual in its slope to the center that it is almost indiscernible unless one is aware of its existence. Despite its innocent appearance, it is one of the most dangerous physical features of that land.

Every two or three years a rainstorm blows in from the Niger River, drenching the land in a sudden cloudburst before dissipating. Because the ground has been baked solid by many months of pounding sun, the water from these infrequent storms is not absorbed, but runs into the centers of the wadis with frightening speed and fills the larger ones to a depth of 15 feet in a matter of minutes. Many travelers passing unsuspectingly through a wadi during a breaking storm have suffered the most cynical fate of nature—drowning in one of the driest lands on earth.

The French built their roads across the wadis on earth and stone dikes as high as 15 feet above the arid ground; these made traveling much safer. The land bridges look downright silly in their barren context, but the high-water mark 12 feet up their sides quells any tendency to laugh.

Getting Around Anefis

We passed no one on the roads that morning and stopped only once to refuel and eat. Hermann managed to drag himself out and gather a little brush for our cook fire before wandering off to socialize with two Taureq children who had appeared in the scrub about 20 yards off, eyes wide and sucking their fingers. As Hermann approached them they vanished, only to reappear in another place and continue staring. Hermann's penchant for meeting people amused us no end and we agreed that he would make a perfect host for a boy's camp on parents' day. Geoff and I were just too tired to care.

At noon the temperature was 105 degrees and by 1 P.M. when we were approaching Anefis it was approaching 115 degrees—hot enough to keep most people inside and too hot to drive safely. However, we had no choice; we had to get while the getting was good.

Scouting the terrain with the binoculars as before, we made another wide arc to avoid the eyes of the police in the small post. The uneven ground was blanketed by thin wispy grass and clumps of dry brush, but the terrain proved no obstacle to our Rover. Because of the flatness, we had to swing out about three kilometers—a time-consuming operation—and it was an hour before we safely circumvented Anefis and got back on the road. But we made it. That left only the fort and police post at Bourem between us and Gao.

Black Market Transactions

Late that afternoon we met a heavy truck going north. It was the first vehicle we'd seen since Bordji-Perez, 250 miles before, and we stopped to chat with the driver. After the usual pleasantries and a vigorous round of handshaking, the driver asked us if we had any Algerian money to sell. For some reason he seemed quite eager to buy it and offered us what he swore to be its equivalent in Mali francs. We still had 200 dinars (about $46) from Algeria and reluctantly agreed to part with half of it for 5,000 Mali francs.

At that time we had no knowledge of the black market and its influence on national currencies. We believed you could change any money from any country in any bank for approximately what you paid for it. It wasn't until much later that we learned that in many countries the official bank rate on foreign currencies is much lower than its actual value; once you've changed your money you're stuck with the foreign cash. You must either spend it all in that country, or exchange it on the black market when you leave.

These same countries forbid import or export of their currencies to force unsuspecting travelers to buy the money they need through the bank at the lower rates. Once we left Algeria, unbeknownst to us, our Algerian money became worthless to anyone but a person traveling to that country; and after that truck driver, we never met another such person.

Hapless Hermann

The driving was rough on Geoff and me, but at least we had youth on our side and were physically fit from years of clean living and good sport. Hermann, on the other hand, was not strong. He was half bald, flabby, and completely unsuited for hardship. Yet despite his physical shortcomings and the terrible pounding he was suffering from the road, he refused to utter a word of complaint.

About 6 P.M. we stopped to refill the tank, not far from two goatskin tents set up in a gully between two mounds of sand. Hermann, his eyes glazed and body dripping with sweat, struggled out of the back and fell on the road, prostrate and breathing heavily. Whether he lived or died was inconsequential to our getting past Bourem by dusk, and we paid no attention to him beyond feeling a vague pity. There was nothing we could do any way.

A Desert Mirage?

As I opened the gas tank and Geoff dragged out the last jerry cans, I had a sudden feeling of being watched and turned quickly to examine the landscape. A flash of blue caught my eye from about 50 yards off to the right, and I forgot all about the tank and the semiconscious Hermann.

Standing there was a Taureq girl, her bearing erect and proud, like a queen in exile—unafraid and almost defiant. She was simply beautiful, about 18 years old with high cheekbones under a smooth dark olive skin that set off her dark, piercing eyes. Her jet-black hair was pulled tightly back on her head and almost completely covered with a light blue scarf; long flowing folds of the same turquoise material embraced her slender figure.

She stood perfectly still and watched us, with her robes rippling in the breeze and afternoon sun and her arms relaxed by her sides—one bare and the other partially covered by a fold of the shimmering blue. There in the quiet of the day, against the background of sand and dusty bush, she looked like a delicate flower—a shining jewel in an arid setting.

Geoff brought the jerry cans around and set them down, following my gaze without commenting and studying her lovely features as though she would vanish at any moment. She never flinched from our staring or took her eyes off our faces. Finally she turned as though satisfied, floated lightly across the sand, moved behind the tents, and was gone.

The spell was broken. We turned to the business at hand and as I poured the last of the petrol out of the jerry can, Geoff helped Hermann to his feet and back into the Rover. I started the engine and we looked for the girl once more, but there was no sign of movement around the quiet tents. We drove away slowly, still looking, and were well down the piste before I stepped on the gas and shifted through the gears.

There are many things I will never forget from that journey through Africa, and surely one of them will always be that Taureq girl in the lonely land below the Sahara.

It often happens that, even in the remotest of places, you can come upon the loveliest of creations. Like the delicate desert flowers, those apparitions appear and then vanish in a moment. You may think you have just seen a mirage, but no, it was real. And you are left to wonder about the miracle of life—and those magical moments that stay with you forever.

Breaking the Rules

There are two types of rules: laws and conventions. Laws are passed by governments and enforced by police. Conventions are standard or common ways of thinking enforced only by your natural tendency to do things the way they've always been done.

To succeed in a tough, competitive, and fast-changing society, you have to be willing to defy convention and try something new or different when the situation calls for it.

Sometimes the ideal solution to your current problem is the opposite of what everyone else is doing. To survive and thrive in your business or career, you often have to offer something that is better, cheaper, newer, and more convenient—all at once.

Be prepared to innovate, to break out of the mold and "go boldly where no one has ever gone before."

Thomas Watson, Sr., founder of IBM, put it this way: "Do you want to succeed faster? Then double your rate of failure. Success lies on the far side of failure."

Or as Dorothea Brand wrote, "Decide what you want. Then act as if it were impossible to fail, and it shall be."

"The difficulties you meet will resolve themselves as you advance. Proceed, and light will dawn, and shine with increasing clearness on your path."
—D'ALEMBERT

CHAPTER 25

A Very Close Call

> "Do what you can, with what you have, right where you are."
>
> —THEODORE ROOSEVELT

THE CROSSROADS AT BOUREM is shaped like a tree, the trunk being the road on which we were driving and the branches the one leading northwest toward Timbuktu and the one going south toward Gao. To reach our goal of the Gao road meant approaching the crossroads, then turning off and cutting across the angle of which Bourem was the center. Then it would be just 59 miles to Gao.

Two hours before dusk the terrain had become a sea of rolling dunes, with just enough silt in the sandy soil to sustain a covering of dark green, tangled clumps of narrow-leafed bush. The sun was touching the horizon when we came out of an S-bend onto a wide sandy expanse flowing straight ahead half a mile to the base of a looming hill. Crowning this hill, huge and shadowed by the setting sun, was the high-walled fort of Bourem.

Not Paying Attention

In our exhausted and inattentive condition, we were halfway across the open plain before it registered that we were perfectly visible from the fort. A uniformed figure had already come out of a building at the base of the hill and was standing, hands on hips, watching our approach. I swung the wheel around and headed toward the road for Timbuktu, my heart thumping and stomach sickening.

A shout came from the uniformed figure and he started waving and motioning us in his direction, but I only increased speed to get away. Suddenly we hit a ridge of sand that tore the tailpipe loose from the muffler in a deafening blare as we lurched onto the Timbuktu road and sped northeast out of sight of the fort.

One Thing after Another

Things were confusing enough with the policeman shouting at us from behind, the muffler roaring, and the three of us trembling with fatigue and fear as we turned off the piste to circle back to the Tessalit road. Then one of the tires started going flat on the front.

Without stopping, we wended our way through the dunes until we came out on the road, crossing it into the sand hills beyond before cutting the engine. We had made a complete loop; even if a vehicle had been sent in pursuit of us from the fort ahead, there would be no reason to suspect that we had turned off the Timbuktu road and regained and recrossed the same road on which we had appeared.

Working frantically, Geoff changed the flat tire while I removed both ends from a condensed milk can, split it down the seam, and bound it around the noisy break in the tailpipe, cinching it fast with spare radiator hose coupling. Our hearts were pounding a mile a minute, our mouths were dry, and our hands were sweating from the nearness of the escape.

The Fort at Bourem

We could have guessed that Bourem was a fort, but had no way of knowing that its strategic location made the danger of detection greater than ever. We would now have to pass in the choppy country under the eyes of the fort. If we used our lights, the police would have no difficulty intercepting us. And the sun was now gone.

The lack of light in the unpredictable terrain was one problem. The loose tailpipe was another, since the muted sound traveled a long way. And our exhausted, stumbling condition was yet a third. But we had no choice. We had to get out of there before the whole Mali army was down on top of us. In the murky dusk, keeping the motor revs low, we started snaking our way through the dunes under the fort.

Lights in the Night

The sand was loose and treacherous the moment we turned off the road, forcing us to use four-wheel drive to creep along the twisting, tortuous terrain. Unable to see clearly, we were steering in the general direction of south and west by keeping the looming fort always on the right. It was soon too dark to see anything so Hermann and I got out and floundered ahead with flashlights to find a way. Twice we got trapped in blind pockets and had to back out, pushing to keep the Rover moving in the clinging grit.

The one thing we had dreaded finally happened. Lights appeared from the fort and people began moving down the hill toward us. When we cut the engine for a moment, we could hear voices shouting and see the lights spreading out as they moved. We were panic-stricken and began trembling in a cold sweat. Keeping the lights off and disregarding the roar of the engine, Geoff stepped on the gas. The Rover churned forward, winding in and out in a switchback pattern in the rough country toward the southbound road somewhere ahead.

Running Out of Time

If each of those dozen lights approaching us represented a soldier with a weapon, our time was just about up. They were no more than 300 yards away and the bobbing line changed direction to follow the sound of the Rover. But the road couldn't be much farther, and the Rover was finally clawing its way ahead without our pushing. Hermann and I ran along with it and then jumped back in just before Geoff roared it up and over a large sand bank.

My heart stopped dead and our jaws went slack with despair. Only 50 yards ahead the way was blocked with a semicircular row of what appeared to be lanterns. The other lights were coming over the dunes to our right and behind us, and to the left was a steep ridge of brush backed by a clay bank. We were trapped.

Fortune Favors the Brave

"Go like hell and keep your lights off!" I shouted at Geoff, but he had already stomped on the gas and the Rover surged forward. Five yards from the first light he gave a blast on the horn and snapped on the head-lamps, swerving to one side.

We almost died with relief at the sight. We were in the middle of a tent camp and heading for a row of cooking fires; the frightened figures of running Tauregs streaked across the glaring beams as children were snatched frantically out of the way. Geoff steered toward a hole in the row of tents and roared out of the camp. The Land Rover bounded along a wide footpath for another hundred yards, and suddenly we bounced onto the Gao road. We had made it.

Moving South

Geoff shifted the Rover quickly out of four-wheel drive, wrenched the wheel over, and once more stepped on the accelerator, taking us lurching and bouncing down the rutted track. We hammered along for 15 minutes, and then turned sharply off the road and parked 50 yards away behind some trees, waiting tensely in the dark. After ten slow and agonizing minutes we knew we had made it. No one was following.

Nothing Left

However, we had made it with nothing left. Twenty mind-numbing hours of nonstop travel had left us with no smiles, satisfaction, strength, or energy. We felt as if a plug had been pulled, and the last drop of nervous energy—or whatever it was that kept us going—had drained away.

After a few more minutes of waiting in the silent blackness, we got back on the road for Gao and drove as if in a trance, with eyes blurred and heads ringing. Geoff finally stopped the Rover in the middle of an open stretch and slumped over the wheel.

"No use," he mumbled. "No use at all. I can't see any more. You'd better drive." A few miles later I also gave up driving. The last shred of energy was gone and I couldn't see the road clearly either. I was dizzy, blind, and driving down a tunnel flashing with hallucinations leaping and screaming from every shadow.

Vaguely remembering the river to be on the right somewhere, I turned off the road and drove until we came to the bank of a muddy tributary. Geoff and Hermann were slumped forward and as I stopped by a clump of palm trees, they jerked awake and looked around to see what had happened.

"We're there."

Without a word or question about the location of "there," we dragged the sleeping bags out of the rear and threw them on the ground. Then everything went black.

> "You become a champion by fighting one more round. When things are tough, you fight one more round."
> —James J. Corbett

SECTION VII

Reflections

> "Before the reward, there must be labor. You plant before you harvest. You sow in tears before you reap in joy."
>
> —Ralph Ransom

You are wiser than you know. You have already had so many experiences in life that, if you could extract from them every precious lesson you have learned, you could make your life into anything you want.

You should develop the habit of looking upon every experience of your life as a building block, handed to you just when you needed it to take the next step.

Earlier, I said that the key to success is for you to set a clear goal and then persist through all adversity until you achieve it. The intense emotions of pride and self-esteem that accompany any great achievement will burn a pattern for success into your subconscious mind. You will be forever internally motivated to repeat this pattern. You'll be set for life!

Take some time to analyze and evaluate your experiences. Write down the valuable lessons you have learned. Then think about the wonderful experiences you have ahead of you. "Act boldly, and unseen forces will come to your aid."

"A constant struggle, a ceaseless battle to bring success from inhospital surroundings, is the price of all great achievements."
—Orison Swett Marden

CHAPTER 26

Lessons for Life

> "Your living is determined not so much by what life brings you as by the attitude you bring to life; not so much by what happens to you as by the way your mind looks at what happens."
> —John Homer Miller

We had made it! We had crossed the Sahara Desert. We had not slept for four days, from Adrar far to the north and to the banks of the Niger River. But we had done it. The first major test of our lives was over. And we had passed.

There was much more to come, but I won't go into that now. I won't tell how we eventually got out of the country of Mali and into Niger with an all-points bulletin out for us on all roads and the army and police under orders to shoot to kill the "spies" and "arms smugglers" who had illegally entered the country and evaded all attempts at apprehension.

I won't give you all the details about everything that happened as we ran the next border illegally, evading police checkpoints and capture and traveling deeper and deeper into West Africa.

Nor will I talk about the other countries we passed through and the experiences we had, not even the time we spent with Dr. Albert Schweitzer at his hospital in Lamberene in Gabon. I won't tell you how we were almost killed under the boots and truncheons of Congolese police and how we escaped death to finally make our way to South Africa, our ultimate goal.

Instead, I'll end this story by telling you what I learned about life and success in the Sahara crossing.

Seven Principles for Lifelong Success

Most of our important lessons in life happen in retrospect, as afterthoughts. It's like backing up, hitting something, and then getting out to see what just happened.

Aristotle once wrote, "Wisdom is a combination of experience plus reflection." Without taking time to reflect, we fail to glean the wisdom that becomes available to us from dealing with a difficult situation. When reflecting on your experiences, learn to extract all the lessons and wisdom they contain.

People who merely have experiences but do not learn from them tend to make the same mistakes over and over. By taking a significant experience and extracting every lesson it offers, you can often learn an extraordinary amount from it and use that new understanding to accomplish great things. As Emmet Fox once wrote, "Great souls learn large lessons from small experiences."

Here are seven principles I learned in the Sahara crossing that you can apply to any challenge you face in achieving anything you desire.

Lesson Number One

The most important step in achieving great success in any endeavor is to decide upon your goal and then *launch.* Take action. Move! Your willingness to step out and move forward toward your goal with no guarantee of success is what separates the winners from the losers.

We set out at the age of 20 with $300 each. Our goal was to cross North America from one side to the other, sail across the Atlantic Ocean, travel the length of Europe from London to Gibraltar, and then cross Africa from Morocco to South Africa. It was a distance of more than 17,000 miles and we made it in 12 months. But the most important step was the first one. All the rest followed from that.

Lesson Number Two

Once you've launched toward your goal, never consider the possibility of failure. The Germans have a saying, *"Immer vorne, nie zuruck."* Always forward, never backward.

Every person who achieves any success does so because he or she refuses to quit when the going gets rough. Your ability to persist in the face of setbacks and disappointment is the true measure of the person you are and the character you have developed to this point.

Your level of persistence is the measure of your belief in yourself and your ultimate possibilities. Your willingness to persist is vital to all great achievement. And persistence is always a decision that you make personally, within your own heart. It is not what happens on the outside that counts. It is always what is happening on the *inside.*

Lesson Number Three

The biggest goal in the world can be accomplished if you just take it "one oil barrel" at a time. Thomas Carlisle once wrote, "Our great business in life is not to see what lies dimly at a distance but to do what lies clearly at hand." If you go as far as you can see, you will then see far enough to go further.

Nothing will ever get done if you think all difficulties and problems must first be solved. If you wait for everything to be "just right," you will never do anything; things will never be just right.

The only time you will ever have is now, the present moment. It is what you do with this moment that determines your entire future. If you live every day and every hour the best you can, the rest of your life will take care of itself. As the Bible says, "Sufficient unto the day are the cares thereof."

Lesson Number Four

Avoid the *naysayers.* Watch out for the negative people around you who warn that you will fail or lose your time or money—that you will "die in the desert."

Associate with positive people—men and women who are optimistic and ambitious. Refuse to listen to objections and reasons why you can't succeed. Work and live only with people who encourage you and want you to succeed. Remember, the people you choose to surround yourself with and listen to will have more of an impact on your life than perhaps any other factor.

Lesson Number Five

Welcome obstacles and difficulties as valuable and unavoidable steps on the ladder of success. Remember that *difficulties come not to obstruct, but to instruct.* Within every difficulty or setback lies the seed of an equal or greater opportunity or benefit. Your job is to find it.

Our trip to Africa was one problem after another. We ran out of money over and over again. We strained every muscle of our bodies trying to ride bicycles across France and Spain. Our Land Rover broke down repeatedly. We suffered from dysentery, heatstroke, and exhaustion. But when it was time, we were ready for the Sahara crossing.

Without the lessons learned from our mistakes, we would surely have died in the desert. When you look back on any great achievement, you will find that it was preceded by many difficulties and lessons. The difficulties are the price you pay for your success, and the lessons are what makes the achievement possible. As the philosopher Seneca wrote, "Fire is the test of gold; adversity of strong men."

Lesson Number Six

Be clear about your goal but flexible about the process of achieving it. Be willing to change and try something new. Keep your mind open, fluid, and flexible. Be willing to accept feedback from your environment and correct your course.

This flexibility is a key quality of peak performers. They are not rigid or fixed on a particular course of action. They are always willing to consider the possibility that they could be wrong, as well as alternative ways to reach the goal.

It's not what you have, but what you do with what you have that determines success or failure. It is not what happens to you, but how you respond to what happens to you that counts. Your ability to respond and adjust to the adversities of life is the real measure of who you are and what you are likely to accomplish.

The Greek philosopher Epictetus once said, "Circumstances do not make the man; they merely reveal him to himself." You find out who you are only when you face a great setback or disappointment and are tempted to quit and to go back. This is the true test; the only question is whether you will pass or fail. The decision is always up to you.

Lesson Number Seven

Nobody does it alone. On every step of our journey people helped us with advice, food, assistance, and money—and especially with warmth, kindness, and generosity. Likewise, at every key turning point in your life, someone will be standing there with an outstretched hand, offering advice, assistance, or an encouraging word. As George Shinn wrote, *"There is no such thing as a self-made man. You will reach your goals only with the help of others."*

We never forgot the kind people who helped us on our trek across France and Spain, the family that fed us and the café owner who befriended us. We will not forget the people in Gibraltar who helped us prepare for Africa, nor the mechanics in Morocco and Algeria who helped with our repairs. We will never forget the generosity of Monsieur Tourneau of Michelin who gave us that precious map that saved our lives when we were deep in the desert.

At the end of our lives what we will treasure most are the memories of the people with whom we lived and laughed and loved. These are the true components of wealth—the true accomplishments of our journey.

So don't be afraid to ask others for help. It is a mark of strength, courage, and character. And don't be reluctant to give generously of yourself to others. It's the mark of caring, compassion, and personal greatness.

Summing Up

The reason the Sahara crossing was so life-changing for me was that after it I never felt there was anything I couldn't do. I felt programmed for success for life—although it took me many years to understand what had really happened and why I felt this way.

In addition, I believe that *everyone* has a Sahara to cross, perhaps more than one. *You* may be crossing your own personal Sahara right now.

Everyone goes through periods of great difficulty—their own private hells and dark nights of the soul. It is by facing whatever life sends you with courage and determination that you grow toward the stars.

Let me end this story with the final verse of "Carry On":

There are some who drift out in the deserts of doubt,
And some who in brutishness wallow,
There are others I know who in piety go,
Because of a heaven to follow.

But to labor with zest and to give of your best,
For the sweetness and joy of the giving,
To help folks along with a hand and a song,
Why there's the real joy of living!

Carry on! Carry on! Fight the good fight and true;
Believe in your mission; greet life with a cheer;
There's big work to do, and that's why you are here.
Carry on! Carry on! Let the world be the better for you;
And at last when you die, let this be your cry:
Carry on, my soul! Carry on!

If you resolve that whatever life hands you, you will carry on, there is nothing that can stop you from achieving the greatness for which you were created. Never give up!

APPENDIX

Becoming Unstoppable

HERE ARE THOUGHTS ON COURAGE, PERSISTENCE, and daring by some of the best thinkers of all time:

"Nothing in the world can take the place of persistence. Talent will not; nothing is more common than unsuccessful men with talent. Genius will not; unrewarded genius is almost a proverb. Education will not; the world is full of educated derelicts. Persistence and determination alone are omnipotent."

—CALVIN COOLIDGE

"Before success comes in any man's life, he is sure to meet with much temporary defeat, and perhaps some failure. When defeat overtakes a man, the easiest and most logical thing to do is to quit. That is exactly what the majority of men do."

—NAPOLEON HILL

"Some men give up their designs when they have almost reached the goal; while others obtain a victory by exerting, at the last moment, more vigorous efforts than ever before."

—HERODOTUS

"Austere perseverance, harsh and continuous, rarely fails of its purpose, for its silent power grows irresistibly greater with time."

—Johann Wolfgang von Goethe

"Few things are impossible to diligence and skill. Great works are performed not by strength, but by perseverance."

—Samuel Johnson

"Never, never, never give up."

—Winston Churchill

"Our greatest glory is not in never falling, but in rising every time we fall."

—Confucius

"There is no failure except in no longer trying. There is no defeat from within, no insurmountable barriers, save our own inherent weakness of purpose."

—Elbert Hubbard

"The rewards for those who persevere far exceed the pain that must precede the victory."

—Ted W. Engstrom

"The most essential factor is persistence, the determination never to allow your energy or enthusiasm to be dampened by the discouragement that must inevitably come."

—James Whitcomb Riley

"If you can force your heart and nerve and sinew to serve your needs long after they are gone, And so hold on when there is nothing in you, except the Will that says to them, 'Hold on!'"

—Rudyard Kipling

"I know of no such unquestionable badge and mark of a sovereign mind as that of tenacity of purpose . . ."

—Ralph Waldo Emerson

"No, there is no failure for the man who realizes his power, who never knows when he is beaten; there is no failure for the determined endeavor; the unconquerable will. There is no failure for the man who gets up every time he falls, who rebounds like a rubber ball, who persists when everyone else gives up, who pushes on when everyone else turns back."

—ORISON SWETT MARDEN

"Do what you can, with what you have, right where you are."

—THEODORE ROOSEVELT

"Always bear in mind that your own resolution to succeed is more important than any other one thing."

—ABRAHAM LINCOLN

"A man can rise above his circumstances and achieve whatever he sets his mind to, if he exercises unshakable persistence and a positive mental attitude."

—SAMUEL SMILES

"Many men fail because they quit too soon. Men lose faith when the signs are against them. They do not have the courage to hold on, to keep fighting in spite of that which seems insurmountable. If more of us would strike out and attempt the 'impossible,' we very soon would find the truth of that old saying that nothing is impossible. Abolish fear, and you can accomplish anything you wish."

—DR. C. E. WELCH

"Men who have blazed new paths for civilization have always been precedent breakers. It is ever the man who believes in his own ideas; who can think and act without a crowd to back him; who is not afraid to stand alone; who is bold, original, resourceful; who has the courage to go where others have never been, to do what others have never done, who accomplishes things, who leaves a mark on his times. Don't wait for extraordinary opportunities. Seize common ones, and make them great."

—ORISON SWETT MARDEN

"Nothing can resist a human will that will state even its existence on its stated purpose. The secret to success is constancy of purpose."

—Benjamin Disraeli

"I am not discouraged, because every wrong attempt discarded is another step forward."

—Thomas Edison

"We will either find a way or make one."

—Hannibal

"Life is either a daring adventure or nothing."

—Helen Keller

"Experience is not what happens to a man; it is what a man does with what happens to him."

—Aldous Huxley

"Obstacles are necessary for success because victory comes only after many struggles and countless defeats. Each struggle, each defeat, sharpens your skills and strengths, your courage and your endurance, your ability and your confidence—and thus each obstacle is a comrade-in-arms, forcing you to become better."

—Og Mandino

"To get profits without risk, experience without danger, and reward without work is as impossible as it is to live without being born."

—A. P. Gouthey

"You must be courageous, and courage is the capacity to go from failure to failure without losing any enthusiasm."

—Winston Churchill

"The credit belongs to the man who is actually in the arena; whose face is marred by dust and sweat and blood; who strives valiantly; who errs and comes short again and again; who knows the great enthusiasms, the great devotions, and spends himself on a worthy cause; who at the best knows in the end the triumph of high achievement; and who at the worst, if he fails, at least fails while daring greatly."

—Theodore Roosevelt

"It's easy to cry that you are beaten and die;
It's easy to crawfish and crawl;
But to fight and to fight when hope's out of sight;
Why, that's the best game of them all."

—ROBERT W. SERVICE

"Courage is resistance to fear, mastery of fear—not absence of fear."

—MARK TWAIN

"Nothing splendid has ever been achieved except by those who dared believe that something inside of them was superior to circumstance."

—BRUCE MARTIN

"Do not pray for tasks equal to your powers. Pray for powers equal to your task."

—PHILLIPS BROOKS

Carry On

It's easy to fight when everything's right,
When you're mad with the thrill and glory.
It's easy to cheer when victory is near
And wallow in fields that are gory.
It's a different song when everything's wrong,
When you're feeling infernally mortal.
When it's ten against one and hope there is none,
Buck up little soldier and chortle,
Carry on, carry on! There isn't much punch in your blow
You're glaring and staring and hitting out blind,
You're muddy and bloody but never you mind,
Carry on, carry on! You haven't the ghost of a show.
It's looking like death, but while you've a breath,
Carry on, my son, carry on.

And so in the strife of the battle of life
It's easy to fight when you're winning;

It's easy to slave, and starve and be brave,
When the dawn of success is beginning.
But the man who can meet despair and defeat
With a cheer, there's a man of God's choosing;
The man who can fight to Heaven's own height
Is the man who can fight when he's losing.
Carry on, carry on. Things never were looming so black;
But show that you haven't a cowardly streak,
And though you're unlucky, you never are weak.
Carry on! Brace up for another attack.
It's looking like hell, but you never can tell.
Carry on, old man! Carry on!

There are some who drift out in the deserts of doubt,
And some who in brutishness wallow,
There are others I know who in piety go
Because of a heaven to follow.
But to labor with zest and to give of your best,
For the sweetness and joy of the giving,
To help folks along with a hand and a song,
Why there's the real joy of living!
Carry on! Carry on! Fight the good fight and true;
Believe in your mission, greet life with a cheer;
There's big work to do, and that's why you are here.
Carry on! Carry on! Let the world be the better for you;
And at last when you die, let this be your cry:
Carry on, my soul! Carry on!

—Robert W. Service

About the Author

BRIAN TRACY IS ONE OF AMERICA'S LEADING AUTHORITIES on human potential and personal effectiveness. He is the chairman of Brian Tracy International, a human resources company based in San Diego, California, with affiliates throughout North America and in 31 nations. Brian has had successful careers in sales and marketing, investments, real estate development and syndication, importation, distribution, and management consulting. He has consulted at high levels with many billion-dollar corporations.

As an internationally renowned business consultant and motivational speaker, Brian addresses over 250,000 people each year on leadership, management, sales, strategic planning, success, personal and career development, goals, time management, creativity, self-esteem, and business development. His exciting talks and seminars bring about immediate changes and long-term results. He is a dynamic and entertaining speaker with a wonderful ability to inform and inspire audiences toward peak performance and higher levels of achievement.

Brian has produced and narrated more than 300 audio and video learning programs that have been translated into 20 languages. These include *The Psychology of Achievement, Fast Track to Business Success, The Psychology of Selling, The Power of Clarity, Master Strategies for Greater Achievement, The Psychology of Success,* and *24 Techniques for Closing the Sale.* These programs are considered to be among the most effective learning tools in the world. They cover the entire spectrum of human and corporate performance.

Brian is the author of 28 books, including several best sellers, such as: *Maximum Achievement, Advanced Selling Strategies, Focal Point, The 100 Absolutely Unbreakable Laws of Business Success, Eat That Frog! Victory!,* and *Create Your Own Future.*

Brian has traveled or worked in more than 80 countries on five continents and speaks four languages. He enjoys a wide range of interests and has a bachelors degree in commerce and a masters degree in business and administration, as well as a black belt in karate.

He is extremely well read in the areas of management, philosophy, business, economics, metaphysics, and history. Brian is an avid believer in controlling one's own destiny, setting daily goals, working hard, and persevering to the end.

He is active in community affairs, serves on the boards of nonprofit organizations, and travels worldwide. He is married with four children and lives in Solana Beach, California.

Brian Tracy International

Brian Tracy is one of the most sought-after speakers in the U.S. and around the world. In the past 20 years, he has delivered more than 2,000 speeches, seminars, and courses for more than two million people.

Brian is a successful businessman who has started, built, managed, or turned around 22 businesses. He has worked with more than 500 businesses as a consultant and trainer, including companies like IBM, MacDonnell Douglas, Northwestern Mutual, Deloitte & Touche, EDP, Federal Express, and Ford. Brian speaks more than 100 times each year for corporations, associations, conventions, and public seminars on the following topics:

Counter Attack – Applying the 12 Principles of Military Strategy to Increase Sales, Cut Costs and Boost Profits in a Tough Economy
High-Performance Leadership—For the 21st Century
Advanced Selling Skills—For the Top Professional
Time Empowerment—How to Double Your Results
Maximum Achievement—How to Get the Most Out of Life
Sales and Service Excellence—Keeping Keep Customers for Life
Superior Sales Management—How to Build World-Class Sales Teams

Each presentation can be customized and personalized for specific clients. For speaking fees and availability please contact:

Mr. Victor Risling
Brian Tracy International
462 Stevens Avenue, Suite 202
Solana Beach, CA 92075
Phone: (619) 481-2977
Fax: (619) 481-2445
E-mail: briantracy@briantracy.com
Website: www.briantracy.com
In the U.S., call toll free: 1-800-542-4252.

Best-Selling Audio Programs by Brian Tracy

To receive more information, or to order any of these exciting, life-changing programs, please call Brian Tracy International at 1-800-542-4252.

1. *The Psychology of Achievement.* (7 hours plus workbook) Perhaps the most powerful personal improvement program ever produced, a worldwide best seller in 20 languages. You learn how to take charge of your life, set and achieve goals, and unlock your superconscious mind. CD or cassette, $75.00
2. *The Psychology of Success.* Discover the ten proven principles for winning with this amazingly comprehensive program. Listen today—you'll see results tomorrow! 7 hour cassette or CD, $75.00
3. *Master Strategies for Higher Achievement.* Think and act better and faster. Increase your personal value and fortune. More than 150 key ideas you can use immediately to get better results in every area of your life. 7 hour cassette or CD, $75.00
4. *How to Start and Succeed in Your Own Business.* Learn how to double or triple your profits with this mini-MBA course. Learn key requirements for business success, strategic marketing, corporate strategy, and how to overcome the challenges of building and managing a small business. 9 hours, $75.00
5. *The Psychology of Selling.* This is the best selling sales training program in the world, in 16 languages. You learn how to move yourself into the top 10 percent of all salespeople: how to get more and better appointments, make better and more effective presentations, overcome objections, and close more sales faster and easier than you ever thought possible. You actually double and triple your sales results within 12 months. 7 hour cassette or CD, plus workbook, $75.00
6. *How to Master Your Time.* Learn how to gain at least two hours of productive time every day! Here are 16 ways to overcome procrastination and focus, concentrate, and maximize your productivity. Get twice as much done in half the time. 7 hour cassette or CD, $75.00

8. *Thinking Big—The Keys to Personal Power and Maximum. Performance.* Learn how to tap into the vast resources of your mind, and unlock your unlimited potential. Practice the ideas in this program and you will become unstoppable! 7 hour cassette or CD, $75.00

All programs described above are unconditionally guaranteed for one year. Phone today to order, or visit us at www.briantracy.com.

Index

A

Abert, Geoffrey F., 208
Accepting the inevitable, 73–74
Action
  "bold," begets the aid of unseen forces, 54, 93, 266
  concrete, 21–22, 268–269
  creative, 147
  daily, 14
  immediate, 38, 64
Adams, Abigail, 240
Adult lives begun, 13, 17
Adventures
  difficult situations as, 50
  zest and joy of, 147
Adversity, adjusting to, 233, 271
Aguelhok at sunrise, 252–253
Algeria
  and the Sahara, 147–154
  border dispute with Morocco, 116–117, 121
  first impression of, 148–149
  Reggane, last town in, 205–209
Allen, James, 1
Alternate route, 122
Anefis, getting around, 254
Antoine de Saint Exupery, 147
Aristotle, 245, 268
Associates, 138, 200, 270
Assumptions, testing your, 33, 36, 37
Atlantic crossing, 29
Atlas Mountains, 107–119
Attacking to the rear, 166
Attitude of gratitude, 68

B

Bad to worse, from, 141
Bailing out for good, 150–154
Barcelona days, 69–81
Baron Pierre de Coubertin, 47
Barton, Bruce, 202
Beecher, Henry Ward, 187
Beliefs, power of changing your, 235
Best
  doing one's, 101
  "laid plans of mice and men," 121–130
  "of times and worst of times," 49–50, 68
Bicycles
  across Africa, 37–39
  as penance and pilgrimage, 66
  discarding the, 85
  pleasurable traveling by, 67
  selling the, 96
Blanton, Smiley, 68
Bon Vivants club, 12, 95
Bond, invisible, 215
Bootstrapping in a new business, 38
Border
  crossing, Algeria, 148
  dispute, Moroccan and Algerian, 116–117, 121
  running strategy, 250–259
Bordji-Perez, 235–244
Bourem, 259–262
Brande, Dorothea, 17, 258
Brave, fortune favors the, 262
Breaking the rules, 257–258
Breakthrough, 103–105
Brennen, Stephen A., 14
Bristol, Claude M., 220
Brotherhood of the road, 127–128
Buoyancy, 36
Bureaucrats, battles with, 79, 83–84
Buxton, Sir Thomas Fowell, 137

C

Carlyle, Thomas, 16, 269
Carnegie, Dale, 69
Casablanca, the road to, 112–113
Castles in the air, building foundations under, 9
Change
  of pace, 131–135
  "your thinking," "change your life," 46
Character
  becoming a person of, 42
  world built to develop, 146
Charell, Ralph, 46
Cheap and lousy stove, 143
Chesterton, G.K., 49–50
Clean, well-lit place, 66–67
Close call, very, 259–263
Collier, Robert, 131
Comfort zone, leaving your, 218
Commitment, acid test of, 51
Common objective, 38–39
Commonplace occurrences, seeing drama and romance in, 65
Complacency as enemy, 181, 195, 230
Confucius, 15
Conquerors, young, 64–65
Convention, defying, 257
Cops, omniscient, 76, 86
Corbett, James J., 263
Corneille, Pierre, 41
Crisis, the first, 23–28
Crossing, "the," 209–220
Crow, Robin, 21
Cup of tea, 144
Currency
  non-monetary, 79
  transactions, black market, 254–255
Cycles and trends, everything in life as, 69

D

D'Alembert, 258
Dale, Arbie M., 166
Deadlines and subdeadlines, setting, 13
Defeat, hovering shadow of, 97
Defection, temporary, 91–93
Depletion, absolute, 263
Desert
  convoy, 190–200, 203–208
  "death in the," 137–146, 189, 270
  diplomacy, 237–238
  etiquette, 238–239
  greatest on earth, 201–259
  heat as enemy, 222–226, 232–233
  heat, designing the days around, 123, 133–134, 204–205
  hitchhiking, 162–164, 167–174
  solitude, 198
  sun, 133–134, 168, 170–171, 178–181, 189
  swimming, 196
  the edge of the, 132
  Wadis, danger of, 253–254
  water, politics of, 236–241
  weather, 197
Destination achieved, 84–85
Detailed plan, making a, 14
Difficulties
  accept, adjust, and respond to, 74
  in business and life, 74
  looking for the gift contained in, 81
Dilemma, facing a, 88
Direct route, 51
Directions, when in doubt, ask for, 86–87
Discouragement, persisting in face of, 99
Dover to Calais, 45
Dreams
  and vision, 107
  destroyed by opinions of other people, 99
  unquenchable drinkers at the fountain of, 65
  working to make yours come true, 2, 8–9
Drucker, Peter, 220
Durrell, Laurence, 41
Dysentery, 139, 152, 174

E

Easy way out *vs.* hard way through, 105
Edison, Thomas, 42
Emergency, coping with, 18–20
Emerson, Ralph Waldo, 43, 201
Emotional intelligence, 243–244
Enduring what can't be cured, 77–78, 118
Entrepreneurs, success rate of experienced, 52
Epictetus, 233, 271
Exasperation, exercise in, 239
Existentialism, 187–188
Expectations, questioning your, 46

F

Failure
  an impossibility, 17, 258, 269
  is not an option, 2
  only in no longer trying, 156
  result of lack of planning and preparation, 109
  specter of, 97, 154
Fair share, 213–214
Fighting when everything's right, 64
Figuig, road to, 142

Finances
- living on limited, 70
- replenished, 102–103

Financing
- credit system, 90
- good Ideas attract necessary, 104
- travel, 12

First aid
- course, vital, 12
- in Spanish machete incident, 80

First night in Africa, 112–113

First step
- as most important, 268
- Vancouver to Montreal, 17–22

Five years forward, projecting, 1–2

Flexibility, 35, 40, 69, 271

Flies, everywhere, 117–118, 162, 189

Foolish, willingness to look or sound, 45

Football analogy on quitting, H. Ross Perot's, 104

Ford, Henry, 146

Fosdick, Harry Emerson, 119

Free lessons, no, 67–68

Future
- creating the, 69
- focus on the, 21
- orientation as hallmark of successful people, 88

G

Galley boy job, 26

Gao, making it to, 262–263

Gibraltar
- days, 83–99
- last leg to, 80–81
- London to, 43–46
- Rock of, 94

Give generously, 272

Glorious fantasies, 11

Goals
- achieved one step at a time, 201–202
- commitment to, 103–105, 155–156
- completing, 220
- launching, 15–16, 31
- method for setting and achieving, 13–14
- seeking way to achieve, 88
- wanting badly enough, 105

Goethe, 42, 155

Going
- away party, 13
- it alone, 206, 210
- with the flow, 135, 161

Good
- experience operates ultimately for our, 121
- giving thanks for the, 186
- "inverse paranoid," 81
- looking for the, 68, 81, 97
- most people as honest, decent and, 112
- unrecognized, 126

Good Friday cleanliness in Spain, 70–71

Good Samaritan, 53–54

Greatness, born for, 9

H

Happiness
- as progressive realization of a worthy goal or ideal, 202
- beaming with, 125
- lessons of, 81

Hard day's night, 126

Help, ability to ask for, 38, 271–272

Heroes and heroines, true, 126

Hesse, Hermann, 81

Hill, Napolean, 2, 15, 154, 221

Hindu proverb, 203

Holliwell, Raymond, 121

Holt, Hamilton, 106

Home sweet home, 94–95

Hubbard, Elbert, 23, 156

Hunger
- lack of in the heat, 227
- ravenous, 44, 54–57

I

Ideas
- attract necessary funds, 104
- resistance to new, 217

Illness, unprepared for, 139–140

Independence above all, 89–90

Inner limitations, personal boundaries determined by, 45–46

Innovate, 257–258

Inoculations, trip, 12, 96

Intelligent plan as first step to success, 35

J

James, William, 118

Joys, finding supreme, 147

K

Knowledge
- not relying on own limited, 176
- skills and abilities, 13

Korda, Michael, 244

Ksar-es-Souk, 132–133

L

Land Rover
- *Bon Vivant's* emblem on side of, 95
- brake failure, 18–20
- damage and repair, 149, 175
- lessons, 86–99
- mechanical difficulties, 109–112, 116
- tires, 126–129, 133, 149, 162–164, 176–177

Language, learning a new, 45
Law of requisite variety, 45
Leadership qualities, 207–208
Leap and the net will appear, 16, 21, 31
Leap of faith
  all great achievements begin with a, 93
  successful enterprise begins with a, 17
Learning what works by trying what doesn't, 78
Lessons
  first real, 21–22
  for life, 267–273
  from crisis, 185–186
  great, 93
  no free, 67–68
Letter, trip-saving, 102–103, 104
Lights and music, 54
Limited budget, living on a, 70
Losing heart, 103–104
Luck, making your own, 244
Lunch
  for everyone, 172–173
  in Limoges, quick, 61–63
Luxury, traveling in second-class, 79

M

Maltz, Maxwell, 235
Map
  lifesaving, 108–109, 272
  one-page, 36
  or plan, any as better than none, 109
  radiator and warnings, 119
Marden, Orison Swett, 40, 101, 200, 266
Marrakech, on to, 113–114
Memories, 272
  currency of, 79
Mental exercise to control mind and emotions, 21–22
Metaphors for life, 118
Mill, John Stuart, 135
Miller, John Homer, 267
Mirage, desert, 256–257
Mistakes, making early, 33
Modern miracle, 109
Money
  accomplishing desired ends with little, 79
  and repairs, 174
  borrowing, 90–91, 171–172, 183–185
  flows to worthy ideas, 104
  gift of, 102–103
  selling food for, 172, 174–175
  "talks," 199
  writing to friends for, 91
Morocco
  and the Atlas Mountains, 107–119
  border dispute with Algeria, 116–117, 121
  last days in, 142–146
Morrisey, George, 157
Murphy's Law, 48
Musketeers, reduced to "two" for a day, 91–93

N

Native capacity, using our, 68
Nature sends peace, pleasure, and happiness to guide you, 81
Naysayers, ignoring, 138, 270
Necessity, virtue of, 50
Never give up, 155–200
New situations require new attitudes, 46
Night train companions, 76–77
No turning back, 246
North African "heaven" near Agadir, 117
North America, traversing, 4–7
Nothing, doing, 60
Nothingness, absolute, 218–219

O

Obstacles
  constant and determined effort sweeps away all, 220
  determining, 14
  lessons and benefits in, 21, 27–28, 155–156, 270
Off to *see* the world, 17–18
One oil barrel at a time, 221–233, 269
Onward or nothing, 246
Open mind, keeping an, 36
Open road, call of the, 3–9
Opinions of others, 99–100
Orphanage for the blind, 123–126
Osler, William, 11

P

Pace yourself, 135
Pain, purpose of, 81
Partnerships as worst form of business relationships, 24
Paying one's own way as character strengthening, 89–90
Peace, lessons of, 81
Permission, giving up asking for, 208
Perot, H. Ross, 104
Persistence
  as most essential factor in success, 99, 269
  test, 27
Personal mission, 8–9
Pfeiffer, Jane Cahill, 33
Plans, bold execution of, 14
Pleasure, lessons of, 81
Political
  pigheadedness of Spanish police, 83–84
  savvy, 244
Poor land, 114–115

Positive change, power of just one, 93
Power, abuse of, 240
Preparation, the, 11–14
Pride, self-reliance as source of, 89–90
Problems
  as stepping stones, 27
  God sends gifts wrapped up as, 81
  successful people constantly seek ways to solve, 88
  vs. facts, 46
Providence, 119
Pyrenees, 69–70, 72–74

Q

Quitting, 91–92
  as habit, 30
  as necessary decision for German traveling companions, 241
  for good, third Musketeer, 150–154
  just before the breakthrough to success, 103–105, 155–156

R

Rage, thirsty, 239–240
Ransom, Ralph, 29, 265
Real
  journey begins, 41–106
  time, operating in, 64
Reality
  cold wind of, 98–99
  the dawn of, 105–154
Reciprocity, law of, 130, 173
Reevaluating and regrouping, 33–36, 166
Reflections, 267–273
Rejection *vs.* acceptance, 104
Relationships, impermanent nature of, 154, 246
Reply at last, 98
Reprieve, 102
Resilience, developing, 38
Resolve to carry on, 151–152
Responsibility
  free of, 31
  revelation, 25
  taking, 166
Riley, James Whitcomb, 99
Road
  code of the, 127–128, 159–162
  wrong, 166
Roads
  get worse, 248–250
  terrible, 115–116
  washboard, 251–252
Rock of Gibralter, The, 94
Romantic speculation, 11
Roosevelt, Theodore, 259
Rough to smooth, 216
Running the border, 245–258, 267

S

Saddened but not destroyed, 101–102
Sahara
  Algeria and the, 147–154
  and Africa map, 108–109
  crossing your own personal, 272, 279
  escarpment, 188–189
  sand storms, 157–159
  Sahara crossing
  routes, 115
  seven principles learned in the, 268–272
  the first attempt, 157–166
  the second attempt, 167–174
  third time lucky, 187–200
Schemes, fitting circumstances to, 11
Schuller, Robert, 104
Schwab, Charles, 107
Schwartz, Robert L., 3
Self-delusion, lure of, 37
Self-reliance as source of pride, 89–90
Seneca, 271
Service, Robert W., 3–4, 64, 126
  poem, "Carry On," 151
Setting out, 43–46
Shakespeare, 41
Shame in living off of others, 90
Shangri La, 66
Shinn, George, 272
Shuttle train, sleeping on the, 60
Silent pact, 215
Sirach, 83
Smiles, Samuel, 186
Solution
  focus on, 46
  no quick, 111–112
  oriented, 22
Something always happens, 103–104
South of France, 64–65
Spanish
  girls, chaperoned, 71–72
  railways, 69–81
  roads, agony of, 72–74
  slums, 72
Spear, Grace, 130
Starting
  again, 29–33
  out, 15–22
Stowe, Harriet Beecher, 27
Stressful situations, 244
Success
  attaining greatest, 68
  clarity as starting point for great, 13
  conspiracy of, 81
  dependent upon choice of friends and associates, 200, 270
  focus and concentration as keys to great, 220